AGENTS IN MY BRAIN

AGENTS IN
MY BRAIN

How I Survived Manic Depression

Bill Hannon

Afterword by
Karen K. Dickson M.D.

OPEN COURT
Chicago and La Salle, Illlinois

Printed and bound in the United States of America.

Library of Congress Cataloging-in-Publication Data

Hannon, Bill.
    Agents in my brain : how I survived manic depression / Bill Hannon;
    afterword by Karen K. Dickson.
       p. cm.
    Includes index.
    ISBN 0-8126-9346-9 (alk. paper)
       1. Manic depressive illness—Patients—Biography.   I. Title.
RC516.H36   1997
616.85'27'0092—dc21
[B]

CONTENTS

The story you are about to read is true. The names of people and places have been changed in order to protect the privacy of my friends and family.

1

KGB Bloodhounds

My name is Bill Hannon. Like thousands and thousands of other manic-depressives type one, when I was extremely manic, I got the delusion that I was a CIA/FBI agent. It was April 1981. I was a twenty-one-year-old college student at the University of Washington in Seattle (UW). I had been in touch with reality, but depressed, for the entire year before that. I had already had manic-depressive mood swings for over four years. I had been normal, happy and healthy until I was seventeen.

In my manic illness, I began a crusade to stop crime. My plan was to get the Washington State Legislature to build a lot more prisons and keep them completely full of criminals. In my manic confusion, I wrote a letter to the governor in which I intended to say something against violence. However, the letter was worded so poorly, so incoherently, that the recipients didn't know what the letter meant. They figured I was mentally ill, and was speaking of violence. They couldn't tell if I was against violence or in favor of it. They thought the letter was possibly some sort of threat. A bit later, I decided that the FBI, CIA, and/or Secret Service had checked out my background so carefully that they realized that I was a good guy, the letter was not a threat, and I was so law-abiding, that they wanted me to be an FBI agent. I was that delusional, that out of touch with reality. Being manic, my judgment was way off. I didn't know that there was something wrong with me. I felt excited, happy, and energetic. However, my speech and writing were hard to understand. I sent a letter to Governor Evans which was meant to say:

Dear Governor Evans,
We are all in too much danger. The penalty for
attempted first degree murder is only three years in
prison. The penalties are way too short like this,
because there is a lack of prison space . . . Please
build more prison space.
Sincerely,
Bill Hannon

Instead, my letter was hard to understand. My intent was just
to describe the general situation in the state, namely, that anyone
with a motive for violence might go ahead and commit a crime.
However, my letter was incoherent. It was more like,

Dear Governor Evans,
Someone could kill you. You better build more
prisons . . . This is a matter of life and death!
Sincerely,
Bill Hannon

This looks alarming, but at the time I thought it was just fine
because I wasn't thinking straight.

I had been manic a year earlier for a four-month period. I
wrote some strange letters to professors at that time. There were
references to violence that were misunderstood in those letters
also. I was trying to say something against violence, but one sentence did not lead to another, and my choice of wording was inaccurate. The inaccurate wording probably reminded the readers of
the myth that mentally ill or confused people are often dangerous.
This myth is widely believed in our society.

The incoherence alone in my letter to the governor probably
would have alarmed any reader who believed in the "mentally ill
people are dangerous" myth. Add in the references to violence
that they could not figure out, and the governor's security guards
apparently interpreted my letter as some sort of threat. They sent
some people around to ask questions about me. I didn't know
about that until a week or so later. I was utterly surprised that they
thought my letter was some sort of threat. I had thought my letter

was a clear statement *against* violence and crime. I also sent a letter to former Vice President Walter Mondale, but I wrote it after the letter to Evans, and I made a point of wording it more carefully when I talked about crime.

I had been a college student, doing a political science internship with a state legislator. When that internship with State Legislator Denslow ended, because the college quarter was over, I was free to lobby the other representatives about criminal justice legislation. I wanted to stop crime. I hoped for some legislation that would establish mandatory minimum prison sentences for each felony, and also would create the necessary prison space. I talked to many representatives—Democrats who were basically against the idea and Republicans who were almost all in favor. The house and senate were controlled by the Democrats. Governor Evans was a Republican. The head of the house appropriations committee was named Steve Leroux.

The appropriations committee was going to have a hearing on appropriations for prisons at the end of March. I hoped to get a chance to speak at that hearing. I had a presentation planned including this song that I wrote:

The Whites kill the Whites,
And the Whites kill the Blacks,
And the Blacks kill the Blacks,
And the Blacks kill the Whites,
And the green grass grows all around, all around,
And the green grass grows all around.

The point of my song was that something needed to be done about all the killing. We shouldn't just sit back and accept it.

Also, too many of the Democratic legislators seemed to be saying that if I wanted to put criminals in prison, I wanted to put blacks in prison, and therefore I was a racist. The Democrats seemed to be saying that criminals should be forgiven if they commit a crime and they're black. This never made sense, especially because black criminals usually have black victims. Most crimes in Washington State are committed by whites, and race should have nothing to do with sentencing.

My idea that I could convince the whole legislature to do something, all by myself, was a grandiose delusion.

My mania led me to falsely believe that Representative Leroux really would let me speak at the appropriations committee hearing. I called four television stations and two newspapers and told them to be at the hearing. I planned to be a big splash on the evening news. I even mailed out postcards to lots of people I had known, saying I was running for Congress in 1982. Being unrealistically optimistic was a symptom of mania. This was the third time in my life that I experienced a freaky and very severe manic episode. I had been normal until I was seventeen-and-a-half years old.

Being manic feels very good. It is very exciting and fun, even though it is bizarre.

The criminal justice appropriations hearing took place on April 3, 1981. One of the television stations I had called was there, and there was a bunch of people testifying. I thought I was going to be on the agenda, but when I got there, the agenda that Representative Leroux had made up did not have my name on it. I was annoyed. I was hyper because I was manic. The hearing started, and people talked about a replacement for the women's prison because the current one wasn't enough fun or something. I began to distribute my handouts. The handouts compared the cost of prisons with the cost of crime. Prisons are inexpensive compared with crime. My handouts had my suggestions for the minimum penalties that people should serve for all the various crimes. I was moving around a lot at the meeting to pass out my literature. That probably was out of order. Also, I kept trying to see Leroux through a narrow aisle which was my only view of him. He kept leaning one way or another. I was just trying to see him in order to pay attention to him when he was talking. Later I learned that somebody thought I was looking for a path to rush Leroux and attack him. I know that I looked nervous because at the beginning somebody told me so. I was just nervous about speaking and from being manic. Of course, I didn't realize that I was manic. I thought I could personally convince the state legislature to build a new five-thousand cell maximum security prison for the state by addressing the committee that day. I was out of touch with reality, and I didn't know it. It was fun and exciting. I was proud of the great knowledge of how to stop crime that I thought I had.

When time was nearly up at the hearing, I yelled out from the audience, "Representative Leroux, you said I could speak, how about a chance?" Everyone just ignored me.

Later, I was near Representative Denslow's office, and he told me that one of the governor's bodyguards had been around asking questions about me. He asked, "What did you say in that letter?"

I said, "Well I wrote, 'Your life is in danger from all the crime'."

"Well, it was poor judgment to say, 'Your life is in danger'."

"Yeah, I guess."

That was the end of that discussion. Later that night, my dad came over and said, "Bill, I've got to talk to you."

I said, "Let me guess, you got a call from the Secret Service (Mondale's bodyguards)."

My dad said, "No. No. I got a call from Dean Carlson (Commissioner of Prisons). He said you were at some legislative meeting acting in a disturbed manner."

I said, "Really?"

"Yes, they thought you were going to rush the chairman."

"Rush him?" I said surprised.

"Yes."

"*Rush him?* That's ridiculous."

He said, "Look, I want you to go see Dr. Dan Holley. He's younger than Dr. Kelly [the psychiatrist I was seeing then], and he can help you."

I said, "Okay, okay, okay, I will."

I didn't argue because I knew I had already accidently annoyed the governor's bodyguards, and it wouldn't hurt to see another psychiatrist on an outpatient basis.

My dad gave me Dr. Holley's phone number. Then I said, "Okay, now get out of my house."

I generally did not get along with my dad. For example, he didn't want me to have a girlfriend, and he got very mad whenever I had a date.

I called the number my dad gave me to make an appointment, and they made a point of getting me in the next day. I went to see Dr. Holley in his office, and decided that not only was he a psychiatrist, but also an agent for the FBI/CIA, or maybe the Secret Service.

He talked to me for a little bit and then said, "I have a drug I want you to try."

I told him I didn't do drugs other than my mood leveler Lithium, and I wasn't interested. He convinced me to take the prescription slip. I had been on Lithium for a full year because I had been tentatively diagnosed with manic depression a year earlier at the age of twenty. Obviously, the Lithium was not working too well at this point.

When I left his office, I went to a bookstore to look the prescription up in *The Physicians' Desk Reference*. The name of the drug was spelled "Sineguan" on the prescription slip that Holley had filled out. I looked it up and found an entry for an antidepressant called "Sinequan." Obviously, the "g" should have been a "q" on the slip. I took this misspelling as a hint that I was not really supposed to take the drug being prescribed. I looked at the list of side effects, and one of them was hallucinations. I decided that Holley had prescribed this drug as a Secret Service trick. I thought the Secret Service knew I would look up the side effects. I thought they wanted to see if I would deliberately induce hallucinations in myself, so that I would have a defense for murder. I thought they wanted to see if I would try to use the insanity defense. Hallucinations show insanity. I was really paranoid. I had the unrealistic fear that the Secret Service was watching me and playing this dirty trick on me. They couldn't arrest me, because I hadn't done anything. So, I imagined, they were pulling dirty tricks on me. I didn't get the misspelled prescription for Sinequan filled. I'm not a murderer, and I didn't want hallucinations.

I know now that it was just as well, because the drug would've probably made my symptoms worse. It was an antidepressant, not an antimanic major tranquilizer. In reality, it wasn't a trick; it was just an erroneous and misspelled prescription.

Over the next several days I lost touch with reality further. I still had no insight into my situation. I thought I was fine, but I really wasn't.

For example, I was reading the University of Washington student newspaper. In the paper there is a classified section for fraternities and sororities. There are usually ads in there like, "Hey Jim and Dave of Sigma Delta Phi, thanks for the great time Monday. Love, your little sisters Stacy, Sandy, Angie, Sue, Dawn, Jane, Laurie and Ann." Well, being manic, I started to think that all those ads were directed at me. I thought of anyone I had ever

known with those girls' first names, and figured they had all gotten together to get in touch with me. I was ecstatic. For one
thing, they were probably in love with me. For another, they had
probably heard about my plans to run for Congress, and wanted
to work on my campaign.

A few more days went by, and I thought the FBI, Secret Service, and CIA had realized that their concern about my letter was
completely unfounded. I figured they realized I was a good guy. I
thought they had checked me out carefully, and had found that I
was very law-abiding. I had even reached the rank of Eagle in Boy
Scouts.

I developed delusions about music. I thought the choice of
songs on the radio, and sometimes the actual words of songs
being played, were being altered by the CIA/FBI to have a special
meaning for me. I figured that my car was bugged, my house was
bugged, my phone was tapped, my mail was being opened, and I
was being followed. By now, though, I thought it was not being
done to guard against something bad I might do, but instead, so
that the FBI could keep track of what I was doing. By keeping
track of what I was doing, the FBI would best be able to help me
get elected to Congress. I was overjoyed. They wanted to get me
elected because they had figured out that I was tough on crime. I
was not violent. I wanted to stop violence. They couldn't overtly
help me, because as federal employees, they couldn't get involved
in politics, I thought. So, they had to help me covertly. This was
all according to my grandiose delusions.

The fact that my house was bugged (or so I thought), let them
know what radio station I was listening to. There was a song on
the radio at that time, that included a line about women that went
something like, "Big, little, or short or tall, wish I could've kept
them all." There was another song that included the line, "Wham
bam thank you ma'am." I combined the two and made it, "Wish I
could bam them all." Then I sent this line, "Wish I could bam
you all," to Geena Andrews, to whom I had already sent postcards
about my running for Congress. I thought she was the one
behind all the girls in the UW paper writing to me. Geena
Andrews was the Vice President of Jewish Teen Group (JTG), my
temple youth group, when I was Treasurer, back in eleventh
grade. I had barely seen her since then, but I had liked her a lot at
the time. She was bright and attractive. At the time, I thought she
would consider this postcard to be code words of encouragement.

The manic, happy mood reminded me of her, and the time I knew her, when I was healthy. In hindsight, I'm sure my postcards were highly annoying. I'm sure she didn't understand them. In fact, she was probably frightened by them.

In a few days, I had another appointment with Dr. Holley. I forgot exactly what we said, but I remember he told me he had been a lieutenant colonel in the Air Force during the Vietnam War. I decided he still was in the Air Force intelligence branch and was my commanding officer. The intelligence community would help get me elected to Congress. It was very exciting. I told him I was going down to Tacoma to visit my friends at the University of Puget Sound (UPS). I had gone to school there for my first two years.

He said, "Take my card along and give me a call if you run into any trouble."

I went down to UPS about nine o'clock at night. I thought a whole caravan of cars was following me down there. I got to UPS and went to the house of some friends. They had just gone to sleep when I got there, but I had called so they knew I was coming. One of their roommates was gone, so I tried to sleep in his bed. I think I just lay there a few hours. Then I got up and started looking for my shoes. After some trouble finding my shoes, during which I woke one of my friends, I went out and drove around for a while. Then I came back to their house and sat in the living room for the rest of the night. My mind was filled with great, fun, optimistic thoughts. It was exciting to be running for Congress, and to feel so good, instead of being depressed. I didn't realize that I was out of my mind. This was a manic phase of manic depression. I had had two previous manic episodes since age seventeen-and-a-half, but since then, I had mostly been depressed. It felt good to sit in my friends' living room and make great, optimistic plans.

The next day, my friends in that house got sick of me, and they sent me over to Jewish House where I knew a couple people. Jewish House was a residential house for Jews on campus who wanted to keep kosher and observe other Jewish traditions. I guess Tim, one of the guys there, was writing a story and needed a new character.

One of my friends in the first house later sent over a note saying, "This is your new character," I guess meaning me.

I didn't really notice. I was too busy talking to them, trying to pick up secret coded information from them, and give other information to them. It was fun. I thought I was finally doing something fun and exciting on this campus rather than hanging out in my dorm room being depressed. Before I dropped out, that's what I did. I hung out in my dorm room and was depressed.

As I talked to the people in Jewish House, I jumped from topic to topic, I'm sure. I remember I kept doing an imitation of an Israeli trying to speak English:

"I eh, don know, eh, how do you say in English?"

Also, I kept throwing my head to one side like you do when you first lift your head out of a pool to get water out of your eyes. Swimming lives on in my mind when I feel good.

At Jewish House, there was a poster on the wall which said, "Consider Yourself One of the Committed." Of course, this meant committed to Judaism, but I kept thinking it could mean being committed to a mental hospital, because my dad had been saying that I was nuts. It was a suspicious poster.

I thought my car had been stolen. Eventually I found out I had just forgotten where I parked it. The people I had been talking to at Jewish House were Tim and Rita. I told them I thought my car had been stolen, and Tim wanted to call campus security, but I told him not to. Later when I was out walking around, Tim called campus security, and I think, reported that I was acting strange, and that I didn't want to call them when my car had been stolen.

I told Tim and Rita that my mission was partly to get my dad put in prison. I decided that my dad had been a CIA agent, and that the campus was a CIA training base. I thought I was a CIA agent in training. However, my dad had tried to restrict me from dating a girl who wasn't Jewish, Melanie Carson. She comes to mind when I'm in the manic, feel-good mode. My dad outranked me in the CIA, but he had attempted to interfere with my civil rights, and that could land him in prison. You have the civil right to date anyone you want. It was an equal opportunity in romance on the basis of religion type of thing. Of course, a civil rights case is usually a civil court action, but I had read it can be considered criminal. I didn't explain it that clearly. I was fairly difficult to understand.

That evening I was in the student union, and a group of campus security guards came up to me and asked, "Are you Bill Hannon?"

I said, "Yes."

They asked, "What are you on this campus for?"

(I had dropped out of UPS a year earlier, and I was now attending UW.)

"I cannot say."

Then they started pushing me and asked, "Why can't you say?"

"I cannot say why I cannot say, and quit pushing me or I'll get you guys arrested."

"What for?"

"Assault."

"Well, we think you're on campus to threaten a professor."

"No."

A few minutes later they left me alone.

I had written anticrime letters to some professors during my manic episode a year earlier. The problems with the 1980 letters to professors arose from my misunderstood references to violence. This was the same problem I had just repeated in the 1981 letters to the governor. Being manic makes a person impossible to understand. People can get the meaning exactly backwards. The likelihood of misunderstanding is increased by the abundance in the media of misconceptions about mental illness. Too often, mental illness only makes the news when some killer is pleading insanity. Most people arrested on suspicion of murder are perfectly sane, and perfectly guilty. On the other hand, most mentally ill people are perfectly peaceful. They are two different groups. Criminals, in their desperate attempt to stay out of prison, end up slandering and libeling mentally ill people by saying they are one of us. They only wish.

Sometime later, after talking to the security guards, when I was out walking around campus Rita called my high school friend David Frish, and my psychiatrist, Dr. Holley. I had given her their names and phone numbers, because I thought she was CIA also. I guess she told them I was crazy.

I spent the evening wandering around campus, looking at the things people had written on their dorm room doors, thinking that the writing contained secret messages to me or about me.

I thought I should send some secret messages as well as receive them. I thought the song "Dirty Water" by the Inmates had to be sung to one particular girl, so I knocked on her door and started singing it.

She said, "Bill, I don't know what you are talking about."

So I left.

I was also looking for Brett Pritchard's house. He lived in a college-owned house the address of which I didn't know. The campus directory just gave the name of the house. I was going to speak to him about the fight against crime. His father was a Congressman.

Also that evening, I crashed a few parties that were going on in dorms. I just walked in. I stayed for just a minute, because I thought I was on a secret mission that I couldn't tell anyone about, and then I left.

Around 10:30 or so I went back to Jewish House and told them I was going to stay there and sleep. I had prearranged to stay in the room of a friend there because he was out of town. He was a friend of mine from my dorm floor freshman year.

I was getting into bed, but first I was stumbling around his room, and I accidently unplugged his clock radio. When I plugged it back in, it flashed 12:00. I didn't know why it did that. It was another clue. My dad would be arrested at 12:00, I thought. I tried to sleep, but I couldn't. Finally, at about 1:00 A.M., I got up and started sweeping the bathroom floor. Using the broom was supposed to symbolize, "Ding dong the witch is dead"—the witch being my father. Then Rita said I was making too much noise, so I left.

Then I decided that the whole campus was a CIA training base, and everybody was supposed to switch dorm rooms to confuse the KGB. I went to the room of the girl I had sung to earlier, and asked if I could sleep there.

She said, "No!" but gave me a sleeping bag, and told me to sleep out in the lounge. That was pretty gracious for someone whom I had never known that well, and hadn't seen in two years.

I took the sleeping bag, and headed to another dorm. I went to the lounge of the dorm, and watched the late night Associated Press news on television. The news was printed on the screen, and would gradually scroll up. I blinked a few times or several times after reading each word or sentence. I thought the CIA could tell what I was reading by shining lasers through the TV screen into my eyes and back to the television. Of course, I thought the information was coded secrets. For example, some of the news was about the National Long Course Swimming Championships.

When it got to the breaststroke, I thought they were telling me that if I did well on this mission, it would make up for all the bad breaststroke races I had participated in.

I thought this was all very exciting and fun. I thought I was very clever. It was good to have a sense of purpose.

I stayed in the dorm lounge for a while, then I left and went walking around campus. A small cocker spaniel started following me. At first I thought nothing of it, but then I thought it was sent to trail me by the KGB. It probably had a microscopic radio transmitting device on its collar. So in keeping with the delusion that everyone on campus was supposed to switch rooms to confuse the KGB, and in keeping with the delusion that the dog was trailing my scent for the KGB, I did what people do in the movies when bloodhounds are chasing them. I crossed water. It throws off the scent. That way the KGB wouldn't be able to kill me.

I took off all my clothes except for my underwear, put my keys in my right hand, and swam across a pond on campus that had a dormitory on the other side. I stopped in the middle to pour mud on my head. I thought to myself, this is a crazy way to make a living. I wondered if being a CIA agent was enough to impress Melanie Carson. I kept thinking about the song that has the line, "Save my life I'm going down for the last time." I pretended to have trouble swimming as I thought of those lyrics. I had no trouble swimming, but it was cold. It was April 12, in Tacoma, Washington.

It was about 6:00 A.M., when I got out of the pond in my underwear, ran into the dorm, and into the men's showers. I took a hot shower to warm up. So far, nobody had seen me. After about ten minutes in the shower, I got out. I walked down the hall and saw someone's name written on his door. It was "Brewster." "Ster" was a syllable that reminded me of a nickname I used to have. The door was unlocked, so I walked in. There was nobody there. I used a towel to dry off, and I changed into some dry underwear that I found in a drawer. They fit. Then I put on some pants and a shirt, and they fit. I thought I had arrived at my new address, the one I was supposed to go to in order to confuse the KGB.

I read the class schedule of the room's occupant, and then I started reading his letters from home. I figured I would have to take on his identity. I was getting comfortable and even turned on a radio. Soon the real occupant of the room came back. (He had been watching the space shuttle launch down the hall.)

He asked, "What are you doing in my room?"

I said, "It's my room now."

He said, "No, it's my room."

"We're all supposed to switch rooms. Go over to the Jewish House and they will tell you about this."

"You're wearing my clothes."

"No. They're my clothes."

"No. They're mine," he said angrily and frustratedly, throwing his arms up in the air. "Oh, God."

"Go over to the Jewish House and they'll explain this to you."

He said, "No," with an angry look on his face.

I said, "Well, then call the police." I thought the police would side with me. He called campus security who then called the police.

They got Dr. Holley on the walkie talkie phone link, and I heard him say, "Yeah, he's a nut case."

They arrested me, and drove me up to McCormick hospital in Seattle. In the police car on the way up there, I started to take off my clothes because I figured they were not mine, but the cops told me to put them back on.

As I got out of the police car at McCormick hospital, I faked an epileptic seizure, but the cops just grabbed me, and brought me up to the psychiatric ward. When I got onto the psychiatric ward, my dad wanted to talk to me, but I wouldn't talk to him.

On the psychiatric ward, I tried to figure out who was CIA and who was not. I also tried to figure out who was a Pacific Lutheran University (PLU) alumnus, and who was a UPS alumnus. I thought there was a friendly rivalry within the CIA between the two schools, since they were in the same town, Tacoma.

I acted bizarre for several days while I was in the hospital. I tried to talk in code. Code, I thought, was usually words that had double meanings. However, I immediately agreed to take medication because Dr. Holley, I thought, was my commanding officer in the CIA, and he said I should take it. He said that I would get out of the hospital quickly if I took the medication. He also said I was schizophrenic. Feeling that that was a serious illness, I decided to take the medication. Of course, deciding that I was schizophrenic was incorrect, but not so surprising at this particular point, because when someone is acutely manic, it's hard to tell if they're acutely manic or schizophrenic. The treatment for the acute stages are similar. As I look back over my medical records, I see that I was given the treatment for mania while I was in the hospital. I had been on mood leveler Lithium, the treatment for manic depression, and hadn't missed a dose. He continued it, and gave me major tranquilizer Thorazine and major tranquilizer Pro-lixin in addition.

Medication eventually proves to be the hero of this book.

Gradually, I got better. Slowly I realized that the hospital was not a rest and relaxation haven for CIA agents. At first I wrote a lot of irrelevant notes to be put on my chart, then I gradually quit writing them. Eventually I wrote postcards to some of the people I had sent postcards to earlier, and told them I was in the psychi-atric ward, so please kindly disregard the previous postcards. I was well enough to realize that I had been crazy.

I was in the hospital for about three weeks. The tranquilizers made me catch up on sleep, which helped me a lot. After about a week, my delusions were gone, and they transferred me to the open ward. There were therapy groups, where we sat in a circle and talked, recreation groups, where we played games, and occu-pational therapy, which is better described as arts and crafts.

When I started to get better, my high school poker friends started calling me and visiting me at the hospital. They lived in Seattle and we were still friends four years after high school.

In the upcoming months of June and July 1981, two of my friends were getting married, Jim Eckhart and Jack Johnson. On one of the last days I was in the hospital, at the end of April, Jim, Jack, Phil Holland, Stan Gold, Dave Frish, and I met and dis-cussed plans for a stag party we would throw for Jim and Jack. Having morals, we opted for a clean stag, where we would just have dinner and play poker.

2

Healthy, Optimistic High School

The previous chapter described a manic episode I experienced during what should have been my senior year of college. I had been happy, healthy, and normal my whole life up through eleventh grade and the first part of twelfth grade in 1975 and 1976. Often since then, I have compared things to eleventh grade. I do this in order to see how far away I am from there, to search for the way back, or to figure out what the healthy me would have done lately, or should do right now. The years 1975 and 1976 were the standard for conduct and thought against which I judged myself when I was depressed in later years. I still suffer from manic depression to this day, but I am much better. I don't judge myself as much. Things are more acceptable in the present.

It is now January 1997. Over the past few years, I've gotten good medical treatment. I don't refer to the past healthy me as much in order to know what to do. I mostly know what to do.

During eleventh grade, life seemed really nice and beautiful. I was still super-jock, super-brain, and super-smooth compared to now. Manic depression had not struck yet, and life was normal and fun. I had always just assumed I would be healthy until I was 65. I had never heard of manic depression.

During eleventh grade, school and surrounding activities were easy and fun for me. As one of my extracurricular activities, I served as treasurer for Jewish Teen Group (JTG). During the summer before eleventh grade, I ran our chapter, because the president, Stan Gold, was in Israel. Stan Gold was a good friend of mine. We had been friends since seventh grade, and he was one of the guys I played poker with every weekend.

Our adult youth group leader, in JTG, was Darren Gollub, and he had been impressed with my leadership abilities in the summer. On the executive board were many great people including Geena Andrews who was the vice president. She was smart, and popular. I liked her a lot, as did most of the guys who knew her. (Years later, as I described in chapter 1, I wrote some bizarre and inappropriate postcards to her when I was manic. These were some of the "I'm running for Congress" ones and the "Wish I could bam you all" one.)

Besides spending time with the youth group, I was also working out for swimming and doing my homework. I had decided to try to get straight A's even if it meant having to do some homework. In junior high, I had a very simple policy; I didn't do homework and I got straight A's. That practice had worked in seventh through ninth grade, but tenth grade showed me that homework was necessary in senior high.

I socialized with a group of poker friends. We had been playing together almost every weekend since Christmas vacation in tenth grade. These were the best and the brightest group of friends I have ever had at any time in my life. Ever since I started experiencing long periods of depression, I have had trouble making friends. It took years to develop these ten friendships. We had gone to Mercer Island Junior High together. We had gone to Mercer Island Senior High together. Many of us had gone to grade school, Hebrew school, JTG, Sunday school, and Boy Scouts together. We were a tight-knit group that had in common honesty, responsibility, some athletic ability, and academic ability. We really enjoyed each other's company.

We played a lot of different poker games and other card games, and had our own slang for much of it. "BHGMFNPW" stood for 'Beacon Hill Guts, Mit Fours, Natch Pair Walks," which meant, "The guts game taught to us by our friend from Beacon Hill where the low card in your hand is wild, fours are always wild, and a pair not involving wild cards is necessary to win the pot if you are unopposed." A "criker" was a hand that tended to drive you up a creek without a paddle if you played it wrong. We would deal the cards and then go around the table stating whether we were in or out. If you said, "GTBITB," it meant: "Got to be in there boys." "Trout," meant you were out. The games were exciting, and people would miss games only if they had a date, or had to work. We played for high stakes and kept the extreme losses or wins confidential to avoid getting in trouble with our parents. Everyone payed their IOU's.

As a high school student, I was naturally living with my family. Let me try to explain them. My dad didn't want me to date from 1971 through 1975, when I was age twelve through age sixteen. I can only speculate as to why. I guess, projecting backwards, my dad wanted me to hang around with him instead of going out on dates. I didn't really date anyone during those years, but whenever I told my dad that I was with a group of guys and girls at someone's house, he said angrily, *"What were you doing over there?"*

"We were talking."

"Well , what were you doing over there?"

"Um, ah, we were talking," I would say, and then I would tiptoe on to another topic.

In fall of 1976, my dad's attitude problem became much worse. He got very lonely and jealous, as I'll describe in more detail in chapter 4 below.

The cause of my dad's loneliness, during the years 1971 to 1975, must have been my mom's manic depression. My mom, Nancy, suffered from manic depression from 1955, the same year that she and my father got engaged, up until she died in 1981. My mom was often sad, distracted, irritable, worried, tearful, dependent, and slow-thinking. This had to be from the depressed phase of manic depression. This would be bad enough to make my dad unhappy in his marriage to my mom. I think it made him want to hang around with me. I did not know my mom had a disease. My parents never told me. Any diagnosis of her had been very vague. We thought the way she was was normal for her, and we were used to it. She didn't seem that much different from other mothers. However, because my mom was less fun than she should have been, my dad wanted attention from me. That is why he didn't want me to date, and instead wanted me to hang around with him. This is my theory.

However, in January 1975, January of my tenth-grade year, things got worse. My mom had a stroke. She lost her ability to walk, talk, read, and write. About the only thing she could still do was shake her head, "Yes" or "No."

As a result of my mom's stroke in January, there was an even greater potential for my dad to want me to stick by him. He even-

tually wanted me to dump everyone else. He wanted companionship. He was married to my crippled mother, which had to be a
strain.

My mom's stroke did not cause me to be depressed (or manic).
I was a healthy tenth-grader in the fall of 1974. During that time
my mom was often irritable as a result of her poorly diagnosed
and almost completely untreated manic depression. She would
often yell at me for no reason. Perversely, the stroke turned out to
be a somewhat positive thing for me. One of the affects of her
stroke was that she was left unable to speak, so she was unable to
yell. So at that time, I felt her stroke wasn't completely bad, and I
looked on the bright side of the situation.

My childhood was happy. I never had a trace of manic depression myself. My childhood memories are mostly good. When I
was younger, even my moody mom was a good mother. I knew
she loved me, and she did nice things for me. She really didn't yell
at me much when I was little. We got along. I was glad she was
home when I got home from school. Once in a while I needed my
dad to give a different opinion on something my mom had said.

When I was little, my dad was also a good dad. He taught me
how to play baseball and how to fish.

I had a happy childhood. There is a study that proves that
manic depression is not related to any abnormalities in personality
before the illness set in. For that reason, I will not go into depth
about my childhood. I was happy and well adjusted as a kid. The
study of personality looked at thousands of healthy nineteen-year-
olds. These were nineteen-year-olds who had never experienced
any psychiatric illness in their lives. The researchers looked at the
ones who became manic-depressive years later. They looked back
at the records of how the manic-depressives had been when they
were healthy and nineteen. The researchers concluded that the
subjects' personalities when they were healthy did not differ from
those who had remained healthy. I was healthy and happy as a
child and adolescent. I didn't get manic depression until I was seventeen. Details of my childhood are irrelevant.

I'll get back to high school. The way I see it now, it was my
mom's depressed, irritable, mood, that made us fail to get along
during fall of tenth grade. I have spent years correcting people's
assumption that I was ever upset about my mom's stroke at the
time that it happened.

Before the stroke, she would scream because I would speak in the wrong tone of voice.

She would call me for breakfast and say, "Biiiiiiellllll."

I would say, "Whaaaaaaaattttttt?"

Then she would get really mad at me for mocking her. She would yell, "You listen to me. Don't you mock me. Don't let me ever hear you talk in that mimicking tone of voice. Do you understand me?"

I'd say, "Yes, Mom."

I was getting yelled at for using the wrong tone of voice.

I know now that the times when she was most depressed, were the times when my parents would go into their room, shut the door, and argue.

Then my dad would tell us, "Mother feels bad, so be *nice* to her."

Also, after the birth of each of my two younger brothers, she stayed in the hospital for a while, because she "felt bad," or so we were told. I know now that she was probably in the hospital for either postpartum mania or depression. We weren't allowed to visit her. Manic depression has a large genetic component. I got the genes for it from my mother.

When my mom had her stroke, when I was in tenth grade, I wanted her to get better so that she wouldn't suffer. Also, I knew that if my mom got better, my dad would act normally, and not act like a pest the way my widowed grandmother sometimes did. I figured that being widowed was like being married to someone very crippled. I figured this caused people to bug their kids. My dad was nearly widowed because my mom was so crippled from the stroke. My dad was in a worse situation than most widowers. He couldn't date because my mom was still half alive.

Also, it was just awful to see that my mom could go from healthy to crippled so quickly. It was terrible to know that we would have to live with her suffering and try to help her, even though helping her was so futile. We couldn't make her better. At temple when we said the mourner's prayer, I felt like we were saying it for my mom.

Over the next year, I gradually ended up ignoring my mom most of the time. I accepted that she was unable to speak, read, or write.

When I was in eleventh grade, it had been a year since my mother's stroke. Mom could just say, "Dee, de, deee, de, deee," in sentences. We could ask her yes or no questions and she would shake or nod her head. Sometimes her tone of voice, expression on her face, or gestures with her good left arm were a clue.

She'd say, "Dee, deee, dee, de, dee, dee, deee," pointing west.

We'd guess, "Something about Dad?"

She'd shake her head "No," and say, "Dee."

We'd guess, "Something about John?"

She'd nod.

We'd guess, "He's at the Felbers?"

She'd shake her head "Yes," and say "Dee."

Many times it was much tougher, and often, we never figured out what she meant.

In spite of my mother's illnesses, Dad was still easy to get along with during eleventh grade. He was a commercial real estate agent, and made a lot of money. He had already accumulated a lot of wealth. That year he went to work and minded his own business. He hired a household helper to come during the day to help with my mom, the housework, and my little brother, Johnny. Johnny was in third grade.

I had an older brother, Steve, who was away from home. He was a freshman in college. Steve had been very upset by my mother's stroke at first, and had hesitated to go away to college for his freshman year because of it. He felt bad about leaving Dad and Mom just eight months after the stroke. However, he knew he couldn't really help her, and so he reluctantly went off to college.

I had a younger brother, Rick, who was in eighth grade. He was upset about Mom's situation, but was gradually adjusting to the idea as well as he could.

I really only saw Johnny, Rick, and my parents during dinner. I ate quickly, and then I went and did my homework. I pretty much ignored Mom.

During the fall of junior year, Dad approved of my activities. These were the JTG youth group, homework, poker, and some pre-season swim workouts which kept me busy. The official swim season started November 15, with practice one hour before school and two hours after. It was a real strain, but it was what we had to do to become successful swimmers. My personal goal was to earn a letter, so I could wear a letter jacket, and be known as a jock. Traditionally, one had to be in the top twenty-four in regions to letter. I swam the 50-yard breaststroke in the medley relay, and the individual 100-yard breaststroke.

Swimming worked out really well in eleventh grade. The positive experience of swimming is one of the memories that would come to mind later during my manic highs. The following year, my swimming ability was to be the first casualty of my manic depression. You can't swim well when you are depressed and unable to concentrate.

In the middle of my eleventh-grade swimming season, two great things happened. My first-semester report card arrived bearing straight A's, even for the honors classes I was taking.

The second great thing that happened in January was that the change in semester put Melanie Carson in my physics class. She was one of the best looking girls in the school, and she sat right next to me. She was half Asian, with long, straight, shiny dark brown hair, and a perfect face. She was so beautiful that I had looked her up in the yearbook back in eighth grade, to find out what her name was. She had never been in any of my classes, even though we had gone to the same school since seventh grade. Now I finally had a chance to get to know her. This was a fantasy come true. Melanie was a lead singer in a local rock n' roll band. She was a good singer, and was popular around school because of it. In contrast to the wild rock n' roller image she portrayed on stage, she was known to be pretty strait-laced, and she hung out with some of the best athletes at school. Melanie Carson would have been a great girlfriend. The following year, she did go out with me once. Later, she was to become a depressive obsession. At that later time, when I was very depressed, I would think that only hugs and kisses from her could cheer me up.

I swam to impress girls like Melanie. I figured that when I got really good, I could invite girls to meets, and I could show off. I thought Melanie and others admired great athletes.

I swam the 100-yard breaststroke at a time of 1:13.5 or so at most of our meets that year. The last meet for me that year was the regional meet that was referred to as "regions." If I placed in the top twenty-four, I would letter, and be able to wear a letter jacket.

When my heat came up in regions, I walked to the end of the pool with the starting blocks. The guys from the previous heat got out of the pool and walked by me dripping wet and breathing heavily.

The starter said, "Swimmers up."

We got up on the starting blocks. I curled my toes over the edge.

"Take your marks."

I bent over and grabbed the starting block.

Bang! I dove in the water and swam as hard as I could. I remember pushing myself to swim even harder. By the third length I could see an opponent to my right out of the corner of my eye. I kept going, and my hands and quadriceps started to hurt like they were supposed to. I pushed myself to the end. At the end, I rammed my fingertips into the wall to stop the clock.

Much to my surprise, my time was 1:10.12. My best time ever. Being relaxed and rested from easier practices at the end of the season had really helped like it was supposed to. I placed twentieth, so I lettered.

I was quite proud of myself, and therefore felt so worthy of attention, that I asked Pete Drexel (star of our team), "Hey Pete, where are all the parties tonight?" Pete was very popular.

Pete said, "Well I don't really know. I'm going straight home after this. I've got to swim tomorrow."

I thought, oh, that's right. The finalists do have to stay rested. Well, at least I can come tomorrow and watch, knowing that the seniors in the breaststroke finals will be gone next year and I'll still be here.

During physics class on Monday I said to my friend Dave, loud enough for Melanie to hear, "The swim season is almost over, I wasn't a superstar, but I did letter."

Then it was springtime, and I didn't need to swim anymore until the next year, and I could buy a letter jacket. I was happy. I was very happy.

Honors Physics was not too hard, but we had to pay close attention in class. This left no time to talk to Melanie, but just sitting next to her was thrilling enough so that physics was fun. Even when we had a minute to talk, I could never think of anything to say, so I'd end up talking to Dave. I also managed to talk to Melissa, Melanie's lab partner, a little bit more than to Melanie. I figured both Melanie and Melissa had boyfriends.

I am now a long way from being in shape like I was then. The medication used to treat manic depression has had side effects including increased hunger. The hunger has made me gain weight.

In eleventh grade, I was 5' 9" and 145 pounds. I now weigh 215 pounds and am the same height.

In order for me to become a great swimmer for the next season, and be the number one breaststroker on our team, I figured I had to swim under 1:07.0 in twelfth grade. Then, I could also make it to the state meet and be a star. There was a summer Amateur Athletic Union (AAU) season that I could swim in. Plus I could run and lift weights. Doing these things over the summer could help me excel during the varsity season in the winter of my senior year.

Doing this was in apparent conflict with the alternative for me for that summer which was being a camp counselor in training, (CIT), at the camp I had attended the previous year. I had been hired as a CIT back in November. It was a big honor to be hired, because the counselor in training positions were hard to get. It would be a lot of fun, and it would be a better atmosphere for a social life and love life because there would be a lot of female staff. Staying home and swimming would make me a great swimmer for my senior year, but would not necessarily give me as good a social life during the summer.

There was a deciding factor. My dad had started to act bizarre. One day at the dinner table he asked, "Do the kids at JTG go in couples or do they come to events there as singles?"

"I dunno," I said.

"Well do the kids *go* in couples?" he asked.

"It depends."

"What does it *depend* on? I don't think kids used to date when I was in school. We didn't date until we were older. We were more normal back then. Romance is foolish when you are young. Dating is ridiculous until you are in your twenties."

Next I thought he was going to ask if my friends were human. He was saying that it was abnormal for teenagers to date.

He also said stuff like, "The people at this dinner table are the best friends you are ever going to have."

I thought that was ridiculous because I already had eight friends who were better friends than anyone at the table then. Also, I thought, is he saying my brothers and I will never fall in love and get married? Won't our spouses be better friends? What a jerk! I thought my love life could only improve at camp because there would be no dad there.

To help me decide what to do, I called my counselors from camp the previous year, and asked them what to do. They all said, "Go to camp."

One said, "You can swim at camp." I thought, yeah right, no coach, no teammates, no wall for flip turns, screaming kids in the way, and algae-infested lake water. Also, no stopwatches, no meets, not enough sleep, not enough time, cold weather, huge waves, and no moral support for swimming.

I thought it was either swim at home or not at all. If I didn't swim that summer, I could plan on being number two breast-stroker behind Jack who would be a sophomore. I would be a senior. It would be the pits. It would forever eliminate my chance to be a superstar. If I could be the number one breaststroker, I'd make it to the state meet doing the breaststroke part of the medley relay, even if I didn't make it in the individual 100-yard breaststroke.

Actually, very few of my teammates were swimming that summer. However, many of them were better than me, and didn't need to improve as much in order to make it to the state meet next year.

As long as my dad was questioning the dating practices of my friends, and therefore of myself, it seemed that for the short term, camp was a better place to be. There, I hoped I would have a better social life, and be more likely to meet someone and fall in love.

I called the head of the CITs, to ask her what we would be doing as CITs at camp. She was an attractive woman, and she was married to the camp director. They were both in their early twenties. I had met them at a group interview. Her husband was a long distance runner. He ran 5000-meter races just for fun. I described my dilemma.

She seemed very friendly and she said, "You can swim at camp."

I said, "Well, it is really tough to practice in a lake."

"We'll have a really big beach area. Our waterfront is going to be twenty yards across."

"Twenty?"

"Yeah."

"Oh, uh, and how deep?"

"Well, it is going to be real gradual. There will be a beginner and an advanced beginner section that goes up to three-and-a-half feet. Then an intermediate part that goes up to four-and-a-half, and then our swimmers area that, we're, well I think it will go up to nine feet," she said in a concerned, sweet, caring, feminine voice.

I really liked talking to her and she seemed to want me to come up there. Nobody as nice as she was telling me directly to swim in the AAU season. I thought it refreshing to see such a young, athletically inclined, well-adjusted couple who were legally married. They were a good role model.

I didn't tell her that twenty yards instead of twenty-five yards is really minor league, and that you can't just sort of kind of maybe have nine feet of water under the floating dock. Nine feet is the minimum for safe diving.

'Will there be time to swim?"

She said, "You get one free activity period each day, and there is free time for an hour every day. How much do you have to swim?"

"Well, at home I'd be swimming four hours per day."

"Would it be okay if you swam only two hours?"

"It would be *okay,*" I said, "but not as good. Tell me a little more about what we are going to do."

She gave me some more information. I told her I would call her back in a couple of days and tell her my decision.

Next I called Joel Stein. He had been selected to be a CIT and was also an athlete. He played football and baseball at a different high school nearby. He had been a camper in my cabin the previous summer. He knew how to get what he wanted out of life, and I trusted his judgment.

I said, "I'm thinking about swimming this summer in the AAU season at home. I could even win districts and make it to state next year in my event if I swim this summer."

He said, "Camp will be fun, you should come to camp. Some fine women are going to be there."

"Who?"

"Lisa Mudek is going to be there, and Jennifer Weinberg, and my friend [a Bellevue classmate], and Terry Lindgren and do you know [several of my other Bellevue classmates]?

"I don't know them."

"Oh they're nice. It is going to be great. A bunch of Mercer Island women are going, right?"

"Yes," I said, "[three Mercer Island girls] will be there."

"Oh, I know them."

"Do you think I should go?"

"Does your coach want you to stay?"

"Well, it would be better."

"Do you have a girlfriend who wants you to stay?"

"No."

"Oh, just come to camp. Do you know what? The head of the CITs said that during prep week we will go to a drive-in movie in a bus, and turn the bus sideways so that we can all see. Isn't that a riot?"

I said, "Yeah, I s'pose."

"Don't you think it would be fun to go to a drive-in movie in a bus, and turn the bus sideways!"

"Yeah, sounds kind of fun."

"C'mon Bill, it'll be fun. You can swim after camp."

We talked for a while.

At the end of the conversation I said, "Joel, thanks for your opinion. I'm going to think about it a while."

He said, "Okay, I hope you come, bye."

"Bye."

I thought it over and decided I'd do it as long as I could swim 3000 yards per day. This should take an hour and fifteen minutes if I did a lot of breaststroke.

I called the head of CIT's and told her I would go, as long as I could swim an hour and fifteen minutes a day. She said that was doable, and so I said I'd see her there. I would put up with the algae, no coach, no clock, no wall, and no meets.

Other things were happening this Spring of eleventh grade besides my debate on being a CIT. The eleventh-grade swim season had ended in early March. After that, I had much more free time. While I did a couple JTG things, actually I started studying even more. I wanted to be able to get into any college. I wanted to have the option of going away because Dad never understood the concept of my dating. I would never qualify for a scholarship based on financial need, because Dad made too much money, but he could afford to pay for any college I got into. I wanted to get into Harvard, Yale, or Stanford. It took good grades to get into those places, and I wanted to graduate from high school with distinction. We had gotten our Preliminary Scholastic Aptitude Test (PSAT) results back in the winter and I, along with almost everyone I played poker with, scored in the 99th percentile. I was a National Merit Commended Student. I was very proud of myself and my friends.

I studied more for all my classes once swimming was over that year. When it was warm and sunny, I studied outside, and worked on my tan.

Meanwhile, I was making no progress with Melanie Carson. I could never think of anything to say to her, and there was no time to say it anyway. After every physics test, almost everyone would tell almost everyone else what score he or she got on the test. Melanie, however, would not tell me, even though she sat right next to me. However, she didn't show anyone else her test paper either. The only person she showed was her lab partner Melissa. I didn't know if that was because she did well and was being modest, because she did lousy and was embarrassed, or if she was just being unfriendly. Her lab partner however, Melissa Jenkins, was friendly and had asked me to help her with her physics homework a few times in study hall. I gladly obliged. After school was over, before camp started, I asked Melissa out. Melissa agreed to go out with me.

I think I asked her out after school was over for the year, because I thought that would reduce the gossip factor around school. Our date crossed clique boundaries. She hung out with the jocks, and I hung out with the Jews.

We went to a movie, and then had a pizza. I had fun on the date and was glad that I was out with someone of her intelligence, looks, status, and warmth.

I don't remember much of what we said; however, *I remember sitting in my car outside her house afterward saying life was great and fun.*

I said, "The biggest problem most people have is deciding what sport to go out for, or who to ask out."

We kissed goodnight and the date was over.

Now that I am manic-depressive, the euphoric manic mood reminds me often very intensely of this last half of eleventh grade, early twelfth grade, and the summer in between. Normal good moods, like the moods I experienced then, didn't happen much after that.

I attended Mercer High graduation in 1976. I felt sad because I was actually going to have to leave town that summer to find a place where I was allowed to have a girlfriend. I had, of course, many friends and acquaintances, one year older, who were graduating. I remember the chorus sang the line "Do you remember the times of your life?" The song made me sad because a lot of the people graduating were staying in Seattle indefinitely, and here I had to leave to get away from my dad, and I was a year younger. If my home had been normal, I could have kept up with swimming and gone on dates while living at home.

My theory is that in my father's paradoxical, contradictory mind, he stopped himself from saying "You can't go to camp," because that would be public evidence that he was clinging to me inappropriately. Then I could have told all my friends and their parents and his friends and the entire world that my dad doesn't want me to have a job. He would have looked bad. It probably also helped a lot that my older brother Steve had had the same CIT job two summers earlier, and incidentally, had *not* fallen in love.

I think that with my dad, it was a bit of an "out of sight, out of mind" type of thing. With me living at home, he would have been attached to me, and would have been jealous when I had a date. Luckily he allowed me to go up to camp. He may have feared the community's reaction if he hadn't let me take the job. He probably felt that he still had long-term control over me, because camp was only for a period of ten weeks. Then I had to come home for twelfth grade.

I kept swimming and weightlifting right up until the day before camp. That was Tuesday, June 15th, 1976.

3

Camp: Good Times

Many of the camp staff took a charter bus. The campers didn't come for another week. Some of the notables on my bus were Lisa Mudek who was already sitting with Joel Stein when I got on the bus. She said, "Hi, Hannon!" enthusiastically.

I said, "Hi, Lisa!"

She had dark brown hair, a very outgoing personality, and a big smile. I liked her, but she seemed to be involved with Joel already. She was going to be a CIT, and was from Spokane.

Another notable was Jennifer Weinberg. She had long, straight, shiny, blonde hair and big blue eyes. I didn't really know her, but wanted to get to know her. She had been a CIT last year, and now would be a full-fledged counselor. She seemed very self-assured and happy which made me like her.

The ride lasted for an hour and a half. I sat by myself just kind of looking around at everybody and doing a little eavesdropping. At one point Terry Lindgren sat in the seat behind me. She was from Bellevue.

We introduced ourselves and she said, "I heard you have to swim every day up at camp."

I said, "I don't have to, but I want to, because I want to be good next year."

She asked, "Oh, what event do you swim?"

"The 100-yard breaststroke."

"Do you swim anything else?"

"No. I'm not really good at anything else."

"How long have you been swimming?"

"Three years."

"Are you very good?"

"All I really did this year was letter, but next year I hope to make it to state."

'Oh, you will."

She said, "I'm a cheerleader, and I play softball, so I know what it's like."

When we got to camp, the first big task was to unload the truck that had all our baggage on it. At one point, I was carrying something small and one of Jennifer Weinberg's friends said, "Bill, will you carry this?"

I said, "No, I'll get it on the next trip."

Jennifer gave me the "evil eye" so I said, "Okay, okay, I'll take it."

At least she knew I existed.

Later that afternoon, we CITs played some "get to know each other" games. The full-fledged counselors were in different cabins, and we got to know them at dinner that night. At dinner we memorized the grace for after meals, and then listened to talks by the head counselor, the program director, the waterfront director, and the music director.

Then we had some free time. Another male CIT and I went over to the training week cabin of some women counselors to see Jennifer Weinberg. It was a little adventure going over to the girls' cabin of these counselors a year older than us. However when we got there, we didn't have much to say, so we soon left. Later, Joel told us that Jennifer had a boyfriend at home. He was a basketball player, and so was she.

Meanwhile, it looked like Joel and Lisa were going to be a couple. I was annoyed at that thought. I was jealous.

Later that night, there was a campfire with someone playing guitar. Maria, a CIT from Olympia, Washington put her arm around me and said, "Let's go to the campfire."

I said, "Okay." I liked the attention, but thought she was a bit forward.

I think we made small talk about the weather or something. She was fairly pretty. We talked for quite a while. We were lying under the stars at the campfire, and her arm was still around me.

After a while, I said, "Do you want to go for a walk?"

She said, "No, thanks." A few minutes later she said, "Do you want to go hear one of my records?"

I said, "Sure."

We went back to the lounge cabin, and she played some song about a psychoanalyst. It went, "My analyst told me, that I was right out of my head." I thought the song was stupid. Who would listen to a song about an analyst anyway? Did Maria have an analyst? I wondered. This was too strange.

She asked me if I liked it. I just shrugged and left soon after that.

The second night, Zack, a CIT, was trying to go to sleep and some others of us were in our beds also. Zack had not slept for two days because he was having some psychological misgivings about being a CIT. I remember somebody walked into the cabin and let the door slam behind him.

Zack said sarcastically, "Could you please slam the door a little louder?"

Joel started laughing and laughing, "Oh could you please slam the door a little louder?" He laughed some more.

Fairly quickly, we all went to sleep, except maybe Zack. I think now that Zack was suffering from depression because that is often accompanied by sleep disturbance. I didn't understand it then. If it was depression, I certainly understand it now. In just six months, I would be massively depressed myself.

For the next five days or so we did stuff to prepare for the arrival of the campers. We got briefed by the waterfront director on how she wanted the swimming strokes taught and how to teach canoeing. We also learned the camp songs, and we went over camp rules.

Starting on the second day of camp, I swam almost every day. I swam 3000 yards. That was 150 lengths across one of the docks in the lake. I always had to have a lifeguard present, but it wasn't that hard to find one. The hard part was making myself find the time and making myself spend it on swimming. I also started doing pull-ups on a rafter in the showers and push-ups on the floor in the showers.

We CITs did go to a drive-in movie in a school bus and park it sideways. It wasn't that much fun. Lisa was already going with Joel, and Jennifer was a counselor not a CIT. I mostly just sat and watched the movie "Clowns."

Another night they showed a movie in the big auditorium. I sat next to Jennifer and put my arm around her. She didn't move away, but after about ten minutes, I got up to get a drink, and when I came back she had moved, and was sitting very close to a female friend of hers, in a way so that I couldn't really reach her. A small defeat. Still, years later, when I felt a manic exciting high mood, I thought about Jennifer, because just being around her was such a thrill back when I was normal in 1976.

Towards the end of the week, we got our cabin assignments for when the campers arrived. We would still live in our separate CIT cabins, but we would be assigned to help lead the campers from a specific cabin. I was assigned to the cabin of a guy who had been my counselor when I was a camper the previous year. Now we would be co-counselors.

One hour of my day was for CIT education. The topics were mostly on Jewish matters. I chose the "Keeping Kosher" class on the Jewish dietary laws. Lisa and I talked to each other a lot on the way to and from that class.

I taught campers how to swim during three other activity periods.

In my free hour I would swim a lot, usually about 1800 yards. I'd then swim another 1200 yards during late afternoon free time, if I could get someone to lifeguard for me. Lisa often was willing to lifeguard. That was nice. Swimming and teaching swimming lessons in the pea soup type of algae we had to contend with in the lake required that I take a shower after every time I was in the lake. This meant I took up to three showers a day. Also, it meant changing clothes about six times a day.

Later in my life, when I was depressed, it was a struggle to get dressed once a day. Now, I still use simple things like changing clothes as a guide when I am fighting off depression. If I can change clothes in two minutes and not let it bother me, then I know I'm not depressed.

It is swimming from that summer and the next fall that would sometimes come back to me when I got manic in later years. Being manic sometimes felt very good, and that summer and fall also felt very good. When I got manic I would often start alternately flexing first my right hand, then my left hand. This is what you do when you swim freestyle. The feeling good of being manic reminded me of the feeling good from the swimming and the great social life in this year of 1976.

Camp led to a relationship which made me the happiest of my life. I began to notice the babysitter who was sixteen. There were some staff who were married and had little kids, and so there was a babysitter on the staff. Her name was Angie Spiess. She was quiet, but always smiled at me. She had long dark brown hair. She went swimming sometimes. One of her swimsuits was made of the same fabric as one of mine.

Down at the waterfront, whenever we were wearing our matching swimsuits, I would say, "Hey, nice swimsuit."

Angie would give me a big smile. She was quiet, but I could tell she cared about the kids she babysat, and I thought that was sweet. She seemed very wholesome and loving.

There was a problem finding time to swim. I tried to swim everyday, unless I was sick or unless there was another absolutely essential task that conflicted. I wanted to be a star swimmer the next winter. I swam in order to have a sense of accomplishment, to be part of a team, and to earn the respect and admiration of others, including Melanie Carson back home.

When I was walking to the beach area with Lisa, we talked about camp stuff. What we talked about wasn't really important. It was just her company that meant so much to me. I just remember that she was intelligent, responsible, and caring. She took her job as a counselor seriously, and really cared about her campers, so maybe she could take a relationship with me seriously if she ever got tired of Joel.

I talked with Lisa a bit about swimming. Sometimes she asked, "How much do you have to swim?"

I said, "Well I don't *have* to swim. I usually do 3000 yards a day. I already did 1200 today, so now I have to do another 1800. I'll still be on the team if I don't swim this summer, I just won't be as good."

Sometime during the third session of camp, I got more interested in Angie Spiess, the babysitter. She seemed to like me and I liked her mature manner. Second and third session, we CITs ate and slept with our cabin's campers, except on Sabbath when we could ask a staff person of the opposite sex to supervise a table with us for meals. On Sabbath, the campers could eat with whomever they wanted. So, I asked Angie to supervise a table with me. The first time we did that, it was nice, but we didn't talk much. I still was more interested in Lisa and Jennifer.

In this last session of camp, I led an exercise activity and more swimming lessons. Teaching swimming lessons was good experience for me. I had to develop good communication skills and good people skills. I had to be fair when judging the campers' swimming abilities, and I had to know how to praise and encourage them. It was good leadership training. Also during the last session, I officiated at a tetherball tournament and I continued to swim.

Meanwhile one CIT, Zach, the guy who had apparently been depressed and was having trouble sleeping at the beginning of camp, remained somewhat troubled. He once saw me look at my watch and know exactly what to do by what time it was, and he asked, "Do you find that a routine helps?"

I said, "Yes, because then you don't have to think. You just know what to do, by knowing what you always do at that time."

In later years, when I was depressed, I often had the problem of not knowing what to do next. I hesitated to do things because nothing seemed fun. I rarely built up a routine of doing things at a certain time because that would require that I consistently thought that those things were important. When depressed, everything seemed pointless and stupid. Nothing seemed important. At camp, I was healthy. A lot of stuff seemed important.

On one Sabbath, I again asked Angie to sit with me. She did, and again, we didn't really talk that much, but she was starting to seem even sweeter.

Joel was really getting jealous because Lisa would lifeguard while I swam. Lisa seemed to like me quite a bit.

Once, I took two days off because I had a cold, so I didn't swim. Then, the next day, I was walking toward the beach with Lisa, and Joel said very sarcastically, *"Oh, I'm so glad your cold is gone."*

I saw Joel and Lisa have arguments, but I wasn't sure what they were about. However, Joel and I were still friends.

He told me that he was so fed up with Lisa that he'd like to get to know Angie Spiess. His saying this helped me realize that Angie was worth paying more attention to.

The next day when I was walking by Angie, I said, "Hi, Beautiful." She blushed and smiled.

The next couple of nights after evening program, when everybody gathered at the flag circle for socializing, I came up behind Angie and put my arms around her waist. She sank back into my arms. It felt good.

About eight days before the end of camp, there was a disco dance. I danced with Angie all night. It gave me a really warm feeling to be with her. We took a break outside to get some water.

She said, "There is this really cool thing you can do. Look up at one bright star, and then twirl around. Keep looking at the one bright star. The other stars will twirl around in a big circle around the one you are looking at."

We both twirled around for a minute. Then we were so dizzy that we fell down to the grass. We lay on our backs and looked up at the stars.

I said, "It's a clear night tonight. No clouds."

"The stars are brighter here than in the city."

"Not as many lights around."

We then went in and danced several more dances. I kissed her on the cheek during "She's Gone" by Hall and Oates. There were several more songs after that. At the end of the dance I gave her a big hug and told her I'd go to her cabin after I got my campers to bed and went to the staff meeting.

I finally got my campers to bed, dealt with the staff meeting, and walked over to Angie's cabin. We spent a lot of time together that night and the next several evenings. It was great having a girl-friend. It was heaven on earth.

Angie had to leave camp a few days early to start tennis practice at her high school. I was going to swim one of those last days, but Lisa wouldn't lifeguard for me and acted kind of cold.

The last two days at camp were spent taking down the docks and cleaning up. I stayed up late the last night saying good-bye to people and didn't get much sleep. I looked forward to seeing Angie after camp because she lived fairly close to me.

4

My Great Fall Falls Apart

When I got home from camp, I called Angie. She called me back a couple days later. We went out to eat. She told me about the classes she had this fall, and her tennis team. I talked about my classes and swimming. We talked about what movies we wanted to see, and also she mentioned a couple plays she wanted to see. We talked about people from camp too. I liked that she acted very mature and sophisticated.

Then we parked in an elementary school parking lot, and made out. It was enjoyable for me, but we were both very sexually inexperienced. It was not very pleasurable for her. This hurt our relationship a lot.

Besides our sexual inexperience, another problem was beginning to develop. My father was getting jealous of my relationship with Angie. I was surprised at the depth of his jealousy and anger. I thought it grossly unfair that my friends had decent people to live with, while I had to live with an ogre. The ogre wanted me to stay home with him rather than go out with Angie. He was lonely because of my mother's condition. As a result, my dad would go into a jealous rage *every time* I went out with Angie. Each evening I spent with her, was less time I had in the same house as my dad. Also, he wanted me to have no commitment to anything or anybody other than him. *On weekday evenings when I was home, I'd be in my room doing homework, and he'd come into my room and ask me to come watch TV with him!* He was anti-homework, anti-Angie, anti-swimming, and he didn't want me to get a job.

My brother Steve was away being a sophomore at college. My dad had begrudgingly let him go because he had decided the year before that he couldn't call off Steve's normal life just because of my mom's stroke. My brother Rick was fourteen and didn't really date. He stayed home and read. My brother Johnny was nine and hung around with my dad. My mom was there too, but, of course, was not much fun. That was not enough companionship for my dad.

On Saturday evenings my dad would notice that I had taken a shower. So after I got dressed, he would barge into my room and start screaming at me. He would scream that Saturday nights were for the family to watch TV together. He yelled that I was wearing out my mom's car by driving to Angie's house. "Driving costs a lot of money," he said even though he was a millionaire. He could have afforded about two hundred cars for our family's personal use.

I offered to use some of my $6,000 of Bar Mitzvah money to pay him for the use of the car.

He yelled, "That's not what your money is for!"

I said, "Should I quit swimming and get a job to pay for the use of the car?"

"I don't want you to do that!"

"Get out of my room!"

"Just a minute, I'm your father!" he screamed. *"Weekends are supposed to be a family time!"*

"Get out of my room!"

He would stay in my room and yell for about five more minutes and then he would finally get out.

My dad was also anti-swimming. At camp, I had sacrificed to swim 3000 yards on sixty out of the seventy days of camp. I had put up with an inadequate workout situation. Now I was at home and could work out in a nice clean pool at the Jewish Community Center (JCC). I installed a pull-up bar in my garage, and continued doing sixty pull-ups and sixty push-ups every day. I had won the CIT biggest boobs award in the male category for my large chest muscles. Now I found out my dad was anti-swimming.

There are ten varsity swimming events. The school record in one or two events usually gets broken every year. One day in early September, I told my younger brother Rick, "My goal is to break the school record in the 100-yard breaststroke."

My dad heard me, and he said, "Oh, don't break any records."

Alarmed, I asked, "Why shouldn't I break *any records?*"

"Don't break any records," he said.

"*Why not?*" I asked.

"*Oh!* Don't break any records," he said annoyed.

This continued for a while and it became very clear that my dad wanted me to quit the swim team so I would have more time to hang around with him. I was appalled.

My mom could understand spoken words and I told her and my dad that I wanted to live with my aunt, uncle, and cousins.

My dad said, "Stick with us. We'll have some fun."

I said, "I don't want to have fun at our house, I'm planning on having fun outside our house with other people."

My mother said, "Dee, dee deeee dee," and motioned to her paralyzed arm. She was agreeing with me.

My father said, "No, stick with us. We'll have some fun."

This sounded absolutely sinister to me.

The next day, I asked my Aunt Brenda and Uncle Mike Felber if I could live with them. I told them that my dad was anti-girl-friend, anti-swimming, and anti-homework. I should have said to them, my father wants me to commit adultery, be a wimp, a couch potato, and a drop-out. The adultery part was because he sometimes said, "Date someone else." That meant date someone I didn't like as much.

My aunt and uncle said that I could live with them, but not if my father objected. My uncle was partners with my dad. Of course, my father objected.

Next I called Jim Eckhart, one of my poker friends. I knew he probably had a spare bedroom at his house. I said, "Jim, this is Bill."

"How's it going?" Jim asked.

"Well, not so good," I said.

"What's wrong?"

"Do you guys have a spare bedroom at your house?"

"Yeah. Why?"

"Ask your parents if I can live there."

"Why, are things tough at home?"

"Well, I have a girlfriend now. Her name is Angie, and my dad doesn't like it when I go out with her."

"Why not?"

"I don't really know. I think he's jealous because he wants me to stick around here with him."

"Is your mom (pause)" he said, before I interrupted.

"My mom, I guess, is the root of the problem, she can't talk normally which I guess is why my dad wants me to stay home and keep him company. He's lonely."

"I see," he said. "Well, I'll ask my parents."

"It's not for sure yet, I have to see how things go."

"Okay, I'll be talking to you."

"Okay. Thanks, bye."

For it to have really been worth it, I thought at the time, Angie and I would have to have been really getting along. Little did I know that my dad would just get worse. At the time, I figured that it was good to put up with my dad because then he would pay for college. He made so much money, that I could never get a scholarship. Most scholarships were based on financial need, and didn't take into account that rich parents might be abusive. So if I wanted any help paying for college, I had to get along with my dad. If I ran away, he certainly wouldn't pay for school. I thought, incorrectly, that college was essential. It is especially true that my dad wouldn't pay for college if I left, since the point of moving out would have been so that I would never have to speak to him again. My dad was a very bad influence. Parents are some of the strangest things that can happen to a person.

The stress of my dad's yelling really only lasted about an hour into my dates with Angie. It took about twenty minutes to drive to her house. I was very much looking forward to seeing Angie, but I was still thinking about my dad's yelling.

I picked her up and I felt we should talk about something light while I was driving to wherever we were going. She never gave me warm greetings. Therefore, I felt I had to warm her up a bit with small talk before I brought up the heavy duty issue of my dad. I didn't want to sit in her driveway and tell her, because then her parents might watch. I didn't want to park somewhere along the way to tell her. Parking somewhere is what we did to make out. I didn't want to confuse the issue. It usually took about twenty minutes to drive to Phantom Lake or wherever we were going.

While we were walking around the lake, I told her, "My dad doesn't like it when we go out."

We were getting along very poorly so all she said was, "Oh."

I paused and waited for her to say more. She didn't.

I said, "I think it is because he is jealous because he wants me to stay home with him. My mom had a stroke and she can't talk normally, so I think he is lonely."

"Oh, that's too bad," said Angie.

Angie's tone sounded quite sympathetic to my parents' troubles. This bit of sympathy was the polite way that everyone responds to hearing that someone is sick. It was very hard to explain to her that I was not sympathetic to my parents' troubles. I didn't try to explain it because sometimes it seemed like Angie didn't like it when we went out either. I wasn't sure why. Also, there didn't seem to be much either of us could do to change my parents.

I just hugged her and said, "Well, I'll ignore him."

I often wished I could live with her family. Yet we were never getting along well enough for me to mention that even as a fantasy. It just wasn't done that much anyway. I was seventeen and she was sixteen.

I tried to get her to talk about anything, to act bubbly. She never really did. We talked about our classes sometimes. Just being with her was pleasant, though, even if we didn't talk much. However, she often seemed a little upset with me. We went to movies and a couple Shakespearean plays, but we were lousy communicators. About all she talked about some nights was the plot of the Shakespeare play we were about to see, so that I would understand the play. Still, I felt it was better to have a quiet girlfriend than no girlfriend at all.

It's her being annoyed that also helped lead to my compromise with myself of seeing her only once a week. If she was annoyed on Saturday night, I didn't want to call her back until Tuesday. Then we made plans for the next weekend. It seemed necessary to give her several days notice. She always agreed to go out with me the next weekend, but there was always some doubt in my mind whether she would agree or not. However, through September and October of 1976, I was still optimistic. I felt things with Angie would eventually work out.

By rationalizing that I really had to do homework on weekday nights, and by rationalizing that I really had to see my male poker friends once a week, I accepted a compromise with myself. I decided that it was reasonable to see Angie only once a week.

In spite of the fact that we had an imperfect relationship, and in spite of all my dad's yelling, this period was actually the happiest time in my life ever. Angie still was more of a plus than a minus. I was so happy, that when I woke up a couple minutes before my alarm rang every morning, I lay there hoping for it to ring! I was looking forward to each new day that much.

I was going to school six-and-a-half hours per day, and enjoying it. I was working out for swimming three hours a day and enjoying that. I was studying three hours a day. Life was really very fun. I was happy with myself. I had pride in everything I was doing except living with my dad. Each day was a new adventure and a chance to achieve something new, fun, and positive. I liked doing well on tests in school.

As my relationship with Angie grew worse, I started going to some parties held by people from my school. I was hoping to run into Melanie Carson. I never did. She was the rock singer who had sat beside me in physics class. I still considered her one of the most desirable girls in the school. She was never in any of my classes again.

At the beginning of November, something awful happened. Someone stole my letter jacket. I left it hanging up unlocked in the general locker room. The season hadn't started yet, so I didn't have a varsity locker. I was depressed for a week. The letter jackets take about six weeks to order, and by then it would've been winter, when it is too wet to wear one of them. I reported the theft to police, but they weren't able to do anything. I was depressed about the loss of the jacket for about five days. I had never felt that bad for five days in a row in my life. Then, I cheered up.

For the next couple weeks, my mood was good. However, I didn't call Angie, and she didn't call me.

Swim practice started then, and I was about the fastest on our team in every event except backstroke. My freestyle had improved markedly because I had swum a lot of freestyle that summer and fall. I had swum freestyle because I had strained my knees several times swimming too much breaststroke. The freestyle kick is different than the breaststroke kick, so if your breaststroke muscles are strained, you can still swim freestyle and that's what I had done. I was optimistic because I was doing so well in practice, that I thought maybe I could win districts and regions, and be declared Most Valuable Swimmer in the conference. Then I would've achieved superjock status. I was swimming with the distance swimmers and lapping them at long freestyle swims.

After not seeing Angie for a few weeks, I became what I thought was indifferent about her. I was in a good mood, I figured, regardless of her. Figuring at least it would stop my dad from screaming, I broke up with her over the phone.

I actually said, "I'm sorry I haven't called you for so long."

Hesitantly, she said, "That's . . . okay," with a strained voice.

I said, "I don't know how to tell you this, but let's go out with other people."

She started crying and I said, "Is everything else okay?"

She said tearfully, "Yeah."

I said, "I'm sorry. You can still call me sometime." She never did.

After our break-up in late November, I was depressed for about a week. I hadn't expected that, and I regretted it. However, I didn't call Angie back. And she didn't call me.

After that week, I cheered up and felt okay. I was looking forward to a good swimming season. I started swimming lots of breaststroke in practice. Unfortunately, my breaststroke had changed because I had swum some breaststroke pull only, (no kick, just arms) with paddles on. This was when I had strained my knees doing too much breaststroke kick. Unfortunately, the paddles had altered my stroke for the worse. I had tampered with success. It usually takes a big effort to change your stroke once it is set a certain way. Now my breaststroke was set the wrong way. Actually, I didn't realize my stroke had changed much for quite a while.

I was in a good mood through the middle of December when we had our first meet. I went 1:13.5 in the 100-yard breaststroke, and did some equivalent time in the 50-yard breaststroke. I didn't swim any freestyle in the meet, so I didn't know how fast my freestyle was. In practice we didn't really get timed. I was disappointed with my breaststroke times. I had averaged 1:13.5 the previous year. I had gone 1:13 point something in our fifteen meets, except for the first one and the last two, during the previous season. I thought all my work in the off season should've made me go 1:09.5.

I came home after the meet. There was no poker game that night. I sat in our den, at first reading a newspaper, and then looking straight ahead absorbed in the question of whether or not to switch events to freestyle. This would mean one less breaststroker on a team that only had three. It would also mean swimming against different teammates, some of whom were my friends. It really would have been a smart move because there were plenty of freestyle events.

My dad was in the room, and noticed I wasn't talking to him and wasn't reading the paper, so he asked angrily, "Are you upset about something?"

I said, "No. I'm thinking about switching events."

He said angrily, "If this swimming is going to make you upset, maybe you should *quit* swimming."

I said, "I'm not upset. It would be good strategy to switch events."

It wasn't good strategy to be discussing swimming with an enemy of swimming, like him, though.

He said, "Oh, don't switch events."

"Why not?" I asked.

"Just swim the event you've been swimming," he said.

I stayed in the room about three minutes silently so he wouldn't chase me and accuse me of storming out of the room. Then I walked to my bedroom and shut the door. I felt totally at a loss, totally helpless. I felt like I would get a lot of grief no matter which way I turned. My dad would give me a hard time for swimming freestyle. I thought that my freestyling teammates would tell me to swim breaststroke, "You're good at it, Bill," is what they would say, but in reality they just feared my competition.

I lost sight of the fact that my dad would give me a hard time no matter what. I think now that in reality I should've swum the 200-yard freestyle, the 100-yard freestyle and the 4 x 100-yard freestyle relay. However, I couldn't put up with any more garbage. The algae and the waves and the cold weather at camp I had tolerated. However, I couldn't sacrifice my comfort any more. I needed help.

I called my coach at home which normally wasn't done. I asked him if I should swim freestyle. What I swam was ultimately his decision, but he was flexible. Everyone wanted to swim what they were best at. They then got even better in it by swimming it in practice and meets. If I was going to swim freestyle, I needed to start doing the distance freestyle practices. Coach was sympathetic. He said it could be okay, and he'd put me in the 500-yard freestyle in the alumnae meet. Talking to him made me feel better in the same way having a good cry helps a person feel better. It's not the most happy feeling.

I would not know it for sure for five years, but this was the beginning of my manic depression. This was the beginning of a depressed phase. The date was December 10, 1976. Everything I'd done up to this point was very athletic, intelligent, and socially sophisticated compared to the bizarre stuff that manic depression would make me do from this point forward.

The first major casualty of the depressed phase would be my swimming. At the time, it felt like my poor swimming caused my depression, but in hindsight it seems likely that my depression caused my poor swimming. There was somewhat of a vicious circle. This is because once manic depression starts by a triggering event, it goes on, and on, and on indefinitely. Then the disease causes sad events. Sad events don't cause the disease. Depression interferes with concentration and therefore interferes with athletic ability. You lose competitions and that is sad. It interferes with concentration and therefore you lose work and school ability. It is depressing to do a bad job at work or school because of poor concentration. A chronic depression that goes on and on causes irritability, which makes you lose friends. Depression can cause suicide, and then you lose everything.

The stressful events triggering the disease were my break-up with Angie and life with my dad. I got the genes for susceptibility to manic depression from my mom. If I would have had a successful, romantic, continuing relationship with Angie, my manic depression may have been delayed indefinitely. I could have avoided the stress of breaking up. On the other hand, having a steady relationship is not the treatment or prevention for manic depression. Relationships can be stressful. Happily married people can get manic depression. Single manic-depressives can get married and it certainly doesn't cure them. Also, breaking up is depressing for everyone. However, most people cheer up in a few weeks after a break-up.

To get the chronic depression or the mania of manic depression, you have to have the genes for it. Fortunately for humanity, only 0.5 percent of the population gets the disease. That 0.5 percent has the genes for it. Another smaller fraction of a percent of the population have the genes for it, but are lucky enough to go their whole life without the disease.

Manic depression is also called *bipolar affective disorder*. Bipolar means having two extremes. Affective means having to do with mood. One extreme of mood is depression, which is a period when there is prolonged sadness, crying, low self-esteem, suicidal thoughts or actions, and many more symptoms. The other extreme of mood, a manic episode, was described in the first chapter, "KGB Bloodhounds." This is when you feel so great about yourself that you think you are an FBI agent, God, Jesus, or John Lennon, for example. You are laughing, you are happy, you don't sleep, and you are totally out of touch with reality.

I have manic depression type one. There is a type two. People with type two do not get as manic. They do not lose touch with reality, but they do get very hyper.

A full 10 percent of the population does get depressive illness. This is also called *unipolar affective disorder.* These people have problems with depression, but do not ever get manic.

A complete list of symptoms of depression and mania can be found at the end of this book.

I inherited the genes for manic depression from my mother. If I had an identical twin, he'd have a 70 percent chance of getting it at sometime in his life. If I were to have children, roughly one out of seven of my children would get the disease. The genes just make you susceptible to it. It usually takes environmental stress to trigger it. Once manic depression starts, though, it has a life of its own. When my manic depression started, the biochemical agents in my brain were present in the wrong amount. My mind's neurotransmitters such as norepinephrine, serotonin, dopamine, and others known or still unidentified were malfunctioning. There are medications which help a lot in restoring the chemical balance, but they are not perfect. Still, medication is the hero of this book, as the reader will see.

5

Depression Slows My Swimming

In practice the next week I swam some freestyle, but mostly breaststroke. I wasn't that depressed yet, I just wasn't too happy. I still swam okay despite reduced morale. I still thought I could do okay in either stroke.

We had a meet that Friday, December 17, which was right before the start of Christmas vacation. We were competing against Kent. They had an outstanding team, but we knew we could keep it close if we swam well. Anyway, I went 1:15.3 in the 100-yard breaststroke. That was a terrible time. I didn't know what was wrong with me. I would learn much later that what was wrong with me was depression.

The next night was the Winter Fling Dance held by our school. It was a girl-ask-guy dance. A girl named Ann asked me to the dance. We went on the date, but I was feeling so awful that I was silently narrating to myself the story of this date, and the story seemed to be a tragedy. The narrator was a cross between horror science fiction narrator Rod Serling and sportscaster Howard Cosell. It was the tragic story of a date which was supposed to be fun, but instead was not. My internal narration went:

Here is the tragic story of a man who was a potential star athlete. He recently swam the unspeakable time of 1:15.3, and can never redo that race. He should be noticing how fancy everyone's clothes are; instead, he dwells on the fact that his date, Ann, needs a tan. He forgets it's December. He should think what a nice cross-cultural, educa-

tional, and adventurous experience it is to eat at a foreign restau-
rant. He should be enjoying it. Instead he is thinking this food is for-
eign, so it won't be any good. He should be feeling very sophisticated,
stylish, and grown up, and should be doing his best to make sure his
date has fun. Instead he wants to go home and cry. He wants to go sit
in his bedroom and regroup, retrench, retreat, or redirect. He wants
to figure out how he has managed to enter The Twilight Zone.

I thought, how could I have a good time when I had swum so
slow? I think I remember wishing Ann would ask me about my
classes, because I was still doing well at those. Also, I could've
told her about my parents if she would have asked. However, I
was too untalkative to bring either of these topics up. I was too
busy bumming out. At the end of the date, she asked me in, but I
declined and just gave her a quick kiss good night. I didn't want
to pretend to be having a good time any more.

I drove home thinking this is now the tragic story of a romance
that could've happened if things were normal, but they were not.

Over winter vacation, I participated in winter vacation swim
practice. Each practice session was up to three hours long and was
supposed to be some of the hardest and most beneficial all year. I
had lost my ability to push myself in practice. Now everyone was
beating me at every stroke. Even a new swimmer was beating me.
I was falling apart and I didn't know why. I should have been
swimming faster.

I also knew I was supposed to be having more fun at the two
parties I went to that vacation. One was a party put on by one of
the CITs from the previous summer. Most of the CITs were at the
party. I remember watching Terry and one of the guys play Nerf
basketball. They were definitely having fun. I was very envious. I
felt they probably had parents that cared about them and liked
them. I had a parent who wanted to crush me. I remember thinking that everyone else at the party knows how to have fun except
me. I again narrated to myself: here were normal people having
fun, and I was not normal. I had the same thought at a New
Year's Eve party, thrown by a classmate that I didn't know that
well. I had the thought that I was not having a normal good time.
In spite of this pessimistic outlook, I did get some New Year's
kisses, including one from Melanie Carson whom I liked so much.
That was the high point of the evening.

We had a meet coming up against our neighborhood rival, an all boys Catholic prep school, St. John's. A fellow student asked me if we were going to win.

I said, "I'm winning my event." Little did he know that as I sat there, I was narrating my life story in my mind, and the story was again a tragedy. It was the story of a star falling apart, never to be heard from again.

I was getting more and more depressed and my school work started to suffer. My swimming suffered also. In the meet against St. John's, I swam 1:16.2 in the 100-yard breaststroke. That was a terrible time. I came in last place. We lost the meet by one point. If I would've gone 1:13.8, we would've won.

When I came home, my dad asked, "How'd ya do?" in a tone that sounded like he was making fun of swimming.

I said, "Awful."

He asked in an annoyed tone, "What do you *mean* awful?"

Remember, he *wanted* me to do awful.

I said, "I went 1:16 in the 100 breast."

He asked in a tone like he was making fun of it, "What's so *awful* about that?"

I said, "It's awful, much slower than last year, and I came in *last.*" Then I walked out of the room. It wasn't proper to be fraternizing with an enemy of swimming. I went to my room and shut the door. I always shut the door.

Later, my dad came in my room without permission and gave his usual anti-swimming speech.

After the anti-swimming speech, I was thankful that I planned to go away that summer. I was planning either to go back to camp as a full-fledged counselor, or to go to Israel on a six-week JTG tour. Also, I was glad I had plans to go away to college the next fall. I felt my dad was really a bad influence on me. I again thought of asking my aunt and uncle if I could live with them during the swim season, but my depression stopped me from taking the responsible action of asking them.

After my father's anti-swimming speech, I usually went to a poker game. It occurred to me that I should swap families with one of my poker friends, or at least live with one of their families, but that seemed foolish because I just had to survive until June. That would be too drastic. I hadn't really heard of that being done much. I should have done it. However, the illness had already started, so it was too late to prevent manic depression. The illness has a life of its own, and environment played only a small part. Depression is a hard illness to talk about, because the depression itself makes it difficult to express oneself.

I went to one poker game and my friend, Jack Johnson, said, "How's it going?"

I said, "Pretty good."

Jack said, "That's good."

"Well, actually not good."

"What's wrong?"

"I need a new family."

"Play cards," said Ed Lundbland.

Jack and I turned toward the table for a second and then Jack said, "Is your mom, (pause)?"

"My dad. My dad is against swimming. I've been swimming lousy, just awful, and that is just fine with my dad."

"Really?" said Jack.

"Yeah, he is jealous of my commitment to swimming, he wants me to just hang around with him. I try to just ignore him. He lets me come here, but he doesn't even want me to play cards."

"That's rough," said Dave Frish.

We just left it at that. Getting away from my dad *would* have been nice, but now I had an illness and I didn't know it. My poker friends, swim teammates, and family didn't know it. The thought of a psychiatrist occurred to me, but I didn't see how it could help.

In swim practice I should have been concentrating on making my muscles hurt as much as I could stand, while calmly trying to catch the guy ahead of me. I should have been concentrating on keeping my stroke right. Instead, I was obsessed as follows:

I am nobody. Here I am swimming behind Jack the sophomore and Kurt the senior rookie, and they are beating me. I'm a nobody. I'm supposed to be the senior expert. I am nobody. I lead off in the lane and they catch me, or sometimes they loaf and don't catch me because they are goof-offs, but they beat me in meets anyway. I am nobody. Come on, pull-exhale, pull-exhale. What type of boyfriend am I to bring home to Daddy when I'm such a nobody that I sacrifice all summer and fall just to swim like an idiot that nobody will ever respect. Jack has such big feet. Try to catch them. I'm a nobody. It was such a gamble to swim that much last summer for the winter varsity season pay-off, just to be slower than the average putz. This pool is crowded. We need wider lanes. Damn cheap school. I'm a nobody. I am a nobody because I still lose to Jack and Kurt in meets. Jack has big feet. C'mon, pull-exhale, pull-exhale. I need to win districts to redeem myself. Too bad I'm rated so far down the list. I am a nobody. Here comes a wall. Do a turn, duh . . . I turn like a peon. Why can't I have a normal happy high school experience and romance? Instead I'm in this dark quagmire far from earth. This is the pits. I am no one.

Thoughts like those would repeat continuously through swim practice and more and more through much of the day.

There was a bright spot to that January. The list of people going on the senior class trip to Jamaica came out. I was going. My dad prided himself on how much money he made, so he didn't want to deny us material luxuries. He had agreed to pay for the trip, even though it meant my being away from him for a week. There were about twenty-five girls and twenty-five guys going. I looked at the list and was pleased to find out that Melanie Carson was going. She was the rock singer. She had been voted "Most Talented" because of her singing ability. I knew her from physics class. She was smart, responsible, and gorgeous. I had thought about her off and on since eighth grade. However, I really didn't know her because we hardly had any classes together. I did overhear her say that her SAT scores were in the 97th percentile. Before that, I hadn't known she was a brain as well as gorgeous. That was great. She had been in my Honors Physics class the previous year but she never let me see her test papers. I hadn't known how bright she was.

A bunch of other cool people were going so it seemed like it would be a fun trip. It would be a great vacation.

Meanwhile the swimming season was going ahead as scheduled for most of the team. I continued to do lousy and was getting more and more depressed. Jack and Kurt were both beating me in breaststroke. This was especially embarrassing because Kurt had not swum since eighth grade, and he was now a senior. Also, Jack was a sophomore.

I even called our last year's captain out of retirement to watch my turns and stroke. He said, "The problem is all in your head." I didn't know exactly what he meant except that maybe I needed a shrink. He was right, as it turns out; I did need a shrink.

I was becoming much less smooth in other areas. At card games, Stan would get upset with me after I didn't show my cards when I had bluffed or just plain bet him out of a hand. The best strategy is not to show your hand when you don't have to. It is nicer and more friendly to show your cards, though. I felt that because I was losing so badly in swimming, I had to make it up in cards, so I wouldn't show, and he would wonder out loud why I was invited to the games. My selfishness could be put under the general category of the irritability symptom of depression.

The situation usually went something like this.

Stan said, "If I drop are you going to show?"

I said, "Maybe. Don't drop."

Stan said, "C'mon it's a friendly game."

Jim said, "It's nicer to show."

I said, "It's bad strategy."

"Just show. I drop," he said, dropping his hand face down.

Then, shoving my hand under some other cards I said, "For another quarter you could have seen them. It's bad strategy to show." Then I pulled in the pile of money.

Stan said, "I don't know why we even invite this asshole. It's a friendly game."

I couldn't see the value of being friendlier. I felt that because I was losing in swimming I had to be sure to win at cards. It is really too bad because Stan and I had been friends for five years at that point and had rarely had an argument. Our friendship survived these games, but the arguments certainly didn't help.

My grades were falling, too. Poor concentration is a symptom of depression. Usually it's because one is so preoccupied with some worry, in my case, it was swimming.

The regional meet was the last chance of my life to make all my hard swimming work pay off. It was also a chance for me to improve my mood. I felt like crying as I got on the starting block. I swam a time of 1:13.9—last in my heat. Then I went in the shower and cried. With the shower pouring on my face, nobody could see that I was crying. This was more crying than the average defeated athlete should do. This was the depressed part of manic depression. I stayed in the shower about ten minutes. Then I went back to where our team was sitting, and tried to give away my swim cap and goggles. I didn't deserve to own them. Maybe one of the juniors could make them go faster next year than I managed to make them go this year. My teammates just ignored me. Nobody would take them. They didn't know what to say.

One of the juniors sat next to me and said, "No, keep your cap and goggles. You didn't do that bad."

I kept saying to him, "How could I get slower than last year? How could I get slower?"

"I don't know. That happens a lot. You weren't that much slower," he said.

"I was a lot slower. I swam 1:10 last year. Watch this heat."

We watched another heat of the breaststroke preliminaries. We saw times of 1:08 through 1:12.

I said to him, "I could have beat half those guys last year. With some modest improvement, I could have won that heat."

We talked some more which made me feel better. I told him to swim distance freestyle instead of sprint freestyle the next year. Our coach was best at coaching distance freestyle.

I went to a couple of swim practices that next week. The practices were to help the team prepare for the state meet. I stayed in my clothes though. I sat on the bench on the side of the pool. It felt better to be there than to be at home alone. At home I would have had for company my mother, one or two of my little brothers, and one of our paid household helpers. I preferred the team. I had begun to sit in my room and talk to myself when I was home. I would go over the same "I'm a nobody" thoughts outlined before, but it was now much worse. After the state meet, swimming was over. There was about a month before the trip to Jamaica. I was badly depressed that whole month.

We were scheduled to leave for the trip to Jamaica on April 2. I was incredibly depressed until the trip. In school, I couldn't pay attention. It was lucky for me that last semester grades didn't count for class rank. When I got home from school, I just sat in my room and talked to myself. I went over and over the swimming season in my mind. I became obsessed with how badly I swam. I didn't do any homework until I had talked to myself about swimming for about two hours. I didn't really talk to myself out loud. I just thought intensely in words, and the words were agonizing. I started falling way behind in school. In the fall I had planned on doing well in school in the spring, because swimming would be over. I should have had more time to do homework. I hadn't planned on being devastated.

In the meantime before the trip, I felt I couldn't justify my existence. I had swum so much and gained so little. I figured I had wasted a lot of time swimming, just proving that I was in no way an athlete. I thought, this is when some people commit suicide, but I would never do that. That would really be admitting defeat.

I thought I would gradually recover, but I was wrong.

6

Melanie Carson

I got up enough initiative to call a guy who had graduated in 1976, who had gone to Jamaica the previous year. I asked him about the trip, and he told me that in the morning you go on tours, and in the afternoon you go to the beach. The trip sounded interesting to me, but not as interesting as I knew it would've sounded if I had felt okay. I asked him how much food cost, and he said $120 would cover food for the week plus souvenirs.

He also said, "Be careful not to get sunburned." I should have kept the sunburn warning in mind.

In the airport gate area while we were waiting, I tried to get Melanie's attention, but she ignored me. It didn't matter that much because I had a whole week to get her attention.

The plane ride was fairly uneventful.

Our luggage was sent automatically to our hotel. We just had to get on our bus to Montego Bay and go to our hotel. We checked out our hotel rooms. Some of our friends were right above us. We saw them on their balcony when we were on ours. We were on the fourth floor and they were on the fifth.

Just for the fun of it, I said, "Hey, we can climb up to your room from ours." I just stood on the rail, but one of my roommates climbed all the way up.

The next thing we knew, there were cops pulling guns on us. Somebody had thought we were burglars when he saw us climbing the balcony. We explained that these were our rooms and we were just having fun.

The cops finally said, "Okay, no problem."

Next we headed down to the bar for a beer. We (my room-mates and about four others) all ordered a beer. The talk turned to how to maintain a supply of beer for the week. There was a liquor store across the street from our hotel. One guy said, "If we each buy a case on one day, we can share and all have some beer."

I said, "I'm not in on that, I'm not going to drink that much."

He said, "Okay."

I finished my beer and said, "I'm going to take off, I might be back in a while." I went to look for Melanie, and her roommates, Paula, Pattie, and Katie. I found them right in the lobby outside the bar. I said, "Do you guys want to take a walk on the beach?"

They agreed and so we went for a walk. I figured being with four girls was a special treat. Still, because I was depressed, it wasn't quite as fun as I knew it was supposed to be. We walked for a ways, and then we took off our shoes and socks and rolled up our pants legs and ran. It was fun.

Paula was the leader. On the way back she walked ahead of us a way, so once at my suggestion we hid in some trees to make it look like we ditched her. She saw us and quit walking so far ahead. I tried to talk to Melanie, but had better luck talking to Katie. Melanie and Katie were close friends, so I wanted Katie to like me, too.

When we got to the front steps of our hotel, some of our group was standing on the steps. One of the guys looked surprised when he saw me with all those girls, especially Katie with whom he apparently was good friends. Katie and he said something to each other, which let me know they were good friends. I went up to my room.

In my room was a bunch of guys. They asked where I had been, and I told them I had gone for a walk with Melanie, Pattie, Paula, and Katie. They seemed a little surprised, but hid it pretty well. We hung around and talked for a while.

That night, we went to sleep at a reasonable hour. We had been up since very early that morning, and we had to be on the tour bus at 8:00 A.M.

The next morning, we got up, grabbed some breakfast, and went over to Ocho Rios for Dunn's River Falls. They were beauti-ful, and we waded in them. I had on a suntan lotion that was sup-posed to have extra sunburn protection. That was before the sun protection factor numbers came out, but I know now its strength was the equivalent of SPF 6. It was a cloudy day, but they had warned that you can even get burned on a cloudy day. We stayed until noon, then we headed back to Montego Bay.

Later, I lay out in the sun with my roommate and swim teammate Jeff. I still had the #6 lotion on. It was still cloudy. That night it was clear that I hadn't gotten much sun.

Later a bunch of us had a beer and compare your sunburn party in one of our school's hotel rooms.

For the first few days of this trip, I continued to talk to Melanie and Katie whenever I could find the chance.

The next morning, we took a tour of a haunted mansion, and then headed for the beach. It was cloudy again, but since I had been repeatedly warned that you can get burned even on a cloudy day, I put on the #6 lotion, and lay out for an hour on each side.

Again that night, I had no color. Some people were starting to get tan and I was jealous.

The next day, I went for it. It was sunny, and I lay out for an hour and a half on each side with no lotion. I got very sunburned. It took about three hours before it hit me, then I started to feel like I was going to faint. Then I got the chills and started shivering. My roommates laughed at first, but then they got concerned. I was too embarrassed and depressed to tell them to call an ambulance, but I needed one. I decided to treat myself. That was stupid. I decided that the chills were from shock, so I thought I needed to keep warm, so I took a hot bath. Years later, I was told that you get the chills when your body temperature is rising even though that doesn't make sense. When you are burned, your skin can't breathe and you overheat. A cold bath would've been right, instead I took a hot bath. My body temperature was probably 105 degrees. I could have died.

How could such a smart guy have been so stupid? Simple. Depressed people are accident prone. When depressed, you can be so preoccupied with one worry, that you neglect all else. In this case it was my obsession with how poorly I swam.

It was about dinner time when I went into the tub. One roommate checked on me, and I said I felt okay. Then they went out on the town, dancing and drinking. I got out of the tub after a while, and just lay on a bed. I stayed in bed until dinner the next day. The morning of the next day one of our teachers who was chaperoning us checked on me, and I said I was all right, just weak and sore.

The day after that, I went back on the tour, wearing long pants and sunblock on my arms. I got some sympathy from Katie and Melanie, which was nice. Katie said, "Does it hurt?"

I said, "It only hurts when I breathe."

Melanie said, "Well, just don't breathe then."

Katie said, 'When do you think you'll be able to go out in the sun again?"

"September."

One evening we saw a nightclub act that included an Elvis impersonator who was pretty good. Melanie went, but I didn't manage to talk to her much.

One day, a bunch of guys were sitting by themselves, each in his own seat on the tour bus. Melanie walked onto the bus and said, "Who wants the privilege of sitting with me?"

I hesitated and said, "I do."

We talked about the tourist sight we had just seen. Having her next to me was a thrill. Now I remember really debating whether or not to hold her hand.

I thought, should I hold her hand for just a second and then let go? Should I say anything about holding her hand while I'm holding it? Everyone was watching. Does that matter?

Just sitting next to her was pleasant. I figured there would be plenty of time for holding hands later. I just tried to keep up friendly conversation.

The next day was kind of cloudy, so another guy and I rented mopeds and went riding up in the hills. There was very beautiful natural scenery, with lots of tropical vegetation.

The last night, I went looking for Melanie at her room. She wasn't there. Eventually I found her in the bar of our hotel, talking to another girl from our school. They were talking about class rank or something and how you could take easier classes and get an A and get higher class rank. I sat down and listened, then the girl asked me where all the really smart kids were going to college like Barry and Eugene. Barry and Eugene were real nerds and carried briefcases to school.

I said, "They're not so smart. They're smart, but they're not *that* smart. However, Barry is going to USC, and Eugene is going to the University of Washington."

"Where are you going?" she asked.

"Well, I don't know yet," I said. "I applied to Stanford, Yale, the University of Puget Sound, and the University of Washington.

Stanford and Yale are hard to get into. You have to have very good grades and test scores."

"Well, you'll get into the University of Washington," said Melanie.

I said, "Yeah, but I'm worried about getting rejected from Stanford and Yale." (I had also applied to Harvard, but had given up on it.)

"What did you get on your SATs?" the other girl asked.

"Well, the first time I took it, I didn't do so hot, so then I took it again and got 690 verbal, 740 math," I said.

"What percentile is that?"

"Ninety-ninth."

Melanie said, "Well, I think you've got nothing to worry about."

The other girl said, "So do I."

I could tell by the look on Melanie's face that she was impressed.

The singer from the band was calling everybody up to dance, so I asked Melanie to dance. We did one slow dance, but I remember thinking it didn't feel as good as it should. I thought, if only my father approved of dating like other fathers. Maybe then it would have felt good. Actually, I needed to not be depressed; then it would have felt good regardless of my dad.

There were three couples from our school dancing including us, so after the first dance I said, "Rotate." We changed partners. I don't know what I was thinking.

The next day, on the plane on the way home, I felt on the one hand that my sunburn was a disaster, but on the other hand, at least I could ask Melanie out when we got home. I felt that if I had been smoother during the trip, we would be sitting together on the way home, maybe even kissing or holding hands.

When we got back to Seattle, my dad picked me up at the airport. I felt unfortunate to be back at our house where I would be subjected to him.

I figure now that the healthy me would have been planning to move out on my upcoming eighteenth birthday. That way, I would not have had to get cash for college from my dad. I could have just worked, and not gone to college. As it was, I was so depressed, I could barely handle the last semester of high school. I couldn't concentrate. I didn't think I could work to support myself. My concentration was too lousy. Given the disease, I needed my dad's money to support me.

At the Seattle airport, when my dad came to pick me up from the trip to Jamaica, I did not know that things were only going to get much much worse, before they were ever going to get any better.

That first week after the Jamaica trip, the whole school knew about my sunburn. I got some sympathy and some teasing. I was depressed, but not too badly. Also that week, I got rejection letters from Harvard, Stanford, and Yale.

I had gotten accepted by the University of Puget Sound in Tacoma, and I had already been accepted by UW Seattle. I would go to Puget Sound in Tacoma, to get away from my dad.

My dad had said, "If you go to school in Seattle, you have to live at home instead of a dorm. If you go away, you can live in a dorm." My dad had said when my mom first had her stroke, "I will still let you kids do whatever you normally would've done."

While dating is something we normally would have done, my dad apparently felt his jealous rages would not get found out by the community. He didn't yell in front of witnesses. If he made us live at home, and go to college locally, denying us a better education, that would be more *public* evidence of his inappropriate clinging, so he had to let us go away to college like we had always planned. He especially had to let me go, because he let my older brother Steve go. My dad begrudgingly let Steve go after deciding that he couldn't keep Steve home because of my mom's stroke. However, my dad often wished out loud that Steve had gone to a college closer to home. Steve went to the University of Pennsylvania. However, as you will see later, my dad almost didn't let me go away to college, because I was planning to be friends with my roommates. He was that jealous of any close personal relationships that I had.

The very good news that week was that Melanie agreed to go out with me. We planned to see the movie *Rocky* on Friday.

At the dinner table I asked, "Dad, can I use the car tonight?"

My dad made me ask permission to use the car even though there were two cars and only two drivers. It was my mom's car that I was asking to use.

He asked, "Why? Are you going somewhere?"

"Yes," I said.

"Where are you going?"

"I'm going to a movie."

"Who with?"

"Melanie Carson."

"Where do you know *her* from?"

"School."

"Is she Jewish?"

"No."

"What are you going out with a girl who's not Jewish for?" he asked.

This was the first time in his life he indicated Judaism was important. At first I thought he was just implying that he thought that I thought it was important. When I was younger, my mother and father both clearly said that it was okay to marry a non-Jew.

I said, "I'm going out with her because I like her."

Boy, was that ever the wrong thing to say! I got up and carried my dishes to the sink.

He got up from his chair, followed me, and yelled, "Just a minute, I don't like the idea of you going out with a girl who isn't Jewish!"

"Why don't you like it?" I asked, annoyed.

"I don't think it's *good* to go out with someone who is not Jewish!" he said angrily, standing near me.

I walked away and he followed me and I asked, "What's not *good* about it?"

"I don't like the idea!"

"Why?"

"You shouldn't go *out* with someone *who isn't Jewish!"* he said following me.

"What about that Newman or that Stein girl you used to go out with?" he asked, naming two girls, each of whom I had gone out with only once.

I said, "I'm going out with Melanie now."

He yelled, "I don't like that idea!"

"Why not!?"

"I don't know if I *approve* of that!"

"Why?!"

He said loudly, "Well, you can go out with her, but don't *marry* her!

"Why shouldn't I marry her?"

"Because life is difficult enough without going and marrying someone of a different religion!"

"Oh."

What a stupid thing to say. If he wanted life to be less difficult, why didn't he leave me alone?

It would be simple. We would have a huge wedding, and we would invite five hundred people. We would invite everyone except my father. I imagined a big wedding and somebody in the back turning and saying, "You know, he didn't even invite his father."

I also thought about which of my friends would let me live with his family. Then I thought, oh, oh, many of their parents are sincere when they say, "You must only date Jews." When my dad says it, he's just jealous. My closest non-Jewish friend had no spare bedrooms in his house, and I had never met his parents. It occurred to me to ask Melanie if I could live with her family, but clearly that would be way too much to ask on our first date.

My mood lowered drastically. I went back to my room and finished getting ready. I had hoped going out with Melanie would cheer me up, because I was really looking forward to it. Now it was leading to more problems. I looked at the situation pessimistically, being depressed. I thought that this would end up like *Romeo and Juliet,* in other words, a romantic tragedy, if I didn't play my cards right. I thought that now things were going to be really difficult. We would have to elope, or just plain run away. How would I explain to my friends that I had been banished from my family? Or that I had dumped my family? I couldn't tell exactly what it would be. It was supposed to be just a date between two high school students. They sing about this all the time on the radio in Beach Boys songs and Beatles songs. Why couldn't it be like that? My friends did not fully understand the situation in my house. Even I didn't know that things would get this bad. My dad had been nice for a month or so, and then he suddenly attacked. Even in the fall when I was dating Angie, he was nice six out of seven days of the week. He only screamed on days I saw her.

This sudden attack by my dad about Melanie depressed me drastically. My dad had made it clear that my life would have to be secret from him, because he planned to be dictator. I was trying to figure out how I would deal with college at UPS. Would I have to keep my love life *totally* secret? Would I have to hang around only with *Jews* there? There aren't even that many Jews there. Would my dad *pay* for college? Would he suddenly quit paying at some unpredictable time in the middle of the four years? I felt awful.

This was my state of mind as I left and drove over to Melanie's house. While I was driving I began to feel somewhat better. Even though we'd be going to different colleges, I thought, we could still see each other on vacations. I thought that maybe I could tell Melanie that my dad had gotten mad, but that I'd just ignore him. As I got near her house, though, I started narrating the story of this date in my mind: the tragic story of how the date would go, compared to how it should go, how I was supposed to be happy and proud to introduce myself to her parents, instead of feeling embarrassed that I was a Jew who couldn't swim well. My swimming failure had not been on my mind that day, until after my dad yelled at me.

When I got to her door, her mother answered, and all I said was, "Hi."

Melanie came to the door and we left and her mother said, "Have a good time." I was so pessimistic about parents that I thought she was being sarcastic. I really thought her mother was being sarcastic.

Melanie and I walked up to my car.

She said, "Is this your car?" in a cheerful voice.

'Um, ah, it's my mom's."

"She lets you use it?"

"Uh, yeah."

I opened the door for her, but then I couldn't figure out if I was supposed to shut it or she was. It was awfully poor form, not at all smooth. Finally she shut the door.

I walked around the front of the car to my side and got in.

I kept thinking of what I would be saying if only I felt normal. Things like, "You look nice. I'm so glad we're together." Instead, I said hardly anything, at first.

I asked her where she was going to go to college. She said, "Pacific Lutheran University (PLU)."

I asked, "Where is that?"

She said, "Tacoma."

I was going to go to UPS, also in Tacoma. I should've been overjoyed that we would be going to school in the same town.

Instead, because I had already obsessed about Tacoma being the pits, I came up with a new pessimistic thought. I thought: Oh no, we'll be going to rival schools. So I just said, "Oh, I'm going to the University of Puget Sound, also in Tacoma." Then I asked, "Why are you going there?" My mood was so low that I think I even sounded argumentative, because I had never heard of it like I had heard of Stanford.

She said, "It's a family tradition. My parents and my brothers went there."

Melanie seemed cheerful which to me was out of place. It made me feel really left out. It made her seem uncaring about or ignorant of what an awful thing it was to go away to college. I was dreading having to leave my friends in order to get away from my dad. Didn't she know what was going on? Didn't she know what a crummy place the world was? Really, I knew that her cheerfulness seeming strange to me was my fault. She couldn't know what was going on if I didn't tell her. On the other hand, graduation was coming, and I was depressed about it, so I just thought that graduation should be depressing for everyone else who was graduating. I had to leave high school without achieving my goal of becoming a swimming star first. To take it lightly seemed out of touch on her part. This is a classic symptom of depression. Happy people like Melanie seemed inappropriately silly.

I said, "I'm not looking forward to graduation, because high school was fun, and college just won't be the same."

The whole date went badly. I was distant, negative, and grumpy, and unable to tell her why. It is hard to break up on the first date. I had most recently been depressed about swimming. My depressive obsessive thoughts switched from my dad and went back to swimming. You cannot choose your obsession, or switch it off. I went on and on about how poorly I had done in swimming.

I remember saying, "Now if you practice and practice at something you are supposed to get better at it aren't you?! Well don't you think so?! I got worse at it!"

Melanie just sat there kind of speechless. My voice was so irritated that it probably sounded like I was upset with her.

I kept on going. I said, "You know I swam the 100-yard breaststroke. My times actually got slower. I actually got slower and slower. Can you believe it?! I was supposed to get faster. Right!?"

Melanie continued to sit there in stunned silence.

I continued, "Well, I got slower. I actually got *slower,* and it is bumming me out."

In Jamaica I was much calmer than this. I was never very visibly upset about anything, not even the sunburn had upset me this much.

I forgot the rule that you're supposed to impress your date, instead of dwell on your bad points. What could be simpler? However, in my state of mind, nothing was simple.

I never even told her about my dad's opposition to our dating. I was paralyzed with depression. When I thought about my dad for a second, I felt like crying, so I avoided the topic. Crying is not a great dating strategy.

We saw the movie and it was all right. When Rocky ate raw eggs, Melanie said, "Maybe you should have done that for swimming."

I knew she was trying to help me feel better, but I felt bad that it was not enough.

We came out and I held her hand as we walked to the car. When I held her hand it felt like she was a really close friend.

She asked, "What do you want to do now?"

The words "make out" came to mind, but I said, "I don't know, let's just drive around."

We drove around a lot, talking. I did not say anything impressive or express any enthusiasm. Finally, we stopped at a McDonald's and I got up the guts to tell her I knew her SAT scores. We talked about that and class rank for a few minutes, but I never got to the point of saying how impressed I was with her or that I thought we had something in common, academic ability, or that we should see a lot of each other.

My brain had only been malfunctioning for a couple of months, and on the one hand I thought I would recover. On the other hand, that night I was so depressed I couldn't bring myself to say anything positive about myself. I just said stuff like, "College just isn't going to be the same. I'll miss my friends."

She asked me a bunch of questions in a friendly way to try to get to a topic that would be easy, pleasant, or relevant. I just gave short answers and she never hit on the root of what was upsetting me, my father.

I drove her home and tried to walk her to the door, but she kept saying, "Good night, good night." Then she went inside without letting me kiss her.

I was so frustrated that I drove around aimlessly for half an hour. I didn't know what to do. There was a card game that night, but if I went there, my friends would ask a lot of questions about the date. So, I just went home.

The next few days I was really frustrated and baffled. I got up enough nerve to ask Melanie to the senior prom, but she said, "I don't think so."

I was really disappointed, so disappointed that I felt very desperate. I even told my dad how bummed out I was. He said I should ask someone else. Then he went into this speech saying that anything that wears a dress should be sufficient for prom.

He said, "You're seventeen so all girls should look the same to you."

I was insulted and told him I had wanted to go with Melanie.

He said, "Ask somebody else."

That was good advice, and I asked Donna Freeman, a long-time friend.

She accepted.

I felt better because I had a date for prom, but my mood was still low. Donna was Jewish, but that is not why my dad approved of her. My dad approved of my going to prom with Donna because he knew I didn't like her that much. In the fall, I had dated Angie who was Jewish, but my dad protested our relationship because he knew we were involved. By my dad's rules, I could date anyone that I didn't like much.

I went to prom with Donna and a couple of my poker friends and their dates. It was fairly uneventful, but I kept wishing I was there with Melanie.

Graduation day came. I graduated with distinction, but I was depressed that I was leaving high school without a girlfriend. That thought ruined graduation for me.

7

Hotel California, Israel

Summer began and I had three weeks to kill. I had been rehired to be a camp counselor at Camp Okranski, but I knew I was in no shape to handle it, so I opted for six weeks in Israel on a tour with the JTG Israel Pilgrimage. This was an excuse to get away from my dad for the summer. It was an acceptable excuse, because lots of people in the community including my poker friends had gone to Israel. Also, my older brother was going there for a year. *My millionaire Dad was paying for my brother's and my trip, but he kept asking me not to go.* The fact that my dad had money was the only reason I was talking to him at this point. I needed his money to pay for college. He was so rich that I could never get a scholarship based on need. I mistakenly thought college was essential.

He said, "Why don't you stay home this summer and get a job carrying out groceries? I think I have been way too free with you kids, letting you do what you want. I think you should stay home and do some work."

I knew that if I stayed home, every night my dad would yell at me not to go out, especially if I was going out with a girl. *By ignoring his begging me not to get on the plane to Israel, I could avoid the daily yelling to stay home each night.*

My dad was rich and proud of it, so he didn't want to deny us material luxuries like trips. However, he kept imploring me not to go. He was lonely.

My crippled mother thought it was a good idea for me to go to Israel. She nodded her head, "Yes," when I asked if she thought I should go to Israel. That helped.

My trip to Israel was, for me, a way to have a secret romance during the six weeks of the trip. My dad may actually have half thought that I was going for the religious, cultural, or educational aspects of the trip. What a laugh. I was going there to have at least a brief romance to cheer myself up. Too bad I didn't know that romance was not the treatment for manic depression.

During the three weeks between high school graduation and leaving for Israel, I played some poker with eight of my best friends and classmates. Also, I obsessed about Melanie. I didn't find much else to do because I was depressed. I wondered what possible validity there could be to Melanie and I not being together because of our religious difference. If Jews thought that Jews should only date other Jews, then Jews were racist. They were prejudiced. They were paranoid. These thoughts about Jews greatly preoccupied me.

During World War II the German Nazis killed 6 million Jews in the Holocaust. Unfortunately, since then, many Jews have felt that any non-Jew is a potential Nazi. Many Jews are prejudiced against non-Jews. They feel that Jews are morally and intellectually superior.

So, I could not really discuss Melanie with most of my friends, who happened to be Jewish, because Melanie was a "goy." Goy is a derogatory word for non-Jew.

My friends would have said, "Why do you like a goy?"

Being so depressed and preoccupied, I wasn't really looking forward to going to Israel, although logically I should have been. Unfortunately, with manic-depressive illness, logic does not play a part. I should have thought, go, have fun, and pretend to be Jewish for six weeks. Instead, a depressed person looks at the worst side of all situations.

I had been told to read a book about Israeli Prime Minister Golda Meir in preparation for the trip. I remember lying out in the sun on my stomach. My sunburn had healed. I was trying to read the book about Golda Meir, but I couldn't concentrate. I remember wondering what could be wrong with my brain. It was horrifying. Still, I thought I would gradually cheer up.

On Thursday, June 23, I started to switch to a manic phase. I had a poker game that evening at my house, and with some luck, I won a lot of money. I remember thinking I could tell what cards people had by reading their faces. A little bit of face reading is normal, but I started to think I could do it extraordinarily well. We played poker until 3:30 A.M., so I didn't get to bed until 4:00 A.M.

Friday evening, I tried to do the dishes, but I was lost in thought. I thought of all the people I knew and their different relationships. It took me four hours to do the dishes for six people, and we had a dishwasher.

My dad came into the kitchen about 10:30 P.M. and said, "Bill, what's wrong? Are you lost in thought?"

I said, "Well, yes, I'm just thinking about the people I know and our family. Mom's not going to get any better is she?"

"Well, no," he said. "It's really doubtful."

This is something that I already had known for a long time, but now I was thinking about it more in depth. I finished the dishes and went to bed. That night I didn't sleep. I just lay in bed thinking and thinking about different people in my life, and what they had in their lives that I did not. I also tried to figure out what made them happier and what made their lives go so much more smoothly than mine. Finally, at about 5:30 A.M., it really struck me that my mother couldn't talk to me. I cried myself to sleep. Being manic is usually like being in a good mood that involves no crying, but when manic, you can switch back and forth between being manic and being depressed. The inability to sleep was a sign of mania.

At about 8:00 A.M. my whole family got up because we were going to a mountain park for an overnight camping trip. At the breakfast table, I told the whole family, "You know, Mom's stroke just hit me last night. When it first happened, we were in Florida, and Dad called us from the hospital and he was crying on the phone. Then Steve, you started crying, and Rick you started crying and Johnny was too young to know what was going on. So I took the phone from Steve, and got the information on where the tickets were, what to do for a cab, and to pack our suitcases so we could fly home that day as scheduled, because we had to be back for school. Then we got home to Seattle, and Mom and Dad were still in Florida. Having no parents around was kind of fun. Mom was in the hospital in Florida, and Dad stayed with her, but I figured she'd get better. I didn't worry; I wanted to go to swim practice. When Mom and Dad got home, I saw how Mom was, and I didn't want her to live like that, but I thought to myself, in the meantime *she can't yell at me*. Mom and I had argued a lot up to that point. Now I realize it's a big problem to have your Mom be unable to talk to you."

My older brother, Steve, said, "I thought it was good that you took responsibility for the tickets and kept your act together. I felt bad for you that you couldn't feel bad with us."

I said, "Well it's not good to feel bad, but I feel bad now. I didn't sleep last night until 5:30 A.M. when I cried myself to sleep. I guess my feelings on this are just coming out now." (This idea that strong feelings or anger coming out long after the incident that caused them is a cause of mental illness, was something I had heard of at that point, so I said it. Now I believe it is a myth.)

Steve said something like, "It's good that you're thinking about it now."

That was the end of the discussion for then. We went up to the mountains. That day, Jack Johnson, one of my poker friends, was having a graduation party at a different spot which was not too far from ours. I was already in a fog. I was switching back and forth from being depressed to being manic.

In the car on the way over to Jack's party, I was crying so hard I couldn't see to drive sometimes. I was crying because I knew the situation in my home would not get any better. My dad would always be jealous of my girlfriends, and my mom would not recover. My mom should be a dear, sweet, capable, warm, friendly, communicative, ambitious mother. Instead, she couldn't talk to me. She could hardly walk, and couldn't read or write. She could hardly do anything. She used to help guide my life and actually did a good job. She could watch over me and be glad if I had a girlfriend. Now she could not do anything like this, like the other mothers I knew. (She was also depressed to begin with as a result of her own manic depression. I didn't know this at the time.) Thinking about the effects of my mom's stroke made me cry so hard that I had to pull the car over because the tears interfered with my vision. I was quite sure that my dad would be acting normally if my mom was healthy. As it was, he was a monster and would stay that way indefinitely. I was going to have to go away to college and stay away as much as possible. Any life between me and a wife or girlfriend would have to be insulated from my dad. This, of course, made me cry also, because it would be so hard to keep

me and my girlfriend insulated from my dad while I was trying
to get my dad's money to pay for college. My brother, Steve,
got away before my dad became unbearable, and Rick was only
fifteen and didn't date much. Johnny was about to turn ten, so
none of my brothers experienced my father's jealous rages. I
worried about Rick and John, what effect my dad's frame of
mind would have on them when they got older. My dad had
money and could pay household assistants, so I could never win
a custody battle for my two younger brothers. They would have
to be physically abused to be put in foster homes. There was
nothing I could do to save them. I could only save myself. As it
turns out, my brothers survived, sanity intact. It was not forsee-
able at the time, though. The thought occurred to me that I
should not go to Israel, that maybe I could just live with another family for the summer.

When I pulled up at Jack's party, it occurred to me to tell Mr.
and Mrs. Johnson what I was going through to see if they could
help. Then I thought, no, this is a party. It would ruin the party.

As I got out of the car, I apparently switched back to the
manic phase, because I quit crying. I joined the party. I remember there was a volleyball game going on. I did well in it because
volleyballs are like tetherballs, and I had played tetherball in my
backyard since I was five. I was also experiencing the manic energy and hyperactivity which made this volleyball game feel extra
good. I had decided that a good mental attitude could help one
do anything well. In a way this is very true. During the volleyball
game, I had a good attitude. Or, at least I felt good. I may have
seemed too hyper. When we weren't playing, I felt worse,
though. It felt good when a girl put some suntan lotion on my
face.

The rest of the party went okay for me until the end. As I was
leaving and fearing a cry coming on again, I turned to one of my
friends and said, "I'm crashing."

He said, "Oh you'll have a good time in Israel, I know it."

I said, "Yeah, it should be good," without telling him the real
reason for my depression.

The ride back to my family's campsite was not totally awful; I
didn't cry too much.

In later years my dad remembered that that night I talked
about the volleyball game in a strange, grandiose way. He said I

was too stuck on how well I had played volleyball. That night, Saturday, I slept about five hours. I normally slept eight or nine.

I don't really remember much from Sunday except that I had a conversation with my dad where he said it was okay to have sex when you were eighteen or nineteen, but it was not okay to fall in love until age twenty-six when you were done with your education. This re-emphasized what I already knew. He did not want me to have a girlfriend until I was twenty-six. Also he was saying a little promiscuity in the meantime was okay. I decided my dad was fired as my dad. I was horrified at the influence his attitude would have on my little brothers.

Sunday we got home from the mountains about 9:00 P.M. I had to wake up Monday, June 27 at 5:00 A.M. to get to the airport by 6:00 A.M. Sunday night, I had to unpack from camping, and pack for Israel. I was hyper by that time. Two of my poker buddies, Jim Eckhart and Ed Lundblad, came over to say good-bye. I was so hyper and manic and busy trying to figure out what to pack, that I didn't notice when they put a folding chair in my suitcase. I was that distracted. They were laughing and so was I, because I was just a bit manic. I finally got packed and they left about 11:30 P.M.

Still, I stayed up until about 2:00 A.M. to figure out some stuff I had to send in to UPS for school. I slept from 2:00 A.M. to 5:00 A.M. That lack of sleep would be a problem.

We got to the airport and everyone who was going from the Seattle area was there. There were a bunch of us. We got on a plane for New York that was loaded with JTGers. My mood at that point was just a little bit hyperactive. It was a fun plane ride to LaGuardia Airport.

Orientation took place at a hotel. Brian Green, an acquaintance from Seattle, started hanging around with me. He was sometimes a pest.

At some point Brian and I walked to a restaurant for dinner with a few girls from Seattle. Later, there was a big orientation meeting where they played "The Star Spangled Banner." This got my attention because it reminded me of swim meets. The big point of the orientation meeting was that if you used drugs in Israel, you would be sent home. They spent about a half hour telling us this.

My mind was filled with distressing thoughts, part manic, and part depressed.

Then there were religious services with just our group number six. Brian wanted to skip them. I said no. He complained that I never wanted to do what he wanted to do. We went to services.

At Kennedy Airport, I was in a much more jovial mood. Thinking funny, optimistic thoughts had me preoccupied enough that I needed Brian's help to figure out which counter to go to in order to pick out a seat on the plane. At one point there was a JTG official who saw Brian and me eating non-kosher hot dogs while wearing JTG nametags.

He said, "That's inconsistent."

I said to Brian laughing, "Hey, we're inconsistent." I laughed some more and so did Brian. We thought it was hilarious.

"We're inconsistent," we laughed. "We're inconsistent."

Later, I remember being nervous going through the security check of my luggage. I was fearful of going to a war zone. My suitcase was a mess because of the way I packed.

The security guard asked, "Is this the way you packed?"

I said, "Yes."

"Do you recognize anything that is not yours?"

I looked at a couple shirts there and had to think a minute if they were mine. I had just bought them and didn't immediately remember that they were mine.

After a minute I said, "No. It's all mine."

Being questioned made me nervous, but that particular nervousness went away when I got on the plane.

On the plane, I sat next to a window on my left and a girl and a guy to my right. I just sat in a smiling, near laughing, stupor. I just sat there laughing and smiling almost the whole flight. Part of what I was thinking was that I could tell what people were thinking by the expression on their faces, because I had so much practice with my mom. My mom could only shake her head "Yes" or "No," say "Dee" in sentences, and let us guess the expression on her face. I thought this face reading technique was a good way to pick up girls. I wasn't laughing out loud, just to myself. This was mania. I thought I could read people's thoughts in great detail. It was a ten-hour flight non-stop from New York to Tel Aviv. The flight left about midnight the night of Monday the 27th, and got to Israel about 6:00 P.M. Tuesday the 28th. You have to add eight hours for the time zone change. I, however, was so out of it, I thought it was Wednesday when we landed.

For a while on the plane the flight attendants wanted us to keep the shades pulled down on our windows. This was to allow people to sleep. Being manic, I, of course, didn't sleep.

I said to the girl next to me, "They don't want us to see the fighter planes out there."

I was serious and I'm sure she thought I was crazy but she didn't say anything. We were still over the Atlantic which shows I had no sense of time. Darren Gollub, our advisor from Seattle, had told us that Israel-bound airliners are sometimes given fighter escorts. Of course, this is only over the Mediterranean and not the Atlantic. In my mind, I was imagining aerial combat, as I had seen in clips of Vietnam aerial combat: air-to-air missiles, aerial bombardment of ground targets, surface-to-air missiles, phantoms in formation and so on. I really thought there might be some of this going on outside the window.

On the news about this time, there was a lot of talk about cults that used brainwashing to force people to join them. I had decided that Judaism was one big cult that was trying to keep me with them. I wasn't afraid of any coercion from JTG, but I thought they had played "The Star Spangled Banner" at orientation deliberately to get my attention because they knew it would remind me of swim meets. I thought it was a psychological trick.

I knew Judaism was escapable, yet there seemed to be a conspiracy going on. I tried to say "This is amazing," to Darren Gollub, who was leading another group in Israel. He was on the plane too, but later he told me I had mumbled, so he didn't understand me.

When the sun rose and we lifted the shades, we could see nothing but blue sky. That minimized my air battle fears at the time. I still looked for other planes, though.

An increased sex drive is another symptom of mania. I was suffering from this symptom. When people started to move around the plane, I noticed a girl sitting a few rows back with an empty seat next to her on the aisle. I sat next to her and started talking to her. Then another guy came up and started talking to me. I talked to the guy for a while and then a JTG advisor came up and the girl said, "Can you get this guy away from me?"

Not taking a hint because I was manic, I just said, "I'm not bugging her; I'm talking to him."

Eventually the other guy said it was his seat I was in, so I left. I had really annoyed the girl. I don't remember what I said. It was probably something overly flirtatious. This is one of the many bizarre things manic people do. This was totally out of character for me.

The girl and the guy in my row both thought I was kind of crazy after that incident. I could tell by the looks on their faces. Just before landing, though, they regained some confidence in me when I acted sane while telling someone what our mailing address in Israel would be. We needed to know it in order to fill out our landing forms for Israeli customs.

We landed in Israel and everybody cheered. I didn't share their enthusiasm. The guy in my row was trying to calm me with friendly small talk. He could see I was hyper. He said, "This landing by this Jewish pilot was much smoother than the landing I experienced by that *goy* pilot coming from Chicago to New York."

He was trying to be friendly. However, he couldn't have said anything worse. "Goy" did not just mean Christian. It meant stupid and immoral Christian. I was not in the mood to hear any more slams on Christians. Melanie Carson was Christian. I just felt sorry for the guy for being a victim of Jewish cult brainwashing, and I tried to be polite and not show my disgust.

Then as we were getting off the plane, I was feeling rather optimistic. I felt I could easily survive six weeks as a tourist. I said, "Well, it looks like we're in Israel and it is Wednesday, and it is a nice day."

The two people near me said, "No, it's Tuesday. It's Tuesday."

I said, "No, no. It's Wednesday."

One of them said, "No, it's Tuesday. It's just ten hours plus eight for the time zone."

I said, "No, no. It's Wednesday."

They just gave me a funny look and gave up.

We were in the baggage claim area when one of our group advisors asked if anyone had not turned over his passport and plane ticket to the advisors for safekeeping. I hadn't, so I brought up my carry-on flight bag and started searching through it for my passport and ticket.

As I was searching my flight bag, a uniformed female security guard wearing a walkie-talkie came up and grabbed my ticket out of my hand and said, "Are you going to Copenhagen?"

I said, "Huh?"

She said, "Are you going to Copenhagen?"

"What?"

"Are you going to Copenhagen?"

"Wha?"

"Are you going to Copenhagen?"

"Oh, uh, yeah, on the way back, we stop in Copenhagen."

"Have a nice trip." She handed my ticket back.

I freaked out. I knew that I had just matched the profile of a disturbed person in an Israeli airport. In Israeli airports they are looking for terrorists. I knew that I was upset about a lot of things and I didn't feel normal. Even though I may have had a smile on my face, I'm sure I looked hyper and nervous. Now I was worried about myself.

I found Debbie Frish (sister of my poker friend Dave Frish) who was in our group and said to her, "Don't play cards with me." She just looked surprised and said nothing. I said again, "Don't play cards with me."

Debbie just looked surprised and annoyed and then said, "Okay, I won't play cards with you."

I said, "No, you see my mom can't talk, she had a stroke and it's buggin' the hell out of me. We can tell what she's thinking only by the expression on her face, so nobody can bluff me."

Debbie said something reassuring that helped for a minute. Somebody else put my suitcase on the bus, and we were off to Haifa.

When I got on the bus, Brian slid over to make room for me to sit down, so I felt obligated to sit with him. I told him that my mom not being able to talk to me was really bothering me.

Brian said, "You should talk to our advisors about this."

I said, "Yeah, maybe," but I didn't want to look for them just then.

"You feel guilty about this."

"No."

"You feel guilty about it, like maybe you caused it."

"No, I'm just pissed."

Brian said, "Yes, you feel guilty."

I said loudly because I decided that anytime was the right time to yell at Brian Green, *"Green, would you listen? I don't feel guilty about anything. The problem is, people think I'm a little different because I don't listen to what they say. Instead, I just watch the expression on their faces, because that's all we can do with my mother. This is a cold, cruel world. You don't think death and war is real? You don't think F-4 Phantom fighter bombers are real? It's not just on TV you know?"*

Brian was speechless.

I kept going loudly, *"Guilty? I have confidence! I am proud of what I can do! The people who are really the best, the most popular, are happy. Why do you think Paula Dehn is so popular? She's always smiling! People want happiness so they're attracted to the people that are smiling! If someone is frowning nobody wants him! Nobody wants frowning! Now my new powers of reading people's expressions on their face could come in handy! Let's say you like this girl.* (I tapped the shoulder of a girl in front of us.) *I could maybe tell what she was thinking."*

Brian said, "Bill, I didn't know you thought this way."

I said just as loudly, *"Sure I do, I'm just as horny as everyone else on this bus!"*

Brian said, "Bill, people are listening."

I said, *"I don't care if people are listening! I'm glad they're listening!"*

I went on and on like this all the way from Tel Aviv to Haifa during the hour drive. I was talking loud, switching from topic to topic and saying inappropriate things.

I remember the point at which we got to our base, a school in Haifa. We got off the bus. I was still carrying on in the loud inappropriate manner. I said loud enough for all sixty of our coed group to hear me, something sexual, and then Brian said, "Bill, I didn't think you thought this way."

To which I said again loudly, *"I'm just as horny as everyone else in this group!"* I was thinking that Brian thought that because I did a lot of homework, I had no interest in a love life.

To which Brian said, "Bill, people are listening."

To which I said loudly, *"I don't care. I'm being honest!"*

Then I finally shut up, and sat at a table so our advisors could talk to all of us. People were crying, because they knew I was losing my mind. Poor Brian didn't deserve all the yelling. Our advisors had planned some orientation for that evening, but decided "everyone" was under too much stress.

This was a manic outburst, about which nothing good can be said.

We went up to our bedrooms. There were seven beds in the room I chose. Brian grabbed a bed right next to mine. One guy tried to say something calming but I was resistant.

Finally we turned off the lights and I said, "Let's tell some dirty jokes." A couple people actually did.

Fortunately, I really slept that night, about six hours. In the morning while lying in bed, I imagined myself a great philosopher commenting on everything from love to Middle East politics. When I got up, I thought it was Thursday morning. It was actually Wednesday.

In the morning, there were services. I got there late and had forgotten my talis (prayer shawl), kepah (prayer skullcap), and prayer book. I felt nervous and out of place.

Then a girl sitting behind me gave me her prayer book and said, "Here." She was trying to be friendly and it worked for the rest of services. I felt calmer. After services I was lost in space again.

I spent that entire day in a fog. I remember only a few things. In the morning we went for a walk to a bank. Everyone was hesitant to go up to a teller, but I went right up to one. I actually made my traveller's check out for the 31st of June instead of the 29th, but it was okay, the teller just gave me a weird look. There is no such day as June 31st. I remember I didn't eat anything at lunch. I just stared into space. I guess people thought I was stoned on drugs.

Evening came and I thought two days had passed, so I thought it was Friday evening, the start of the Sabbath. It was actually Wednesday. I refused to go to dinner or get out my bus fare. (We were going to go somewhere after dinner.) I thought our advisors were playing a trick on us by telling everyone it was Wednesday when it was actually Friday. In JTG groups, you observed the Sabbath strictly. This meant you didn't ride on a bus on Sabbath, and you didn't spend money on Sabbath. Spending money is like doing business. If you obey all the strict rules of Sabbath, you are supposed to rest and not do anything resembling business. I thought I was the only one who had caught on to the advisors' trick of saying it was Wednesday when it was Friday. All the other guys went down to dinner. When I asked them not to go, they thought I was crazy.

Also, the advisor, Sam, who heard me ask them not to go, got really mad.

He said, "Now I'm really getting pissed at you!"

I said, "It's Friday. It's the Sabbath."

He said, "No. It's Wednesday!"

Brian said, "It's Wednesday! What would your dad say?"

I said, "Forget that."

They went down to dinner.

Sam came up to my room a couple of times and asked me to come down to dinner. I found out later that he had concluded that I was on LSD. I refused to go down to dinner and told him I was looking through my luggage for my toothbrush.

Another advisor, Ted, came up and into my room and said, "What kind of drugs are you on?"

I said, "I'm not on drugs."

He said, "Last night you were on some."

"Flying on that plane was a wild experience," I said, momentarily remembering that only one day had gone by.

"You're flying now"

"Yeah, right."

I had been fumbling with an injector razor, but I couldn't figure out how to inject the blade. I had never used that type before. I said, "Would you do this for me?"

He put in the blade for me.

Then he asked, "What are you doing?"

"I'm looking for my toothbrush."

He went away for awhile, and I went to the bathroom and shaved. Then Ted came back.

He said, "Why don't you come down and have dinner."

"I don't rush on the Sabbath."

"It's not the Sabbath, it's Wednesday the 29th." He showed me his watch, and I looked at it, but I didn't know where to look to see the date. I thought he had set it back anyway as part of our advisors' game of seeing if anybody really knew what day it was.

Ted said, "What kind of drugs are you on?"

"None."

"C'mon what kind of drugs are you on?"

Not to be argumentative, I jokingly said, "Let's see, cocaine."

Ted didn't take it as a joke though. He believed me and said, "Did you read the rules?"

"Well, actually, I think I just signed them without reading them."

"Don't you think you should read before you sign?"

"Well, I know what the rules are. Why? Are you interviewing me?" I asked.

"Interviewing you for what?"

"For the job of JTG Israel Pilgrimage Advisor for next year," I said totally seriously. I thought they were interviewing me because I was the only one who figured out their day-switching trick.

Then Ted went back downstairs.

I gave up on finding my toothbrush and finished getting dressed in clothes that were slightly nicer because I thought it was Sabbath. I went downstairs a few minutes later. Everyone else had already left for somewhere.

Then I saw Ted, and caught him talking about me to a secretary who was down there. I heard Ted say, "And then he's got this razor thing that he doesn't know what to do with, and he thinks we're interviewing him."

Ted was laughing and thinking it was funny when I walked up and asked, "What are you doing?"

Ted looked flustered for a second and said, "Let me get you something to eat."

"I'm not hungry."

"C'mon, eat"

"No."

"C'mon, have some."

"Why?"

"We don't want you to skip meals."

"So?"

"C'mon"

"Okay, fine," I said, disgusted.

He brought me a tray of food from the kitchen and I started to eat. Then he asked me, "Is anything bothering you?"

I said, "Yes. You're bothering me."

"I'm your JTG advisor."

"You don't act like it," I said, as I started to eat.

"What do you mean?"

"You're not observing the Sabbath," I said, eating some more.

"It's Wednesday. What kind of drugs are you on?"

"I'm not on drugs."

"You said you were."

"I was just kidding," I said, taking some more food.

We talked a little more and I finished eating. I started to walk out the door. Then Ted grabbed me suddenly by the arm to stop me from going. I broke away from his grip, and wondered why he was starting to get rough, but waited for him anyway. He spoke to someone in the kitchen in Hebrew too fast for me to understand.

Then Ted started talking in Hebrew outside to a middle-aged man who, I theorized, was a member of a right-wing Israeli extremist organization. I thought they were planning to force me to join the extremist organization. I thought they wanted to brainwash me into helping them fight the Palestinians and other Arabs.

Ted and the middle-aged man quit talking and the man said to me, "I am your friend."

Of all the nerve. I thought, I'll make those decisions! I punched him in the nose, medium strength. I will decide who my friends are.

Then I walked over to the gate to the street which was open, and started to walk through it, but the security guard shut it. The guard said in an accented voice, "*Too* morrow, *too* morrow you will go out."

I made some half-hearted attempts to climb over the fence, but the guard pulled me down.

I thought this must be a concentration camp simulation exercise. Many Israelis were survivors of the Nazi Holocaust against the Jews, so I thought that now these fascist Israelis were holding me prisoner as an initiation. I said to Ted, "This isn't funny. I want to go for a walk."

Ted said, "No." Then he started to talk to the middle-aged man and another man in Hebrew. I was thinking, here are some racist, fascist, right-wing extremist, militaristic, Jewish Israelis who think Jews are the master race, and they are going to try to force me to join them. They want to brainwash me into helping them kill Arabs. Being an Israeli is like being a Nazi. They are so racist, they think intermarriage is a crime.

I thought about Melanie and Katie.

I was thinking, if only the rest of the American kids would get back here and help me.

Giving the Nazi salute, I yelled to the men there, "They were all saying Heil Hitler, Heil Hitler, but you knew they were full of shit! They were all saying Heil Hitler, Heil Hitler, but you knew the invasion was coming!" I went on like this for a while. The men stopped speaking in Hebrew and looked at me for a second. I stopped speaking and then they started back up again in Hebrew. I couldn't understand Hebrew when spoken quickly. I started up again, "They were all going Heil Hitler, Heil Hitler, but you knew they were wrong!" I went on like this for a while.

One man (there were now several men) said, "How can you say this about a man to whom I lost twelve cousins, three aunts, and a brother?"

I pointed to each of the men present and said, "Nazi, Nazi, Nazi, Nazi, Nazi, Nazi."

This prompted more talk in Hebrew, and then four of them grabbed me and tried to drag me inside. I struggled, but they managed to get me inside. I didn't punch any of them because there were too many of them. When I was inside, they said I should go up to my room, but I wouldn't go. I continued to call them Nazis. After a while, I was afraid they were going to beat me up because I called them Nazis. They wouldn't let me walk away. Four of them grabbed me and dragged me into a room. I would've killed them if I could have. None of the now ten men except Ted, who was in tears, were people I recognized. I thought I was being kidnapped. As I was being dragged near the secretary I said, "Call the police."

One of the men said, "Vee vill get you ze poleez."

In the room there were ten men there, so I was afraid to fight. I thought that this was probably what it felt like to be gang-raped. I thought they were going to beat me up and torture me. It would be like being a prisoner of war, only nobody would know where I was. America did not know that Israel was capturing people like this. At least during the Vietnam war, we knew the names of most of the people who were captured, and we knew that they were somewhere in Vietnam. My captors made me sit in a chair. There were three of them standing really close to me and seven others in a small room. They were all looking at me and talking in angry, hurried tones to each other about me in Hebrew, which I did not understand. I was so scared that they did not even have to hold my arms when they gave me a shot of a drug, which I have since learned was the sedating, major tranquilizer Thorazine. I thought the shot was to brainwash me into joining them in their fight against Palestinians and other Arabs.

I woke up in an ambulance, tied to a stretcher.

I said, "All I'm going to do is live. All I'm going to do is live."

I meant that as long as they let me live, I would cooperate.

One of the men was in the ambulance and repeated, "Nobody is trying to hurt you. Nobody is trying to hurt you."

I thought, yeah bullshit, then why are you kidnapping me? Where are the U.S. Marines when you need them? Will the United States go to war with Israel to save me? Israel could just report I died to cover up my capture.

The ambulance stopped and they pulled me out on the stretcher. I looked over my shoulder and saw a sign that said "Rambam Hospital." (The signs there are often in both Hebrew and English.) I thought, what are they taking me to a hospital for?

Then there were people surrounding me wearing white coats and speaking in Hebrew. I was too intimidated and drugged to say anything. Next I was in an elevator, and then I saw a sign that said, "Psychiatric Ward." I thought psychiatric wards were for murderers. Did I murder anybody? No! Then I thought, wait, the Soviet Union puts political prisoners in psychiatric wards. Israel must do so also. I'm a political prisoner!

The next thing I knew I woke up from what seemed like a good sleep. My contact lenses had been in overnight, so my eyes felt thick and dry. I took my lenses out and tried to find something to put them in. An orderly took them and I panicked. I was afraid he didn't know what they were. I was afraid they didn't have contact lenses in Israel. I was motioning to my eye and then this other guy with blonde hair said, "Hard or soft?"

I was so relieved. They knew what contacts were enough to say "Hard or soft." I also felt for a minute or so that JTG was taking good care of me because I hadn't been sleeping well.

When the guy with the blonde hair said, "Hard or soft?" though, I thought that meant he knew English very well, and I could talk to him like I would talk to an American. This was a mistake. A few minutes later he took me into a room to talk to me. He said with only a mild accent, "I am Dr. Ancell."

I said, "Hi."

He asked a lot of stuff including, "Do you take pills? Are you on any medication?"

I said, "No."

"Your father was against this trip?"

"Well, uh, yeah."

I don't remember the whole conversation, but several times he said, "Talk slow, I don't understand when you speak so fast."

I thought he was trying to tell me to relax, and not be nervous. I didn't understand that he meant he really had trouble understanding me. His English was not really very good. I knew he was a psychiatrist at this point, and I thought he just wanted me to relax.

He said, "Your mother is sick and that bothers you?"

At first I thought he meant something else happened to her. I said, "Really, what happened?"

"She is crippled and can't speak."

I said, "Oh, yeah, that's right, she can't." It felt good to talk to a psychiatrist. I don't remember what all I said. I had heard of psychiatrists and counseling before, but I didn't really know anything about them.

Later he said, "We'll talk more later."

I remember saying I wanted to leave.

An orderly named Greg kept following me around as I looked for an exit, saying, "The doctor will decide when you can go."

I kept saying, "The doctor has decided." Thinking of myself as the doctor, as the captain of my own ship.

The next thing I remember, I was sitting on a table in a small room on a different ward. I was arguing with the people there and calling them Nazis. They took my blood pressure and then forcibly gave me an injection with the sedating, calming, major tranquilizer Thorazine to put me to sleep.

There were usually about four people surrounding me when I was yelling, otherwise I might have started punching. I still felt I was a political prisoner. I thought I might be in this hospital for life. I thought that if I was not going to be in here for life, maybe they wanted to make me stay in Israel for life. There is no way I wanted to stay in Israel for life.

One time when I was yelling, about eight male patients (it was an all male ward) surrounded me and one said, "I'll kill you. I'll kill you."

Someone else said, "You must come with us."

They forced me over to my bed and started taking off my pants. I thought they were going to rape me. I yelled, "Greg!"

He told them to stop touching me, but then he gave me an injection of major tranquilizer Thorazine in my butt. It put me to sleep.

About the only time manic-depressives might get violent is when they are being forced into treatment. When you are manic, you feel fine and don't think there is anything wrong with you; therefore you don't see any need for treatment.

On one of the first few days, Dr. Ancell showed me the showers. In Nazi Germany, poison gas showers were used to kill Jews. When Ancell showed me the showers, I thought that he was saying that the Israeli fascist Jews could kill me, an American Jew, if they wanted to. I was in their control, and I had to do what they said. I knew it was a regular shower, because I had already used it, but it still felt like a death threat.

After a few days, the major tranquilizer Thorazine had made me sleep enough to be calm enough to cooperate with the staff. I started taking the drug in pill form when they told me to.

However, there was this huge muscular homosexual patient who kept harassing me. He kept wanting to borrow my shoes because they were Adidas. Adidas were imported to Israel and so they were expensive. He also liked shaking my hand with a very strong grip, and once in a while he would make sexual suggestions.

I would say, "No, you do that with girls."

He then would smile and say, "Oh, yes."

There was one female aid I liked to talk to, but she didn't know much English. She would sometimes say, "I don't understand," but because she said it in English, I thought she knew English. Eventually, after a few days, I started using the Hebrew I had learned at Mercer High.

One of the first things I remembered how to say was, "I don't know Hebrew," in Hebrew. This would confuse the patients and the staff into thinking I knew Hebrew, because I said it in Hebrew. Being in the hospital like this was an intensive crash course in Hebrew under duress. I had to remember all the Hebrew I had ever known, or life would be more difficult. Eventually I figured out there were two options, either I speak to them in Hebrew and they speak to me in English, or, I speak to them in English slowly, using big pauses between each word, no big words, and no slang. They would usually respond in English. I didn't get this really mastered until about July 5.

A typical exchange went something like this:

I said very slowly, "When do we get our snack?"

"Ten o'clock," said an Israeli patient.

"Is it always bread and tea?"

"Yes."

At first, when I could have a conversation that successful, I was happy. That was progress over the first few days.

I still had some delusions. The staff played the radio for us sometimes. The radio played American rock and roll. There was Fleetwood Mac's "Don't Stop Thinking about Tomorrow," which

I thought meant I could get out of the hospital tomorrow. This conflicted with "Hotel California" by the Eagles with the lines, "We are prisoners here of our own device," and "You can check out any time you like, but you can never leave." Early on, I thought the Haifa municipal radio station played these songs specifically for me, to give me a secret message. This is the first time I ever heard the song, "Hotel California."

The psychiatric ward was a strange place. One patient there went quickly through everyone's dresser drawers, ransacking them.

I said, "Hey, what are you doing?"

He said, "*Shut up!*" in a threatening tone, so I shut up. Later, I figured he was having nicotine fits, and was looking for cigarettes. Now, I think he was manic in addition to suffering from nicotine withdrawal. I've never seen such a nicotine fit.

Another guy was in for what I now guess was extreme depression. He couldn't shave himself, so somebody was doing it for him.

Around July 2, a staff person said, "Your father is coming here."

At first I thought he meant my father would be a patient here, and that seemed appropriate, so I said, "He will be a patient here?"

He said, "No, he is coming to visit you."

I thought, oh no, what could be worse, I travelled all this way to get away from him, because he was driving me crazy, and now he's coming to "visit" me. Like he's concerned with my well being? I was thoroughly annoyed.

A couple of days later, I realized by talking with the other patients, that I would get out eventually if I cooperated. I figured I had better cooperate or I could be given electroshock or a lobotomy like in *One Flew Over the Cuckoo's Nest*. My dad came that day, and I pretended to be glad to see him, thinking that if we appeared to be getting along, I would get out sooner. I still had some fear of a conspiracy to hold me against my will indefinitely, so it was good that my dad wanted me out of there. We talked for about ten minutes.

I told my dad, "You are the father of the problem."

He said, "What?"

"You are the father of the problem."

"You're kidding me, Bill, aren't you?"

"Just forget it."

I felt that given my vulnerable situation, I was in no position to start yelling at my dad.

Another thing my dad said was, "Your doctor says you're doing better today."

This made me try to think of who my doctor was, because at times the staff all blurred together. At times all the patients and staff blurred together because they almost all had dark curly hair, dark complexions, spoke Hebrew, and smoked cigarettes. To this day, hot temperatures plus cigarette smoke reminds me of that hospital. My dad's comment about my doctor was helpful, because it made me figure out which person was my doctor.

I realized then that Dr. Ancell was my doctor and started paying closer attention to him. I did get out of the Israeli hospital sooner because my dad was there. A funny thing is, I found out later that Dr. Ancell was from Mexico, so if I would've taken Spanish in high school, it could have been useful. His first language was Spanish. I had switched from Spanish to Hebrew in tenth grade, partly because I figured that as a Jew, I would have more use for Hebrew than Spanish. Little did I know.

Dr. Ancell and I needed to communicate better because for a long time he thought I was "hearing voices," having auditory hallucinations. He had asked me, "Are you hearing people speak to you?"

I said, "Yes, I'm hearing my friend say 'have a good time', also my aunt, also Jim Eckhart saying 'Don't do anything I wouldn't do.'"

I just thought Ancell meant hearing in the sense meaning remembering what people have said. It didn't occur to me that he was asking if I was having auditory hallucinations. However, from my response he decided that I was having auditory hallucinations. I found this out much later.

I communicated well with one patient. He had lived in California for one summer, so he knew English well. He interpreted for me a few times when I was speaking to other patients or the staff.

While in the hospital, I longed for something familiar, even my calculus book. I felt this sure was a long way from Melanie Carson's arms. And it was no way to start out life as an adult and high school graduate.

On July 5, my dad said we might be leaving on July 7. That was hopeful. Most of my paranoid symptoms were gone by then.

The major tranquilizer Thorazine they had given me, at first in shots and then in pills, had worked. And my delusions about reading the expressions on people's faces were gone also.

On July 7, early in the morning, we left. Fortunately, my dad was good at trying to get me the best medical care available when I was acutely sick. It was a good thing that he had enough money to pay Dr. Ancell to fly all the way back to Seattle with us. That way Ancell would be sure I was okay on the plane on the way back, and he could talk to the doctor I would start to see in Seattle.

It was a long flight, but it was sure good to be back in America. It was good to hear people speaking English, and to see a variety of hair colors and encounter some people who weren't smoking. However, I felt like I had been recaptured by the enemy, my dad. I had almost escaped on a nice tour of Israel, but I had blown it. I would have preferred to rejoin my tour group, but they wouldn't take me back. We switched planes in New York and flew to Seattle from there. I was glad to be on a plane loaded with Americans. I was very glad to be back in America, even if it meant being in a psychiatric ward.

We went home to my house after we got to Seattle. My brothers and my mom were very relieved to see that I was okay.

I said, "Ahnee low meshugana, ahnee American." That's Hebrew for, "I'm not crazy, I'm American."

My brothers were relieved that I was making sense.

Then we went to Helgerson Hospital in downtown Seattle. I was put in the psychiatric ward and met Dr. Ronald Kelly. I begged him to let me show him that I could fall asleep without drugs, but he insisted on giving me some major tranquilizer Thorazine. As it turns out, I did need the Thorazine or a major tranquilizer of some kind. It was what Ancell had been giving me in Israel. It would have been better in combination with mood leveler Lithium, but for the short term it was good medical practice. I was on Thorazine for three months.

Dr. Kelly and Dr. Ancell then had plenty of time to talk to each other. Ancell had flown all the way back to Seattle with us, from Israel, at my dad's request and expense.

I slept that night and I woke up in the morning. The hospital in America was much nicer than in Israel. I had my own room rather than having to share it with five other guys. Also, the food was better. Familiar brands of familiar foods in familiar wrappers written in English. Not so much yogurt, eggs, and greens. More meat and potatoes. Land O' Lakes butter and milk. Wheaties. Corn Flakes. Cheerios.

I participated in occupational therapy, better described as arts and crafts. It was led by nice American women who all obviously thought I was sicker than I was. They talked baby talk to me until I talked to them for a while. I found out later that they had been told that I was hallucinating regularly. When I read my chart years later, I saw they wrote that they observed me having some hallucinations. They were mistaken. The way I moved my eyes or something made them think I was seeing things. Some manics hallucinate, others don't. I'm one who doesn't.

Earlier I had been asked, "Are your poker friends with you in the hospital?"

I said, "Yes," but I meant they are with me in spirit, and they want me to get better. It hadn't occurred to me that they were asking if I was having visual hallucinations.

Their idea that I was having hallucinations was a mistake. It is a serious symptom that I didn't have, and I don't want to be thought of as having had. It does not change the diagnosis, because some manics do hallucinate. Sometimes the manic knows what he is seeing is not real, and sometimes he does not know. However, they could have told me to point to where my poker friends are sitting right now, name them, say who is dealing, say what game they are dealing, and tell what I had just bet.

I would have said, "Are you guys crazy? Why are you asking me all these bizarre questions?"

Looking back, I didn't see or hear anything out of place. I could have only hallucinated some very ordinary pieces of furniture in very ordinary places.

Of course, I had plenty of delusions. Delusions are ridiculous conclusions drawn from normal sights and sounds. The flight attendant wanted the shade down, so I thought she was hiding fighter planes. Some men thought I was acting strangely as a tourist in Israel, so I thought they wanted to kidnap me and brainwash me. The Haifa municipal radio station played "Hotel California," and I thought they were sending me a personally harassing secret message like, "Our minds are definitely twisted," from the words of the song.

For a while, I kept up the mistaken attitude that although I had been confused, most of the problem I had in Israel resulted from a misunderstanding due to the language barrier. I didn't know I had a definable illness. I just thought I had been under too much stress and had not gotten enough sleep.

On July 12, they let me out of the hospital for the evening because it was my eighteenth birthday. All I could think about was that now, being an adult, I could get stuck with the bill for my hospitalization. Now I had to be nice to my dad so he would pay for it. This was just when the healthy me should have been dumping my dad.

On about July 13 (the dates matter because I was counting the days until I could get out) my dad and my brothers, Steve and Rick, came to visit me. My dad made a horrendous statement, "So much of this could've been prevented if our family just had closer relationships. If Bill could've told me he was having problems before he left, this could have been solved much more easily."

I had flown all the way to Israel to get away from my dad because he did not want me to have a girlfriend. He wanted to be the one closest to me. I went to Israel to get away from my dad because he was driving me crazy by wanting such a close relationship. I thought that in Israel I'd be free to have a girlfriend for a while without getting yelled at, and I'd cheer up. Now my dad was pulling this junk.

I tried to explain that a more distant relationship between him and me would have made my life easier, that he was demanding too much attention. I didn't lay it on thicker and heavier because I was afraid that if I argued with my dad, I would be forced to stay in the hospital longer.

Steve and Rick were there and I didn't want to offend them. My dad said we should start hugging each other to be closer. We never did before. We weren't Italian. I didn't mind hugging my brothers although it felt strange. I wasn't going to hug my dad, but my brothers seemed like they'd be mad if I didn't, so I did. My brothers didn't know that my dad didn't want me to have a girlfriend.

For years after that, my dad would force me to hug him by basically threatening to quit paying for room, board, and tuition if I didn't.

On July 15, 1977 I was discharged from the hospital with no current delusions, but I didn't know that I had been out of touch with reality. I knew I had been confused about which day it was, but I thought the whole thing had largely been a misunderstanding because the group leaders had wrongfully accused me of being on street drugs, and because I didn't know Hebrew.

Dr. Ronald Kelly had, up to this point, failed to tell me my diagnosis. I had asked, "What's wrong with me?"

He had said, "Oh don't worry, we'll have you out of here soon." He wouldn't answer the question.

Many years later, in 1989, I requested a copy of my medical records, and I saw that he had written in 1977 that I was schizophrenic. He failed to tell me that, even though I had asked him directly. I consider that awful, even if it was a bad guess at diagnosis. The patients' bill of rights in effect in most states requires that a patient know his diagnosis. He also got the diagnosis wrong to begin with. I consider that bad medical practice.

Dr. Kelly's failure to diagnose correctly, and failure to discuss the diagnosis with me, delayed the beginning of my recovery from 1977 to 1982. I was properly diagnosed and started getting better care in 1982. I started cheering up then.

Years of manic-depressive misery could have been minimized if Dr. Kelly would have recognized that mood leveler Lithium needed to be tried right away. I also would need antidepressants in just a few months, but Dr. Kelly never prescribed them or told me that depression was treatable. I had never heard of antidepressants. I experienced a lot of depression and mania during those years that could have been avoided with Lithium, antidepressants, and major tranquilizers. Dr. Kelly could have told me how to recognize mania in myself, and it would have prevented a lot of problems, including two hospitalizations. If he would have told me about antidepressants, I likely would have graduated from college in four years instead of six, and I likely would've had a better social life. He never talked to me about my symptoms.

I didn't hear about antidepressants and didn't realize that they would help me until February 1982. When I realized how much they helped, and that Dr. Kelly had failed to mention them, I wanted to sue him for medical malpractice. However, the doctor I had then was unwilling to testify against Dr. Kelly, so I was unable to sue.

I now have the medical records from this 1977 episode. In the records, Dr. Kelly also complains that I hadn't admitted that I was mentally ill. This is a lie.

I had asked him, "What is wrong with me?" I had also asked, "What is my diagnosis?"

He never answered.

Dr. Kelly never discussed my symptoms with me. He never named any mental illness that I was supposed to think I had. He never named any illness I was supposed to admit I had. As a result of his lack of information, I thought I was just confused from not sleeping enough. He never even said the words "mentally ill" to me. Another problem is that he would often, in the hospital, treat me like a baby.

For example, when I was feeling better, I would ask, "Tell me why I can't get out today. How long will I be here?"

He would say, "There, there, now, everything will be okay." He wouldn't answer the question. This clearly indicated his intent of never carrying on a rational conversation with me. My barber and my dentist talk to me more than my psychiatrist, Dr. Kelly, ever did.

This was his chance to start a rational, intelligent discussion with me about what had gone on. Instead, he never discussed the incidents on the night I was put in the hospital. That night was the first time something went drastically wrong with me. Discussing such incidents was the key to making a proper diagnosis. *It doesn't take a legal or medical genius to know that it was Dr. Kelly's duty to ask me what I was thinking, and why I was doing what I was doing on the night I was put in the hospital.* He never asked me.

Dr. Kelly did continue the major tranquilizer Thorazine, which for the short term was decent medicine.

Throughout this book, medications will always be preceded by adjectives like "major tranquilizer" or "antidepressant." I want the medications I discuss to be crystal clear. At times, they will not be living up to their descriptions. Often they will fail because the doctor made errors in the prescribing strategy. At other times they will fail because they are far from perfect under the best of circumstances. By the end of the book, the drugs are successful. Drugs become the heroes of this book.

8

Dr. Kelly Pretends To Practice Outpatient Psychiatry

I got out of the hospital and was free at last, but I still had to live with my family. I asked my Aunt Brenda and Uncle Mike if I could live with them, but they again said no because of my father's objections. They did not believe me when I said my father did not want me to have a girlfriend. It was too heavy an accusation for them to believe.

I went to a poker game with my usual friends, and said something like, "I'd like to tell you guys what happened, but I'm not really sure."

I left the card game relatively early to make sure I got enough sleep. I wondered what my friends had been told about me, but I didn't have the assertiveness to ask. I was afraid that they had heard only official fifth-hand rumor, and I didn't know what the rumor was. I still couldn't tell them about Melanie, because they would have said, "Oh, it doesn't matter, she's a goy."

I was on a lot of major tranquilizer Thorazine so it was hard to talk, and still I had heard nothing about my diagnosis. I hadn't figured out what all went wrong the night they put me in the hospital.

I told some people that the explanation for the events in Israel was that I was confused. I said mostly it was a misunderstanding from the language barrier and from the Israelis thinking that I was on drugs. I said I was also confused because I hadn't slept much in five days. It's true I hadn't slept much in the five days prior to being put in the hospital, but that was as much a symptom as a cause. I figured it was nervous exhaustion or stress.

I saw Dr. Kelly three times as an outpatient that summer. His treatment did not help me at all. I sat in a chair and talked, facing him. He just wrote down what I said. I saw him for a half an hour. Here is what a typical session with him was like.

At the beginning of the half hour he asked, "How are you?"

I then talked for five minutes. I told him about myself, Dad, Mom, my brothers, Melanie, school, Israel, swimming, or my friends. He wrote down what I said. He didn't say a word. He did not give me any information.

Then he asked, "How's your family?" Again, I spoke for about five minutes. I told him about myself, Dad, Mom, my brothers, Melanie, school, Israel, swimming, or my friends. He wrote down what I said. He didn't say a word. He did not give me any information.

Then he asked, "What have you been doing?"

I spoke for about five minutes. I told him I had been running, playing tennis, and playing poker. He wrote down what I said. He didn't say a word. He did not give me any information. After a few more general questions like this, the half-hour session was over.

He said, "Okay, time's up, bye." At the time, I thought that was standard practice. I didn't know any better.

During my five-minute answers to his general questions, I displayed symptoms of depression from being dragged down by major tranquilizer Thorazine. And, I described symptoms of mania and depression from the recent past while answering his questions. However, Dr. Kelly apparently missed the significance of the symptoms I was describing. At that time, I didn't know they were symptoms of a specific disease. I hadn't heard of manic depression before, so I didn't know what it was. I know now.

Occasionally with great effort, I could get Dr. Kelly to answer a question. I asked, 'Why did they put me in the hospital the way they did? Couldn't they just have let me catch up on sleep? Couldn't they have told me that they wanted to take me to a hospital?"

After I asked him three times, he said, as if he was quite annoyed at the question, "You took a swing at the tour director."

When he said that, and after I had talked to many people other than Dr. Kelly, I became more sure that the people who dragged me into the room were not right-wing Israeli extremists trying to brainwash me into killing Arabs just because I was Jewish like them. Eventually, I figured out they must have been the cooks and janitors who worked at the school we were staying at, and one of them was the tour supervisor.

Eventually, by gathering information from people other than Dr. Kelly, and by thinking about it enough, I figured out what happened. I did this by talking to a lot of people who had been on the trip, including Brian Green, when they got home. I realized that there was something seriously wrong with me. Also I remembered the stress I was feeling from my home situation, and figured that that was a major cause of the problem. So I wanted a word for what happened, and all my dad would say was that I was "sick." He acted like it was outlandish for me to want another more specific word. I wondered if nervous breakdown was the word, and asked some people what word they had heard, but nobody knew a specific word.

I asked Dr. Kelly, "What is the word for the problem I had in Israel?"

I paused and Dr. Kelly remained expressionless in his chair. He kept writing.

I asked Dr. Kelly again, "What is the *word* for it?"

I paused. Dr. Kelly kept writing. He kept looking down at his yellow legal pad. He was ignoring me.

"Dr. Kelly, is there a *word* for it? Is there a *name* for the problem I had there? *Dr. Kelly, is there a word for it? Is "nervous breakdown" the word?*"

He finally acted startled, quit writing, sat up in his chair, adjusted his hearing aid, and said, "'Nervous breakdown' is not the word." He went on to say, "What happened to you has no known explanation and it is very rare. All it can be called is a severe thinking disturbance." His tone was that of a spectator rather than a concerned caregiver. His tone seemed to be asking: What are you asking me for? He lied when he said that there was no word for it, after he already had written down a diagnosis. He had written that I was schizophrenic, and that I would need medication for an indefinite period. I know that he wrote that, because as I've mentioned, in 1989 when I started to write this book I requested a copy of my medical records from 1977.

Schizophrenia was the wrong diagnosis, but he could have at least said, "Well it is either schizophrenia or manic depression, I'm not sure." Actually he could not honestly be sure of anything, because he never asked me what my symptoms were. There is a list of symptoms for both diseases, and you either have those symptoms or you don't. He never showed me the symptom lists. He gave me medication for only three months instead of an indefinite period. I needed to know my diagnosis. There is literature to read about schizophrenia that can help a patient. However, you will never find this literature if your doctor has not said the word "schizophrenia" to you. You won't know what to look under at the library.

At the library I could have learned that schizophrenics usually hallucinate, don't have trouble sleeping, have their delusions and hallucinations in the presence of normal mood, may have no emotional fluctuations at all, think that outside forces are controlling their mind (not just giving messages), or think that they can broadcast their thoughts. All of these symptoms would have helped rule out schizophrenia in my case. Maybe I would have read about manic depression in the same section of a book. Instead, Dr. Kelly lied by saying that he couldn't imagine a diagnosis.

Maybe he thought hearing the word "schizophrenia" would hurt my feelings. That would be redundant. My feelings could not have been hurt more than they already had been. I was already "a person who has been in a psychiatric ward." One more word would not hurt me. Sticks and stones may break my bones, but a diagnosis will never hurt me.

If Dr. Kelly had been a good doctor, he would have questioned me closely about my episode and the months leading up to it. He would have discovered that I was manic depressive. Then he would have told me my diagnosis, and given me mood-leveling Lithium. Lithium is the treatment for manic depression. It is not the treatment for schizophrenia. He never prescribed this drug for me. He also should have told me about antidepressants. I would need antidepressants in a few months, but didn't get them for four-and-a-half years because Dr. Kelly failed to tell me about them. I didn't hear about them for four-and-a-half years. I suffered greatly because of his laziness.

As I said earlier, my barber and my dentist talk to me more than Dr. Kelly ever did.

At the back of this book is a list of symptoms of mania and depression that psychiatrists, psychologists, general physicians, social workers, and people can use as a guide to recognize manic depression. People with the disease should seek treatment from a competent psychiatrist.

To qualify as manic or depressed, you usually need just four of these symptoms at the same time. To experience depression after a serious loss or other tragedy is normal, but the depression should last only two weeks or so. If it lasts longer, treatment is recommended.

Just for reference, a good doctor would have also talked to a few of my friends to find out my medical and psychological history. Dr. Kelly just talked to my dad. A doctor can't get an accurate psychological history of an eighteen-year-old by talking only to one parent. The doctor needs to talk to the patient's friends, with the permission of the patient, of course.

During this August of 1977, I needed something to do. It was summer. Classes at the University of Puget Sound didn't start until a few days after Labor Day. We were due for orientation a few days before Labor Day. In the meantime, in August, I did some lawn work at home, hung out with my friends, and took a speed-reading course.

That summer, my friends stuck by me. I told them there had been something seriously wrong, but there was no explanation for it other than the stress from my family situation. I didn't know about the genetic aspects of it; I thought it was environmental.

Throughout the summer, I still thought of Melanie Carson, and looked forward to being in the same city as her, Tacoma, without my dad. In the same pattern as before my trip to Israel, I was hanging around while being totally preoccupied with Melanie. I was now in the sort of depressive zone that major tranquilizer Thorazine drags you down into when it is trying to pull you down from mania. Mania is like being way too far up. Depressed is way too far down. Thorazine calms you enough from mania to sleep at night, but drags you down a bit during the day. It's sort of like depression. I was preoccupied with "I am a loser" thoughts.

The day before I left for college, Phil Holland and Jim Eckhart, two high school poker buddies, came over to say good-bye. We had been friends since we were little kids. Now I was actually leaving them and my other friends in order to improve my social life and love life. It was absurd. If I could just get to school, I would be at a place where I wouldn't get yelled at for having a date. I told my friends that I would visit and write. I felt like crying as they left my house. I had said good-bye to my other friends earlier. Some were going away, but many were living at home and going to UW. I wanted to go there too, I had told them, but I had to get out of my house.

9

College Freshman Half There

On the way down to the University of Puget Sound, I was alone in the car with my dad. I was sitting there not saying anything and he was driving. He asked, "What are you thinking about?"

I said, "Nothing."

He took his foot off the accelerator threatening to turn the car around and asked angrily, "Are you *mad* at me about something?"

Terrified at his threat of turning the car around, and not wanting the yelling which he usually gave me after asking if I was mad at him, I said, "No, no," and I slid as far to the right in the passenger seat as I could.

"*What* are you thinking about then?" he asked, speeding up.

I said, "I'm thinking about what happened in Israel."

"What are you thinking about *that* for?" he asked angrily. "Are you afraid it's going to happen *again?*"

"No. I'm planning how to tell my roommates about it."

"You don't have to tell *anybody* about this."

"But I want to tell my roommates."

"What do you want to tell *them* for?"

"I'm planning on being friends with them."

He said angrily and loudly, *"You don't need any friends! I never had any friends when I was in college!"*

I said, "I want to have friends."

He said, taking his foot off the accelerator and slowing down, "Maybe you're not ready to go to college yet. Maybe you should stay home."

I was shocked and horrified. I knew he was jealous of my potential relationship with my roommates. I said, "Okay Dad, fine. I won't tell them."

My dad then sped up a bit. Then there was a moment of silence, but he wouldn't leave me alone. He asked, "What are you thinking about now, honey?"

"*Nothing.*"

"Are you still thinking about the *same thing?*"

"*Yeah. Why?*"

"*Oh, I'm taking you home,*" he said, taking his foot off the accelerator.

"*Dad, Dad, Dad,* I won't tell anyone."

"Okay, don't tell anyone," he said speeding up again.

"Look, *honey,* I'm your best friend. I'm paying for your *education.* You don't need any other friends."

"Right, Dad, but I think I should be friends with my roommates."

"Oh, I'm taking you home!" he said angrily as he took his foot off the accelerator. He started looking for a place to turn around.

I couldn't believe it. I felt coerced. I started to feel the same way I felt when I was held by the four guys who grabbed me the night I was put in the hospital in Israel. I felt I needed my dad's money. I probably could have started getting social security disability if I would have known what my life was going to be like, and if I would have known my diagnosis. However, I just knew I wanted to go to college, so I needed my dad's money.

"*Okay, okay, Dad.* I won't say a thing to them."

He sped up again.

He asked, "What did you want to tell *them* for?"

"They'll ask what I did this summer."

"Tell them to mind their own *business!*"

I said, "That wouldn't be very friendly. I want to be friends with them."

He said loudly and angrily, "What do you need friends for?! I never had any friends when I was in college!"

Taking his foot off the accelerator and starting to turn the car around again he said, "Maybe you're not ready to go away to college yet, because you're supposed to be going there to study, not make any friends."

I started to consider the possibility of actually not telling my roommates about Israel, but I swore I would survive to tell this story.

Being in the depressive, obsessive state that the tranquilizer Thorazine drags you into, I really was stuck on planning on what to say to my roommates in an hour. I couldn't switch gears fast enough to think of something to say to get more control of the present situation. The healthy me might have said, "Do you want me to call my three siblings and my three uncles and tell them you don't want me to go to college because I'm planning to be friends with my roommates? Or would you like to just drive 55 miles per hour? Quit slowing the car down, or I will tell them."

Or the more responsible, healthy me may have had confidence in my ability to hold a job. I might have calmly said, "If you turn this car around, I'll get my Bar Mitzvah money from you. I'll get an apartment. I'll get a job, skip college, and I'll never speak to you again."

Instead I felt that college dorm life was my only way to gradually recover. I felt stuck and totally coerced. I felt I needed my dad's money. I didn't think I could hold a job until I gradually recovered.

My dad said, "Are you afraid that nobody loves you because of what happened in Israel?"

"No, no, Dad, I was just thinking that my roommates will ask what I did this summer."

"Tell them to mind their own *business!*"

"I want to be nice to them."

"You don't need to be nice to them." He paused for a few moments, thinking, and then said, *"I'm taking you home!"* while taking his foot off the accelerator.

"No, no, Dad. I won't talk to them, I promise."

"You're going down there to study, not make friends."

"Right."

He speeded up.

"Is the problem that you think I don't love you? Are you afraid I think you've been a bad son to me?"

"No. The opposite."

"Maybe you should stay home just this quarter, I could make steak *every night*. We could take you home and make you feel appreciated, so you know we care about you. Is that the problem, that you don't feel appreciated?"

"No, no, Dad. I was just looking forward to school."

"Look, you have to study a lot. You don't need any friends. I'm the best friend you are ever going to have."

"Dad, yes, I swear I'll just study and not make any friends, I won't tell anyone about what happened in Israel as long as I live," I said, trying to figure out how I was going to live like that.

He then put his foot back on the accelerator and said, "Okay, just study."

I felt relieved when he put his foot back on the accelerator.

This is a greatly abbreviated version of the half hour of abuse I suffered on the way to college. His threats of not letting me go to college scared me so much that I never told my roommates about my "severe thinking disturbance," as Dr. Kelly had called my manic episode. This violated the rule that says you tell your roommates everything significant, whether it be good or bad, if you expect to be friends with them. One of my roommates from then is now a psychiatrist and was interested in psychology then. He could have suggested counseling then, and I might have gotten diagnosed earlier. Thanks to my dad, I didn't take the initiative to go to counseling, because I felt I would've had to keep secret the fact that I was going and the reason I was going. I told my roommates that my drugs were for hay fever. I tried to be as friendly to my roommates as possible. I told them the other things I did in the summer. We talked a lot about other stuff. Once my roommate Wayne asked, "What did you do this summer?"

I answered, "Well, early in the summer something happened that I don't want to talk about. Later I took a speed-reading course and hung out with my friends, played some poker, did some movies."

"Did you work at all?"

"No. Actually not. What are you going to major in?"

"Maybe biology," said Wayne.

"Maybe physics," said Al.

"For me," I said, "maybe physics or chemistry."

We kept talking about potential classes, what we did in high school, where else we applied to college, our SAT scores, and lots of other stuff.

My roommates, Wayne and Al, were a little too polite and never pressed me to find out what happened.

Even though I knew my dad was just jealous of my sharing personal information with other people, I didn't want to risk my four years of room, board, and tuition by disobeying him. I felt I needed his money. I mistakenly thought going out and working full time right after high school was a losing proposition, even under the best of circumstances. Also, once I didn't tell my roommates, there never was a perfect time to tell them about my nervous breakdown. My dad's threats had made it genuinely hard to talk about even though I had been looking forward to telling about it. It was like running away from home, but not having permission to cross the street.

Wayne was from Olympia, and Al was from San Francisco. Wayne was interested in biology and psychology. He is the one who is now a psychiatrist. In high school he was on the debate team, and was a good student.

Al was interested in computers, spent a long time in the computer center each day, and was somewhat less sociable than Wayne.

As time went on, I developed a pretty good, respectful friendship with Wayne, but Al kept to himself more. One thing I used to say to Al was, "You're on drugs." (He was not on drugs.)

He would say, "I'm not on drugs."

I would say, "Oh, you are too."

"I am not on drugs."

"Oh, yeah you are."

It could go on awhile, or end there. It was in the nature of a hassling, razzing kind of joke.

This was the result of my being accused of being on drugs in Israel, and also sometimes in the winter and spring of twelfth grade.

I was accused of being on drugs occasionally in twelfth grade because I looked out of it. I was depressed, and I had bloodshot eyes from swimming and wearing contact lenses. People said to me, "Hey, are you on drugs?" in an interested and joking manner. That was usually at a beer fest, so being stoned was considered great, because it was 1977, and marijuana was considered cool.

Just for the record, I've never used illegal drugs, and I've never been drunk.

I soon returned to the depressed phase of manic depression. I was very unhappy. I tried to be as sociable as possible in an effort to cheer myself up. I was still depressed about my swimming performance in twelfth grade. Also I was still depressed about not being the boyfriend of Melanie Carson.

I thought then, if only my dad wouldn't have gotten so mad when I went out with her, we might have been together. I never would have gone to Israel. I thought one day I would get my act together and I'd be able to call her at Pacific Lutheran University across town, and say the right thing. However, she had said no to going to prom with me. I had asked her out again after prom in early June and she said no to that also. By that time she had probably heard that I had suffered a nervous breakdown. She would just say no again if I asked her out again. There was no point in calling her. I had bugged her too much as it was.

Few of the women at Puget Sound looked as good as I remembered her to be.

Thinking things would straighten out in my life, not knowing that I had a chronic illness, I decided to take pre-med classes. Many people at Puget Sound were pre-med, as were several of my poker buddies at home. I decided it was fashionable to be pre-med, so I'd be one too.

My concentration was poor. When I was alone and tried to study, I really had problems getting any school work done. I would worry about swimming, about Melanie, about my "severe thinking disturbance" in Israel, and about the fact that I still had to get along with my dad. It would take me three hours to do a one-hour assignment. The negative, depressive, inappropriately pessimistic thoughts dominating my head went something like this:

Here I am stuck at this crummy place. These women are ugly. They average about a three on a ten-point scale. None compare to Melanie Carson. This is a crummy place. Also, Melanie is not as sleazy as these Puget Sound women. This is a crummy place. Why couldn't I have been born Lutheran? I'm a loser. Why did I go and take Hebrew for my language requirement? Just because I already have some. I'm in a rut. It clearly has no point. This is such a disaster. The one cute Jewish woman here is clearly not religious and dates Christians. That's very good, yet I keep thinking that my friends and relatives would disown me if I did. My love life is a disaster.

I got a string of thoughts like this between maybe *every paragraph* of reading homework. I really thought a romance with someone who I thought was attractive was the only way to cheer up. I did not yet have insight into the phenomenon of depression affecting how attractive people appear to be.

I was friends with my roommates and the people on my floor, but because I was depressed, nobody seemed as fun as people seemed when I was well. I ate meals with my roommates and floormates, and we would try to make each other laugh, but I had a pretty low percentage of successful jokes. We went to movies together, partied together, and hung out in our dorm rooms and talked. There were a lot of interesting people on my floor. It was fun getting to know people from all over the region.

I got some okay grades because I took easy classes. Fall quarter ended a couple days before Thanksgiving. I went home. We had Thanksgiving with my aunt, uncle, and cousins, the Felbers.

I saw Dr. Kelly again. I asked him again what the cause of my problem in Israel was, and he basically shrugged his shoulders again. I accepted that as good medical practice at the time! As a result of what he said, I believed I had nothing definably wrong with me.

In the winter, I was on the swim team. I lettered for swimming the 1000-yard freestyle in meets. This did not boost my pride though. Nobody else wanted to swim the 1000. The team was very minor league. My high school's records were faster than the UPS school records.

In the spring, I felt that I should possibly tell my floormates of my "severe thinking disturbance." I felt they would know me and understand me better if they knew. Yet it seemed stupid and negative to tell, and I remembered that my dad had told me not to tell.

At the beginning of the school year, I had told my resident advisor, "I am on medication for a severe thinking disturbance. Without it I kind of flip out. I'll be on it until the prescription runs out, and then I won't be on it anymore."

She said, "Okay," and she didn't question me further.

This was because as our resident advisor, she had asked us to tell her of any medication. Nobody else heard me tell her. Now, I decided I needed help in deciding whether or not to tell my friends. I decided to talk to her about it. I tried knocking on her door, but she was never home. I sent her a note through campus mail, saying I wanted to talk to her. I didn't say what about. I wanted to be sure to talk to her, but keep it confidential, not make it sound like an emergency, and not make it look like she necessarily would be able to convince me of what to do without really listening. All these requirements seemed huge at the time, because I was severely depressed. I was not assertive enough to make this easier. I knew that the difference between telling and not telling could be a big deal. Maybe they could give me moral support for dealing with my dad, but maybe they would think less of me.

My resident advisor stuck her head in my dorm room when there was about three people standing there and she said, "Bill, did you want to talk to me?"

I said, "Oh, uh, I don't need to talk to you anymore." Which was not true, but I had to say that, because then everyone would want to know what we talked about.

She said, "Okay." Then she left.

Predictably, Wayne then said, "What did you want to talk to her about?"

I said, "Oh, nothing."

After that I was too unassertive to ask her to talk to me again. I figured I already had bugged her too much. Even though I hadn't bugged her. I knew that the happy me of old, who should be the present happy me, would have handled the situation, tactfully, efficiently, and gracefully. I knew the "severe thinking disturbance" and the present unhappiness making it difficult to talk about, were related, but I did not know how. I could not imitate the happy me. I didn't know that my unhappiness was due to a definable disease. I thought it was due to my environment. I thought my crummy home environment was bugging me long distance, and I thought my lack of a girlfriend at college was a natural justifiable reason for feeling down.

Wondering what the happy me would be doing was a legitimate medical question, but it was also a symptom. All day I hesitated to move because I wondered what the happy me would be having for lunch, what the happy me would be saying right now, what the happy me would be studying right now, and what the healthy me would have been studying five minutes ago. This could ruin a whole day and was a symptom.

That year I got a B average by taking several courses that I almost could have tested out of, because I had learned the material in high school when I was well. I learned just a little bit in college. I couldn't concentrate; my mind was too filled with depressive, obsessive, negative, and pessimistic thoughts.

It was a very sad and boring time.

10

Summertime and I Can't Reach My Bootstraps

The summer of 1978, I got a job as a lifeguard and swim instructor at the Mercer Island Jewish Community Center. I liked teaching little kids, but my attention was not always what it should have been, because I was depressed. Also, for lifeguarding, it would've been much safer for the kids who were swimming, if I was all there.

Once there was a four-year-old on the deck who taunted me, "Bet you can't catch me." I was thinking so poorly that I, blindly enforcing the rule against running around on the deck, picked her up and threw her in the pool. Then I looked away. A few moments later, I looked back, and she was struggling with her head under water. I jumped in and saved her. She could've drowned. She had come to the pool every day and was always in the water, so I thought she could swim, but then I realized she had always been hanging on the wall in the shallow end.

Also, I was a jerk to my co-worker Mark Daniels. Sometimes he wanted me to work his shift for him, but I usually refused. More hours gave me more stress, I felt, and lowered my mood further it seemed. I really was not very nice to him. I couldn't get any satisfaction out of doing a favor for another person. I was crabby and irritable, a symptom of depression.

Feeling crummy at work and elsewhere, I felt I had to do something to make myself feel better. In my free time, (I only worked about twenty-five hours per week) I read self-help books. I read *How To Be Your Own Best Friend, Looking Out for #1, Win-*

ning Through Intimidation, Your Erroneous Zones, Grief, and *How To Take Charge of Your Life.* I liked reading these books. They seemed to be on my side. However, my mood remained depressed after I read them. In other words, these books didn't help. They may help some people, but they didn't help me. They didn't help me regain the smoothness, happiness, or confidence I once had.

I didn't consider a psychiatrist, because I had concluded psychiatrists couldn't really do anything. This conclusion was based on my experience with Dr. Kelly. I figured I was sleeping fine, so I didn't need major tranquilizer Thorazine, so I didn't need Dr. Kelly.

My lifeguard/swim instructor co-worker Mark apparently had some smoothness. He was a former swim teammate of mine at Mercer High. He was a year younger, so he had just graduated. All he could talk about was women. He went out with a different woman every night. He told me some wild stories about the women he met.

I went out with a few women that summer. I didn't go out with any woman more than once, except one.

Towards the end of the summer, Mark invited me to a party with a bunch of his friends. I went, and at that party I met Beth Tasa. I talked to her with a group of people for a while. She told about a skiing wipe-out she had that broke her leg. It was healed, but she still had a scar. Other people were talking about how drunk you should get on your nineteenth birthday, because then you could celebrate the fact that you could drink legally. I thought she was cute and seemed smart. I thought it was impressive that she had been a great skier.

A few days later, I called someone else who was a mutual friend of Beth's and mine, and asked her for Beth's phone number.

I asked Beth out to an amusement park. We went about 3:00 P.M. We held hands the whole time we were there. We went on some rides and saw some shows and displays, and I won her a big teddy bear at one of those games that gave stuffed animals as prizes. I had to throw a hoop over the bear, and the hoop had to go all the way down. Mine did.

We talked about school and our friends and what to major in while we were walking around.

About 9:30 P.M., we sat down a little way away from all the distractions. We sat in a small area that was grassy and we leaned against a fence and talked in greater depth. We talked about college. She was going to be a freshman. She was a good student and was going to Vassar. I told her about my mother, and about what a problem my father was. She was touched. Then we kissed. She really kissed like she meant it. It was great.

The next time I went out with Beth, we went to dinner at a fancy restaurant. That was nice. We dressed up. I felt so mature and sophisticated. I thought this could be leading to a serious relationship if it weren't for the fact that she was going to Vassar in a week. Then we went to Phantom Lake and walked part of the way around. After that, we headed back to Mercer Island and parked somewhere.

The third time we went out, we saw the movie *Heaven Can Wait*. Then we parked in the parking lot of a big outdoor swimming pool until a cop pulled up and kicked us out of the park, because you're not supposed to be parked there after 11:00 P.M. We went home.

Beth had to go off to school in a day or two, so we didn't see each other again that summer. We exchanged school addresses, and promised to write, and take good care of ourselves.

11

Sophomore Space Cadet

I spent most of the school year of 1978–1979 in my dorm room preoccupied with inappropriately negative, inappropriately pessimistic, depressive strings of thoughts that went something like this:

Oh, I just shouldn't have said that to Tracy at lunch. Debbie heard that and now she thinks I'm weird. I'm such a jerk. I would be such a good boyfriend if I knew a woman was right for me. She would have to be able to make me happy. None of these women really make me happy. I'm such a jerk that they wouldn't like me. If they did like me, they'd be stupid. I don't want a stupid girlfriend. With a stupid girlfriend, I would be miserable. No matter who she was, she'd be mad at me for being inattentive, for not caring about the silly stuff women care about. I don't like the same things they like. It would be better if this radio played better music. Some women like to go dancing. How can they dance at a time like this? Can't they see the world is a crummy place? The former motivated, happy me could attract women. Now I can't handle the pressure. Why couldn't my dad approve of my dating? I'd have to keep it a secret. Maybe he'll die and I'll inherit money. Women still wouldn't like me; they would know the money was inherited and not earned. I'm such a loser. I need to get a normal life like everybody else. I need to get normal.

Worries like this preoccupied me during classes, and when I was trying to study, so much that I hardly learned anything. I also was so preoccupied that I hardly *did* anything, such as be sociable enough to go out and meet people which is the only way to start dating.

During Christmas vacation, I called Beth and asked her out, but she didn't want to. I think it was because of my low grades. I think she was real unimpressed when I told her about them.

The rest of the year was a disaster. There was no learning on my part. I just sat with a book open. No dating, just a few women on my floor who tickled me and one who hugged me. A little jogging, I thought it would cheer me up somehow. No work, I was too busy attempting to study. There were a few guys and women I hung around with. They played backgammon a lot. *They* thought it was fun. I didn't see how they could be so easily entertained. I thought *they* were out of touch with reality. Didn't they see life was horrible?

Let me tell you about one of my female friends that tickled me, Esther. A few of us were standing outside her room, when she gave us a little tour of her room. Esther said, "That is our make out couch."

I said, "Oh, let's try it."

She said, "Any time."

To this I didn't say or do anything. I knew she probably meant it. However, I figured that she only liked me because she didn't know me well. If she knew me well, she wouldn't like me. When she got to know me, especially the low academic grades part of me, she would reject me, which would just bum me out worse. I also figured it was wrong to get involved with her when she thought that I was something that I was not. I was a loser. Romantic attraction did not seem entirely normal. I had low sex drive from the depression part of my disease. I tended to think of only the negative aspects of relationships. I did not know I had a disease of negativity. I figured that if I could live my life since high school over again, I would do things right and be happy. However, I felt that in any case, I had to have a girlfriend that was as attractive as the ones from high school. Otherwise, I'd be compromising myself, stooping below the standards I had set in high school. Esther seemed below those standards. In high school I had a better outlook on life. Everyone looks less attractive when you are depressed.

I was still often preoccupied with swimming in twelfth grade, and Melanie in twelfth grade. I thought that the key to being happy as a sophomore in college, was to go back in time and straighten out twelfth grade. Then, I'd be happy as a sophomore in college, because I could look back on a happy twelfth grade. I thought, only then could I be proud of myself. The going back in time idea was quite absurd. I didn't really see a chance to cheer up, because I didn't really see a chance to go back in time. I thought maybe something nice might happen to me, and then I would cheer up. I didn't know my brain chemicals were stuck in the depressed phase from a disease. I was still undiagnosed.

In my classes that year, I got two F's, one B, and the rest C's. My grade average was below C level. I declared economics as a major because it was something I could use without graduate school.

12

Introduction To Getting Fired

Summer came and I went back home. My older brother, Steve, was working at a summer camp in California, and my younger brother, Rick, was working as a counselor in training at Camp Okranski. So at home with my parents were just my youngest brother, John, and me. This meant my dad would demand a lot of attention from me as usual. He did get me a high-paying construction labor job, though. He was the friend of an executive in the construction company.

I worked as a construction laborer at a new maximum security prison they were building. I tore apart wooden forms for concrete after the concrete was dry. Sometimes the forms were partly buried, so we would have to dig to get them out. Other times the job involved carrying big girders from one place to another. Early on, my foreman got the idea that I didn't like him. I guess now, it was because I didn't smile at him or talk to him much. He transferred me to the supervision of another foreman. I had no idea why I was transferred. I thought the other guy just needed the help. Then the other foreman didn't like my attitude or productivity level, either, I later found out. These were more symptoms of my depression. My work and the people I knew and worked with seemed unfun. This was the "nothing is fun" phenomenon of depression.

A co-worker of mine named Ron once asked me, "Do the students at the University of Puget Sound all have high intelligency?"

I said, "'Intelligency' is not a word."

I was such a jerk.

Another instance of my bad mood was when Ron and I were shovelling off a foundation that had gotten covered with mud. Then a guy who I suspect, in retrospect, was spying on me for management came and watched. A few minutes later, I slipped in the mud and fell on my back.

Then George, the guy who I think came to spy, said in a friendly tone, "You aren't going to get a lot done lying on your back."

Ron said, "Yeah, that's what I keep telling him."

I got up and George said, in a friendly tone, "Your mother is going to have more laundry to do now that you fell."

I turned away and said nothing. I'm sure now, that he thought I was rude, when he was just joking around. I turned and thought to myself that he was ridiculously silly for being so jovial and thinking everyone has a normal mother who does laundry. It would be so nice if I had a normal family again, but I thought George was way out of line. I didn't get how everyone could be so happy all the time. George must have felt slighted when I said nothing, and that, in retrospect, probably contributed to my getting fired for bad attitude.

The foreman told the supervisor, who told someone else, who told someone else, who told my father's friend, who told my father "Bill has the worst work attitude I have ever seen." My father came home from work and told me this. It was the first time I had heard about them being unhappy with my work. I was so grumpy and unapproachable that they didn't even want to approach me to say that I was grumpy and unapproachable.

The next day I told my original foreman that if he didn't like how I was doing, he should tell me, yell at me even. I told him not to tell my father. I ended up working there another couple weeks before I got "laid off." The foreman said, "We don't know if you or the dirt will go flying when you shovel."

After some pondering of the situation, I decided I should tell people about the situation with my mother, whenever the topic of mothers came up, in case someone thought my mom did laundry. Now I realize that it was depression's irritability that made my co-workers not like me. The depression was biological, not environmental. I know now that the healthy me could have talked about my mom at the right time, shovelled and done my laundry at the right time, and made my co-workers like me. The healthy me was not there. I had lost a $10.00 per hour job. That was a lot in 1979.

Early that summer of '79, I went out with Beth Tasa once, but I think she wasn't too impressed when I told her I had flunked a class. She wouldn't go out with me again.

Early in the summer, I called Melanie Carson once and asked her out. I forget how I got the nerve to do that. I may have been optimistic about earning $10.00 an hour then. She said no to a date, but I did talk to her for a while, and that was nice.

I remember telling her about my construction job.

I said, "You know the wooden forms that they pour concrete into?"

She said, "Oh, you do those?"

"Well, I take them apart once the cement is dry. Then I stack up the wood. Also, I do a lot of shovelling. The foundations get covered with mud when it rains, so we have to shovel them off. What are you doing this summer?"

"I'm singing in the band that I've been in for a while. It's fun, and I like the other people in the group."

"What songs do you do?"

"We do a bunch including that new Beach Boys one, "You Need Good Timing," We do some disco, and some old Beatles songs."

"Sounds good. I remember you have a great voice. How's PLU?"

"I like it. I'm studying nursing. I don't want to be in smokey bars my whole life."

"Yeah. I'm majoring in economics. I figure I can get a job using that, without grad school."

"Yeah."

We talked a bit more. I forget what all about.

"Well, really nice talking to you," I said.

"Good luck."

"Bye."

It was a pretty nice conversation. Still, thinking about her for so long was depressive obsession. I didn't have insight into the symptoms of depression.

13

Satisfactory Progress Towards Flunking Out

Labor Day came and I went back down to Tacoma for school. I lived in a single room in a good dorm. The floor was half freshmen, and half upperclassmen. Having a single was good for privacy, of course. There were no restrictions on visitation privileges. In other words, women could spend the night. Having a single could be lonely though. Sometimes I would sit in my room for hours, trying to study and feeling all alone. I kept playing *Simon and Garfunkel's Greatest Hits* album over and over again. I guess I could relate to the song "I Am a Rock." It includes the words, "I am an island."

Once that quarter, I went to see one of the psychologists at school. My dad had wanted us all to get counseling to talk about my mother's stroke. I would not go with my whole family, as my dad had requested. Instead, I went once to talk about my dad's behavior and the psychologist asked if I had ever been to counseling before, and I said "Yes."

I told her about the events leading up to my experience (manic episode) in Israel, the incident in Israel, and the aftermath. She asked how depressed I was now, and I said that I was not depressed. That's how little insight into my own condition I had. I thought that depression was something you had immediately following a seriously bad event. You felt like crying all day, and then you gradually cheered up. There was no recent seriously bad event. I didn't feel like crying all day, and I was not gradually cheering up. What I had was not going away, so I thought it couldn't be depression! I thought that my poor concentration was due to having to deal with a crummy father and no girlfriend. I was used to my unhappiness and thought it was normal for my particular life. I told her about the current problem with my dad. I was afraid that he still wouldn't approve if I started dating someone steadily.

She had just asked if I told anyone at the University of Puget Sound about my experience in Israel, when time for the psychology session ended.

I told her, "No. I didn't tell anyone because my dad told me not to."

A few days later, on the phone, my dad started interrogating me about the visit with the psychologist. I told him I went because he wanted me to go, but I wasn't going to tell him what we discussed. I didn't figure going to a psychologist would really help, so after he started interrogating me, I figured I didn't want to go. The interrogations weren't worth it. So I quit going. That was stupid.

That does point out a classic dilemma in counseling. You go to talk about your abusive parent or spouse, and then the abuser attacks you for going.

Talking to the psychologist about my nervous breakdown and the events leading up to it in 1977, made me think about Melanie Carson some more. So I wrote her at Pacific Lutheran University. I told her how I had felt on the one night we went out in April 1977. This was a reference to our date after the senior class trip to Jamaica. In the letter I told her how mad my dad had gotten because she wasn't Jewish. This was the date when I wanted to tell her how impressed I was with her SAT scores, and that we had academic ability in common, but I had been too depressed to speak. I told her how depressed I had been. I told her how much I liked her. I told her that I had wished I could've run away from home to a place where they would approve of us being together. I wrote that I was not planning to live with my father the next summer or ever again.

Melanie wrote back saying religion is important and that my father had a valid point about it. Melanie also wrote that she had been recently diagnosed with a potentially crippling disease which she did not name. That was bad news. She had recovered from her first attack 99 percent. That was good news. She also wrote that she had no desire to go out with me. She said it was nothing per-

sonal and not my religion either. I was glad she had at least written me back.

I had a habit of going to the library to study, but being unable
to concentrate on homework, I went over to the newspaper section of the library, and read the newspapers from various cities. In
the newspapers there were crime stories. I think these crime stories
fit in with my depressive view of the world as a crummy place.

Half my dorm floor was occupied by women. There was one
junior coed on my floor I had eaten dinner with a couple of
times. She was very pretty. Her name was Wendy Taylor. One
night I was studying in my room and I went out to the lounge on
our floor to see if anybody there wanted to go down to the snack
bar. There were a couple people there, but only Wendy said she
wanted to get a snack. So we walked downstairs and over one
building to the snack bar. We got our snacks and sat and talked
about our classes.

The next weekend there was a dance. I was in the hall of our
dorm floor talking to some of my floormates. I was debating
whether or not to go to the dance.

Wendy said, "You should come. It will be good."

Our group talked a bit more. We discussed what band would
be playing and other social alternatives for the evening. One guy
was considering studying even though it was Friday night.

Wendy stood next to me for a while, and we discussed going to
the dance. Then she put her arm through mine and said, "Let's
go. It will be fun."

I said, "Sure."

We walked arm in arm all the way to the dance.

We stayed together at the dance and people-watched. Her arm
was around me the whole time. She told some risqué jokes and
she told me a line in one of the songs that I hadn't caught. The
line was, "Go tell nasty limericks to your mother." She laughed.

We people-watched some more and then we went outside to
get some fresh air. We left and took a long walk, arm in arm, to a
wooded area of campus. I told her about the situation with my
parents. I told her about how jealous my father got when I was
living at home and had a date. She talked about her more normal
family and her career goals.

Wendy and I got across campus to the wooded area nearby.
She said that the woods would be a nice area to spend the night. I
kissed her, and she kissed back.

After a while, she said, "I was serious about spending the night here."

I said, "Well, let's go back to my room. I have a single."

She said, "Okay, but let's stay here a while first." Eventually, we walked back to my room.

I said, "I don't want to get you pregnant."

She said, "I'm on the pill."

"Good."

We had sex. It was my first time. In bed I was a bit passive, which was probably the result of having low sex drive due to depression. Everything worked well enough, and it was a pleasurable experience. I knew how to please her because I had read *The Hite Report*. We slept together two more times and my eagerness improved.

We also talked a lot while we were in bed. She told me about her brothers, her parents, her past boyfriends, and life in France where she had lived during high school. It was great having such a close personal friend.

She had one older and two younger brothers. They all played basketball. One of her younger brothers was totally in love with her and treated her like his girlfriend. She said that was annoying.

Her father was in the U.S. military and stationed in France. Wendy went to an American high school there. She told me she had been a homecoming queen candidate in high school, but she didn't win. I thought it was quite an honor to be with her.

Wendy also said that she used to teach Sunday School, but she said her minister would probably disapprove of this pre-marital sex we were having.

I told her a little about my brothers, and in the back of my mind I wanted to tell her about my nervous breakdown in Israel, but on the other hand I was glad it was far in the past, so I could skip it.

I told her about my poker friends at home and some of my friends on campus. She was a good listener and was definitely a plus. She was a bright spot in an otherwise dreary autumn.

Wendy and I didn't really have a committed relationship. Nobody really knew we were seeing each other. Even though I was sleeping with her, I still experienced the depressive symptom of second guessing of what I should do. Instead of just intuitively building a relationship, I would question myself when I was thinking of going down to her room, or thinking of what to say. This was in addition to my usual excessive, depressive attempt to second guess what music I *would have been* listening to during the day, what clothes I *would have been* wearing to class, or what food I *would have been* having for lunch, *if* I felt okay. I always tried to imitate a happy person, a happy Bill, but I didn't know what a happy Bill would have been like anymore. Again, I thought feeling bad was just environmental. I couldn't see the beauty of having a great dorm room, and a girlfriend, at a decent college in a free country.

That quarter I dropped the class "Introduction to Drama," so "Market Structure and Pricing Policy" and "Intro to Film Arts" were my remaining classes. I got D's on the mid-quarter tests in both. I was unable to concentrate or feel motivated. My mind was filled with too many depressive obsessional worries. I decided, when I got these results back, to quit school, or at least take a year leave of absence. I told the school administration that I wanted to take a leave.

The Assistant Dean of Students, when I told her I was flunking out due to poor concentration, looked at my high school grades and my SAT scores and said, "There is no problem here."

Ideally, a more informed dean would have looked at my awful college grades and insisted that I have a couple meetings with a psychologist before I quit. The purpose of this would have been to check for clinical depression. Clinical depression is not that rare. There *was* a problem. I was flunking out because I couldn't concentrate. I was clinically depressed and I didn't even know it. I thought my mental situation was "normal" for what I just thought happened to be my particular situation. The psychologist I had seen earlier that quarter may have been able to diagnose me. I, an uninformed twenty-year-old, didn't know that mental health professionals were of any value. I thought "depression" was not the word for my situation.

I decided not to tell anyone that I was quitting. I had some friends who would've tried to talk me out of it. Some might have even suggested counseling. I didn't think counseling would help. I didn't want anyone to try to talk me out of it, so that's why I didn't tell anyone until there were just a couple weeks of school left.

I had read so much about crime in the newspapers, and I had heard about enough criminal incidents on campus, that I decided

I wanted to be a cop. Four years of college were not necessary to become a cop. As a cop, I could do some good in the fight against crime. I could help put criminals in jail. The idea itself was not crazy, but I eventually became crazy and kept the idea. I felt I was having academic problems because school was boring, and I needed something exciting.

Because Wendy and I were not in a committed relationship, and possibly because I was getting a little manic (hypomanic), there was a sophomore woman who lived one floor below me, who I had noticed, and asked out.

We went out to dinner once. She was a good listener. She was the first person I told about quitting school and becoming a cop. She was really beautiful, and seemed really sweet. She told me about her family and they seemed nice. She seemed really mature which I liked. Her name was Betsy Straka. There were about two weeks left in the quarter when I went out with her. She didn't let me kiss her good night, but she made a lasting impression.

About this time I started telling my friends that I would be quitting school and going to work somewhere. They seemed disappointed, but didn't really try to talk me out of it. I think Wayne, my roommate during freshman and sophomore year, suggested counseling, but I was erroneously sure that it wouldn't help. It could have led to a psychiatrist who could have given me the proper medication.

I told Wendy that I was quitting on the day before my last final. She seemed disappointed. I promised to visit her.

I took my final and then left school.

14

Manic Delusions of Law Enforcement

It was December 1979. I gradually got manic. This manic episode in the winter of 1979–1980, was similar to the one I described in the first chapter of this book which took place in spring 1981. During both manic episodes, I had the delusion that I was a CIA/FBI agent. According to my rough estimate, up to one-fourth of all Amerian manic-depressives type one, get the secret agent delusion. Roughly half think they are Jesus Christ, God, or the Virgin Mary. Other common delusions of grandeur include the thought that you are the reincarnation of John Lennon, a big business tycoon, or a great rap artist. One woman thought that she was the reincarnation of Noah.

When I got home after dropping out of college, I started looking for jobs in the want ads. I answered an ad to be a cab driver and got the job. I remember they checked to see if I was a rapist or other violent criminal before they hired me. I drove a cab for two weeks until it was clear that I was hardly making any money. I kept getting lost. I was too distracted with my manic thoughts of trying to save the world from crime.

I gradually became a manic fanatic at fighting crime. I was going to the library to look up the Washington State Criminal Statutes. I thought the law that restricted cops from using their guns in situations where other people can use guns was unconstitutional. I felt it was unequal protection and therefore against the Fourteenth Amendment. The cops were being discriminated against. The way I talked about how I was going to get that law declared unconstitutional, made my dad and my brother, Rick, think I was crazy.

I heard of a drug dealer on Mercer Island, who also threatened people with knives and took sexual advantage of women when they were unconscious. Consistent with my reckless, dangerous, crime fighting urges, I told the cops I'd volunteer for an under-cover drug buy. The Mercer Island police force needs the help of citizens, so they liked the idea. I went to the dealer's house with money with the serial numbers recorded to buy drugs, but he wouldn't sell any to me, because he had almost been caught earlier, and he didn't know me.

During this time, I often said stuff at our dinner table loudly, for example, "The whole Washington State Legislature has violated their oath of office! They've stopped cops from using their guns when other people can! They have violated the Fourteenth Amendment! All of the legislators should be removed from office!"

My dad started to suggest I get a shrink to get this "thing" taken care of. I didn't know what "thing" he was talking about. I wouldn't talk to him, which to me was normal, but to him wasn't. My mom was in the hospital for being manic at that time. She had been opening up all the windows in the house even though it was winter, and she had been trying to wheel herself in her wheelchair down the icy road with one hand and one foot to get to Temple Moses.

Dad said, "Mom's doctor wants you to come into the hospital, just to get started on some *medication*, to get this thing cleared up. These things can be genetic."

I had no idea of what my dad was talking about when he said, "This thing that needs taking care of." I thought it was perfectly reasonable to think that I could impeach the whole legislature. When he told me about this plan of putting me in the hospital, we were behind a closed bedroom door or in the car when nobody else was around. I thought this was just another form of abuse he was trying to keep secret. I thought he was trying to put me on mind altering drugs to control me.

In order to get away from my dad in general, I was going to move into my grandfather's old duplex. My grandfather was in a nursing home for a while and then he moved in with my dad. My grandpa's place was very run-down and I was going to fix it up, or so I said.

When my dad was talking to me about my "thing," he would alternate between extreme anger, and telling me how much he loved me.

Once when we were alone in his car, driving to go visit my grandfather at the nursing home, my dad said in an inappropriately familiar, affectionate, voice, *"I'm* the one who is your best friend. I'm the one who will go *all the way* with you."

"Dad, would you just drive?"

Furiously, my dad screamed, pulling the car over, "Now listen *you,* you better listen to me. You are *sick!* You are out of your mind! I'm helping you with a problem! Nobody else is ever going to help you!"

"Dad, you better drive, or I'll get out and hitchhike."

Then he started driving again, but kept up his twisted speech.

He'd get mad when I would ignore him. I thought that he was the only real problem in my life. I thought that if he would just have a heart attack and die, my life would be a breeze. I thought he was the crazy one. I thought he was trying to get me to like him.

When talking about my mother, he found great amusement in the idea that, *"If* she *could* talk, what she *would* say would be irrational." About me he said, "We'll put you in the hospital, and then you won't be mad at me. You'll be back to your old self!" He was smiling as he said this. He said this with great contentment and enthusiasm.

I sat there thinking that he was a fool for not realizing that my old self hated his guts just as much as my present self. I didn't see how my Mom's situation applied to me. Finally one day he threatened to have me taken out of our house in a straitjacket. Then I moved out into my grandpa's house.

I tried to get more involved in fighting crime, and giving the police more power. Even though the American Civil Liberties Union usually tries to restrict police power, I tried to get them interested in expanding police power. I felt the cops were being persecuted. The American Civil Liberties Union said that there has to be a victim of the law concerning unjust use of guns by police before a suit can be filed. There would have to be a case where a cop was convicted of using his gun at the wrong time. So a lawsuit was out. I instead decided to write a book accusing the Washington State Legislature of violating their oath of office. They are sworn to uphold the constitution, and I felt the law about when police can shoot was unconstitutional. It didn't let the police use their guns often enough.

I drove down to the University of Puget Sound and told my friends, including Betsy Straka, about my plans for a book. The book would say that police are a persecuted minority. My friends' reactions seemed favorable the first time I went down there.

My friends at home were beginning to think I was going crazy because I was so obsessed with fighting crime.

I had read in the paper some statistics about how much time people served in prison for various serious crimes. The amount of time was surprisingly short. These included an average of two years and eight months for rape for a first offender. The average penalty for kidnapping when the person was returned unharmed was about eight months in jail. To spend more than a year in jail, a burglar of businesses had to be convicted four times. The average time served for murder was about six years. The reason for these short times served is that there is not enough prison space. The state and federal government chooses not to spend money on keeping criminals locked up, so they let them go.

I decided I could save the world from crime by convincing all the state legislatures and Congress to build more prison space and keep it full. I would do this same kind of thinking during my manic episode in 1981, as I described in chapter 1. The parole boards were really just rationing out the available prison space; that's why they let people go. They weren't letting people go who had been reformed, or who had been punished enough. They were just too cheap to keep them locked up longer.

I started calling up state officials telling them they were too easy on criminals. I called state prison guards, probation officers, prosecutors, legislators, and I also called Brett Pritchard, the congressman's son, a few times. Then I started driving to Olympia to talk to state legislators. I told them we should build more prisons to fight crime. I also told them a lot of other right-wing stuff like we should balance the federal budget. I guess I seemed sane because people talked to me.

I decided the best thing to do to save the world from crime was to run for state legislator as a Libertarian from the Tacoma area. It was 1980, so it was an election year. I thought I might as well also declare my candidacy for President of the United States in 1996. I knew you had to be thirty-five to be President, and 1996 would be the first election when I'd be thirty-five. I would run on the Libertarian ticket. The Libertarians believe government should maintain law and order, but should not be involved in anything else. Some Libertarians therefore believe that the government-run currency system is wrong. For one thing, it's run by the government. For another thing, it's not based on the gold system. They believe that everything should be done on a barter system. The previous summer I had read a Libertarian book, and I was trying to adhere to its principles. I felt the government was focusing too much on other things and not enough on crime control.

I thought I could make a lot of money on the stock market by investing in companies that would be involved in the building of prisons after I convinced the country to build more prisons. So, I got possession of the stocks that my dad had saved up for me since I was born. I had to threaten to sue him in order to get them. Then, I sold some of them. I bought stock in Kaiser Cement, Fluor Construction, and Caterpillar Tractor. I thought companies like this would be involved in the construction of new prisons. I also started buying silver coins. I thought I could start an economic revolution that would make gold and silver the standard for money. Craziness.

I went down to the University of Puget Sound and stayed for a day or two with my friend Randy Harold. I told all my friends from my dorm floor freshman year and others about my plans to save the world from crime. At first I think they listened, but later they thought I was crazy.

I was under the impression that the head of the criminal justice committee of the legislature was going to let me speak at a hearing of the committee. I started to get some paranoid thoughts. I remember saying to one of my friends, "Those legislators are going to want to shoot me after I get done speaking to them, because I'm going to make them look so bad."

He said, "They won't shoot you, they just will disagree with you."

I said angrily and sarcastically, "No, it can't happen here. It can't happen here!" By that I meant that their shooting me *could* happen here in America.

I was also paranoid. I thought I was about to be rich and famous, and someone would try to steal my stocks. So I split them into two groups, and put them in two separate safety deposit boxes in two different banks.

Another thing I did that was out of the ordinary was to go to my high school biology teacher during a class and ask him for one of the finger prick things I knew he had. We had used them for blood typing. I was going to use it to prick my finger during my speech to the criminal justice committee to dramatize crime victims. I thought the blood would be a good dramatic touch. I'm sure he was somewhat annoyed, but he gave me a couple of them.

I also had come up with the statistic for my speech, namely, that one year's worth of Washington State's crime victims would fill the King Dome more than four times.

About this time, my Mercer Island friends Stan Gold, Dave Frish, and Tom Spano arranged a meeting with me where they tried to convince me to see a psychiatrist. They didn't like my grandiose delusion that I could save the world from crime.

Stan asked, "What's your occupation?"

I said, "I am an author and a politician."

Stan said, "You're *not* an author *or* a politician."

"I am, too."

"Why did you flunk your courses?"

"The economics they teach is garbage. It is not based on the gold standard."

"You flunked all your courses, not just economics. The old Bill Hannon would have gotten straight A's."

"I had more important things to worry about."

They pointed out that I had a history of psychiatric illness.

I said, "There was never anything wrong with me in Israel, and I should sue whoever tarnished my reputation by saying there was."

The argument we had went on for about fifteen minutes before I told them to go to hell, and left.

I even took a couple steps towards trying to gather evidence for the lawsuit against the people who said I was crazy in Israel.

My dad also was trying to get me to see a psychiatrist. He said he would pay me to go to one. He would pay the bill, and he would also pay me. I went once, and I told the doctor that my dad wanted me to be committed to a psychiatric ward because I wouldn't talk to him in light of his attitude towards my dating. When I told the doctor that my dad was paying me to come see him, he picked up the phone to call my dad, but I wouldn't give him the number. I told him he did not have permission to talk to my father. I thought that if he heard my dad's side of the story,

I'd have to come back several more times to convince the doctor of my side of the story. Also, I didn't want it to turn into a counseling event where I had to learn to get along with my dad. The doctor told me to come back another time, but I never did.

My delusions got worse. I started seeing all sorts of popular culture as having hidden meanings for a peaceful Libertarian revolution where the government cares about law and order and not about much else. I also thought we should convert to a monetary system based on gold. I thought that the movie *The Wizard of Oz* really meant "the wizard of ounce," ounces being ounces of gold. I felt that the yellow brick road that we are supposed to follow in the movie actually was made of bricks of gold. The author had been saying we should be on the gold standard, which was my opinion. Actually, though, others have interpreted this movie this way, but I thought it was a big deal. There were a bunch of other movies that I felt had hidden meanings. I can't remember them all. One was *Rocky Horror Picture Show*. I felt that the song "Let's Do the Time Warp Again," meant let's go back to the gold standard and let's cut back the huge increase in government spending that started with Roosevelt's New Deal.

The movie *The Sound of Music* confirmed to me that the hunt for liberty in the United States must include listening to popular music. *The Sound of Music* was a musical about people seeking freedom, so I started playing all my music, looking for more clues about freedom. An example of music that had secret coded meanings to me, was Steely Dan's song "Josie" which to me sounded like "Georgie." Georgie was George Washington. I thought Steely Dan was saying that we had to get back to the principles that our country was based on. These were more Libertarian than Democratic or Republican, I felt.

Another song which became my anthem was Led Zeppelin's "Stairway to Heaven." I had interpretations for this whole song. The words all pointed to the need for a peaceful Libertarian revolution. The words, "If there's a bustle in your hedgerow, Don't be alarmed now, It's just a spring clean for the May-Queen," were, I felt, talking about a rape. The words, "There walks a lady we all know, who shines white light and wants to show," were referring to the Statue of Liberty.

I had my records strewn all over my living room floor because I changed records so often trying to find all the secret meanings in the words. I didn't have time to put them back in their jackets.

The next thing I did was write some letters to some University of Puget Sound professors. I hand-delivered the letters. The purpose of the letters was to convert the professors to crime fighters and Libertarians. Some of the letters were misinterpreted as threats. They were pretty incoherent, because I was manic, and there were references to violence that they did not understand. Here is one of them to Professor Cable, a math professor. The change in his name to "Capable" was on purpose then.

Feb. 12, 1980

Dear Mr. Capable,
    I wish you were more capable of seeing the truth in the fact that no matter how well the flood gates are engineered, a few well placed sticks of dynamite ruin the whole Deal. It could spell the end of an ERA. If you don't remember that computers are just big abacuses and that we use the Arabic numeral system, you should resign.
Sincerely,
Bill Hannon
P.S. I think that before this decade is out, we should set free our notion the goal of even having an abortion. This means young, old, males, females, and return the fetus safely to the womb.

What I meant by dynamite ruining the whole Deal, was that the penalty for vandalism is so small, that you could blow up a dam and probably get only thirty days in jail for it. I capitalized Deal to refer to the New Deal, which spent government money on things other than law enforcement, like dams, many of which we don't need. I capitalized ERA because then it means Equal Rights Amendment. The Libertarian book I read was against the ERA. The book liked the liberty of being free to discriminate. I was against the ERA because I felt it could put women in combat infantry platoons where they would get sexually harrassed by their fellow American male troops. Imagine a coed group stuck living together in a trench for two months. Also, I felt the ERA didn't allow for real differences between men and women in other areas such as pregnancy. The ERA to me also represented civil rights hysteria. This is the same hysteria that seemed often to let dangerous criminals go free.

The part about the Arabic numeral system was to tell Professor Cable, who was Jewish, to quit being so concerned about Arabs and to start being more concerned with crime at home.

The bit about abortions was me, trying to sound like President Kennedy. The "before this decade is out," was also my trying to sound like Kennedy, when he was speaking of when we should send a man to the moon. However, I was saying that if there was more peace in the land (less crime), and better sex education, there would be a lot fewer unwanted pregnancies in the country. Therefore there would be fewer abortions. This was my unintelligible way of saying: Make love not war.

The letter looked incoherent and like a threat to this math professor who I never had for a class. The part about the dynamite scared him and he called the police.

Another example of a letter I sent was to a Professor Martin whom I had had for a class two years earlier and liked.

Feb. 12, 1980

Dear Mr. Martin,

Your assignment is to call a session of the joint (Oh pardon the pun, this has only a little bit to do with Indian Hemp Peace Pipe smoking) heads of departments to discuss my first degree. If you fail to deduce the sensibility of this, may you be exiled and have troops *March through your department on their way to a battle that you don't really want any part of. Pardon the dangling precipice, I no be real educated.

Sincerely,

Bill Hannon

*You may have to beware the ides.

In this letter, my first degree referred to the honorary degree I thought I would deserve from the University of Puget Sound soon. The troops marching through his department would mean troops in the great anti-crime war that may be needed if new prisons were not built soon. Marching through his department was like Hitler going through Belgium in World War II. That neutral people suffer was my point. The ides of March is the fifteenth. I felt the country could be in chaos by then if something was not done to stop crime. Naturally Martin didn't understand what I meant. He misinterpreted the part about troops marching through his department, and the ides of March, as a threat of harm to himself, by me, so he called the police.

I gave out about eight or ten letters to professors. I hand-delivered the letters to these professors at their houses. I did this because I thought my message was so important, and hand-delivering them added a personal touch. I didn't realize until later that they found that to be alarming. Not all of the letters caused alarm, but a few more of them did. My wording was so confusing that people got the exact opposite meaning.

About this same time, I was also giving out my interpretation of "Stairway to Heaven" as campaign literature to several people I knew on campus including Brett Pritchard and my old camp counselor who went to school there. On the top of the interpretation of the song were the words "BILL HANNON FOR LEGISLATOR IN 1980, FOR PRESIDENT IN 1996 AND AGAIN IN 2000." I just walked in and handed it to them. Then I said, "I got to go." I'm sure now they thought I was crazy.

I also mailed some valentines to Betsy Straka. That was February 12, 1980. Then I went back home to my grandfather's duplex on Mercer Island.

I had just gotten new locks put on my part of the duplex. I figured that too many people had the keys to it. It was just in time, I found out, because my dad felt that as the landlord, and as my father, he had the right to barge in at any time. On the thirteenth, the Tacoma police called his house and asked to speak to me. I wasn't there so they talked to my dad. They told him I was wanted for creating a public nuisance, for writing threatening letters. My dad went to the county court house and got a commitment petition. Then he came to my door with some county social worker and tried to get in. I wouldn't let them in the door and threatened to have them arrested for trespassing. They threatened to have me forcibly committed. I didn't know that the cops wanted to talk to me until much later that evening.

I then called a lawyer and made an appointment to see him that afternoon. I couldn't find my way to his office though. So I came back to my duplex, gathered my perishable food which consisted of a carton of milk, and drove down to the University of Puget Sound again. This time I went to a lawyer's office near campus and calmly explained that I needed to sue my father for harrassing me. I told the lawyer that my dad thought I was crazy because I was lobbying the legislature, and I wanted the harrassment stopped. I forget what the lawyer said, but I think I sounded sane enough to him. We decided to wait and see what happened.

Then I went and saw Randy Harold, one of my friends from freshman year. I told him what was happening and he sounded annoyed and said, "You can't stay here forever."

I went and visited with my friend Gary Cunningham and talked with him for awhile. I told him that Tacoma was the last bastion of civilization left on earth. At the time, I didn't know that the police wanted to arrest me for creating a public nuisance.

After talking to Gary, I took a walk across campus to go visit some other friends, and then campus security and a Tacoma police officer came up to me and said I had to come with them. They said the Dean of Students, Harry Arvidson, wanted to talk to me. So I went with them, and I had no idea what it was about. We went to the Dean's office.

Mr. Arvidson asked, "Did you send threatening letters to several professors?"

I said, "No."

He asked, "Is this your handwriting?"

"Yes, but they're not threatening."

Then the cop asked, "Well, what are they supposed to think when they get a letter like that?"

"Just what it says."

The cop said, "Well, right now I've got a warrant to take you to jail and charge you with creating a public nuisance. We would, but in reading these letters, Dean Arvidson thinks you may be having some kind of psychological problem."

I said, "No, I'm fine."

The cop said, "Maybe you're using some kind of drugs."

"I've never."

Dean Arvidson said, "Well, right now I can offer you the choice of undergoing an overnight psychiatric evaluation and doing what they say, or getting arrested for creating a public nuisance."

"Well can't I just pay a fine or something?"

The cop said, "No. You have to go to jail."

Arvidson said, "We thought this had something to do with Vice President Mondale's speech tomorrow."

"Why? What is Mondale saying tomorrow?"

Arvidson said, "We don't know what he's going to say. He's giving a speech here in Tacoma at Pacific Lutheran University tomorrow. Did you know that?"

I said, "No." That was the truth.

The cop asked, "Do your letters have something to do with that?"

"No. My letters were trying to convert the professors to my way of thinking." I then went on about my plan for the economy that included a massive barter system with Tacoma as one of the centers. My plan seemed so farfetched that it was clear to Arvidson that I was crazy. He started crying.

Eventually he got himself together and then he asked, "Do you want to undergo a psychiatric evaluation?"

Thinking it would look bad for a crime fighter like myself to be arrested, and thinking that the psychiatrist would find that I was okay, I said, "Yes, I'll get the psychiatric evaluation."

The cop walked with me out to the car in which Arvidson would drive me to the hospital. The cop and I waited in the car for Arvidson.

While we were in the car the cop said, "This is a drag, Mondale coming to town. I have to escort some protesters who will be protesting him."

I knew then that he was checking to see if I was a threat to Mondale.

I said, "Oh, really," in a bored tone.

Arvidson came to the car and the cop got out. Then Arvidson drove me to Beasley Hospital in Tacoma. I then went to admitting. They had me turn over my wallet and keys to them for safekeeping. I remember saying that if they lost my safe deposit box keys, I would end up owning the hospital. On the admitting form they already had listed as my diagnosis manic-depressive. I had never heard the term "manic-depressive" before. I wrote on the form that the Dr. Grisso who was calling me manic-depressive should lose his license for calling me manic-depressive without even seeing me.

As I went into the locked psychiatric unit, I remember asking the aids who greeted me if there were any criminals on the ward.

They said, "No. We don't let them on this ward."

Then they showed me which room would be mine, and a nurse said they would start me on mood leveler Lithium. I started laughing because I knew Lithium was an element on the periodic table of chemistry. I wondered if it was like Helium which is supposed to make you talk funny. It just didn't sound like a drug. I had never heard of it as a drug before. It sounded like a joke. The nurse thought my laughter was inappropriate. I refused the drug. After all, I don't do drugs. Especially since I felt there was nothing wrong with me.

I went to bed that night, but I didn't sleep. Instead I looked at the spots of light on the wall and tried to figure out what they meant. In the morning I met with Dr. Grisso for the first time. I told an aid to come with me as a witness.

I yelled at Grisso, "What if I hadn't scored in the 99th percentile on my verbal SATs, and couldn't read that you had diagnosed me manic-depressive without even seeing me?"

I forget what he said, but I told him he should lose his license for diagnosing me without seeing me. The whole session was mostly me yelling at him.

Later I started thinking that I was actually put in the psychiatric ward to undergo the psychological screening necessary to become a CIA/FBI agent. I decided that the Secret Service had done a background investigation on me after they heard about my "threatening" letters around the time of Mondale's visit. I decided that they discovered I was so clean, that I was qualified to be an FBI agent. Plus, I figured, they knew the true meanings of my letters, so they understood I had some good ideas about stopping crime. I thought I was in training to become an FBI/CIA agent.

I also viewed the whole psychiatric profession as corrupt, mainly because I thought they wanted me to get along with my father. I thought they, in general, tried to get people to get along who shouldn't get along. It would be wrong to expect me to get along with my dad, because he was such a bad influence.

The nurses' notes I obtained from Beasley Hospital to help write this book say that on February 14, I got served with papers telling me of my seventy-two-hour hold by the court. To be held in a hospital against your will in Washington, you have to be deemed a danger to yourself or others. I was being held three days pending the outcome of a hearing. I needed the treatment, but I didn't know it. I was a danger, because of my driving 85 mph in a 55 mph zone or through other accidental means. Sometimes they take just a little evidence as qualifying you as a danger to yourself or others and you get committed and you get well. Other times the court fails to commit people who need it. Then the people often end up in a severe car accident if they are manic, or they can kill themselves deliberately if they are depressed.

The nurse report says my speech was rapid with occasional inappropriate laughter. Also I was "guarded" in my responses to questions. This guardedness, I remember, was because I didn't know who on the ward to trust. I didn't know who was an FBI or CIA agent, and who was not. I didn't know who had security clearance and who did not. I thought that some people on the floor really were regular patients and nurses, and I thought others were FBI/CIA. The civilian staff, I thought, misinterpreted a lot of my CIA-directed speech as crazy thinking. There was no point talking to them.

On February 15, I decided that there must be some codes I had to think of to be a CIA agent. There was a T-shirt that a friend of mine at Puget Sound had, that looked like it said something in Hebrew if you looked at it right side up, but if you looked at it upside down it said, "Go Fuck Yourself," in English. I thought this could be a code phrase.

There was a very quiet female patient. I went up to her and kissed her and whispered in her ear, "Go fuck yourself." The nurses sent me to the quiet room for ten minutes.

Every few hours that I was in the hospital, a nurse would offer me medication, and I would refuse. I would refuse because I thought there was nothing wrong with me.

Sometimes they would say, "You'll feel better if you take it." This was ridiculous because I felt fine. Manic people almost always feel fine. Unlike when I was depressed, I finally had a sense of purpose. I was CIA/FBI in training. I was excited. The nurses should have known that I felt fine. This was in spite of the fact that I hadn't slept at all since being admitted.

The nurses eventually convinced me to accept some medication by telling me, "You haven't been sleeping. These will help you sleep." I knew a person could go insane from not sleeping, so I took the medication those nights. Unfortunately, the nurses did not catch on and keep telling me that the drugs would help me sleep. Nor was any nurse willing to stick her neck out and say that if I took the medication, I'd get out of the hospital sooner. It was really very ineffective nursing practice. Manic people have increased sex drive. I wanted to get out of the hospital to find a partner for sex. I knew I couldn't have sex in the hospital.

Nights not on medication, I didn't sleep. The whole ten days that I was in Beasley Hospital, I only slept on two nights. (The two were the nights the nurses said, "Medication will help you sleep.") I would go to bed on the other nights, but I would not sleep. Instead I would look at what the street lights from across the street were projecting onto the walls of my room. I thought the CIA was actually doing the projecting, and the shadows and the lights had a secret meaning that I was supposed to pick up. It was eerie, but a great adventure. I remember one interpretation of what I saw was a man and a woman standing close together. As the night wore on, I decided that they were close enough together to make love. I interpreted this to mean that to be a CIA agent, you needed to be married because the CIA often works in husband and wife teams. I had heard this from someone I knew at the University of Puget Sound. His parents could not tell him what they did for a living; they would often take long trips; they wouldn't say where they were going or when they were coming back; and they lived in a suburb of Washington D.C. So, he figured his parents were CIA agents. I figured I had to get married, so I could work in a husband wife team like that.

So I wrote to Betsy Straka, who I had gone out with once. I asked her to marry me.

Another bizarre thing I did for a while in the hospital was, I wouldn't eat the food from the tray for me if the handwriting spelling my name was a little off. I told the staff that there were dangerous chemicals in the food. The real reason I wouldn't eat was because I thought the handwriting being a little off was a message to show that everything about my identity must be exact. I thought, whoever on the hospital staff was CIA, would know that I got the message if I didn't eat. Instead, I ate some food from the refrigerator that was in the lounge of the ward.

To get my identity straight, which was what the food thing was all about, I figured they had taken hair samples off the electric razor I had borrowed from the staff. I also consented to a blood test and said I should be tested for syphilis because I thought this test was mandatory for marriage. I thought the blood test would help to identify me also.

The 1980 Winter Olympics were on television, and Eric Heiden kept winning gold medals in speedskating. I thought, though, that the whole thing was staged and put on the television in the ward by the CIA. I thought it was supposed to be a message to me that I could win gold medals like the Congressional Medal of Honor, or the Presidential Medal of Honor if I did succeed in drastically lowering the crime rate by getting more prisons built and keeping them full.

I kept requesting to leave both orally and in writing. I wanted to leave to have sex. I could still give my anti-crime speech to the legislature, even if I wasn't a CIA agent. The nurses told me there was a hold on me. They never explained that it was a court-ordered hold, and a judge would decide at a hearing if I could go. They also didn't explain that if I did get committed, they would get six orderlies to tie me to a bed, and give me shots. They wrote in my records, that I have now obtained, that my speech was rapid and incoherent. I'm sure it was. After all, I was speaking in a code that only the CIA was supposed to understand.

In spite of all this, I felt good. Being manic is like being in an energetic, happy mood.

Another delusion I had about the CIA, was that my Uncle Mike Felber, who had died about a year earlier, actually hadn't died, he had just gone undercover as a CIA agent. Also I thought, another uncle, Adam, who had died before I was born, must be deep undercover in U.S. Army Intelligence. I remember telling all these things to my cousin Laura Felber over the phone. She said that can't be true, because she saw her father's body, and she had seen pictures of Uncle Adam very sick. I'm sure it was a very weird experience for her, talking to me.

I had paranoia about the drugs Dr. Grisso wanted to give to me. He wanted to give me major tranquilizer Haldol, which I interpreted as Hell Doll. I figured the drug would turn me into a Hell Doll, which was, I figured, a guy who had had a sex change operation who now had the body of a woman. This woman would then go around sleeping with prospective agents to gather information. I thought Wendy Taylor, the woman I had been sleeping with at Puget Sound, may have been one. I thought this along with the general information that you can be blackmailed for non-marital sex, so I had to be careful.

For exercise, and to kill time in the ward, I would walk the full length of the ward, back and forth, for hours. I would often flex my hands alternately like I was swimming freestyle. I felt good. One day I was clenching and unclenching my right fist like you do when you donate blood. I donated blood a week after my high school trip to Jamaica. I would do these clenching motions for about twenty minutes before I realized where they were from, where I had done them originally. The walks on the full length of the ward were every day I was in that hospital, except the two days that I took medication. The two days I took medication, my speech and motor activity were slowed down.

My mood and outlook were great. I was happy. Not only was I making the swimming motions with my hands, but I was also thinking about fun times at camp and in high school, times when I was happy. I had finally been lifted out of depression and it felt great. It was very hard to convince me that there was something wrong. I thought about touch football games at my grade school playground when I had been in junior high—the athletic prowess, the toughness, the cleverness. I thought about the strategy and tactics needed to win skills competitions in Boy Scouts. I thought about the socializing during JTG overnight conclaves when I had been in senior high. I felt the thrill of doing well on tough tests in high school. I thought my studying had paid off, because now I was a CIA agent in training. I now considered myself equal to my poker buddies. I had not felt equal to them since high school. They were still undergrads, and I was a CIA agent in training!

I was writing a lot of notes to be put in my chart while I was in the hospital. They were supposed to have secret meanings for those on the staff who were CIA agents. Also, I composed some letters to friends, and sent a few. Here is an example. This was part of a letter dated February 17 to Stan Gold, but I never sent it:

> . . . I would like to get out of here soon, though, who do you think I am? Alexander Soldie Nitze type? May bee I will put out the white cross = amphetamines for those who live and graves for those who die. Let's stay behind door number one. What've we got? We got a lot, we've got a team that's red hot. Sizzlae. If you go shadow dancing, Do it Right! No need to blitzkreig the combat zone type environment. War is not healthy for children or other human beings. Nation shall not lift up sword against nation, nor shall people fail to burn their draft cards. I heard when the old coach at Mercer initiated new members, they would get their

head dunked in a toilet, and I love my hair. I'll keep it
and wash it whenever and however I feel like it. I
don't need Brett either. And I wany my money . . .

Obviously, I was jumping from topic to topic with no apparent
connection. In my mind somehow, there was a connection, but it
is not apparent to the reader, and the nurses took it as evidence
that I was manic.

On February 20, I had a hearing. Two county deputies drove
me to the hearing. At the hearing I requested Dr. Kelly (my first
doctor) instead of Dr. Grisso. The judge granted that request, so
on February 22, I was transferred to Helgerson Hospital in Seattle. I thought Dr. Kelly already knew me so he'd be more likely to
let me go. I had mistaken Dr. Kelly for a competent psychiatrist.
(A competent psychiatrist would have kept me for two to three
weeks, on medication, but I didn't know that.)

Dr. Kelly decided I had to stay in the hospital. He was competent for not letting me go, but if he or Dr. Grisso had been better,
they would have told me, "You will get out of the hospital in
three weeks, at the latest, if you take the medication." They didn't
tell me that, so it took five weeks.

It could have been only three weeks if they would have
explained that being committed meant being tied down to your
bed, and having the drugs injected, while taking the drugs by
mouth meant getting out in three weeks without getting tied to
your bed. Instead it was five weeks.

So on the 22nd of February, I arrived at Helgerson Hospital
under the "care" of Dr. Kelly. When I first saw him I launched
into a speech about my idea that I was going to sue the people
involved with putting me in the hospital in Israel, because they
were mistaken, and now the fact that I've been sick before was
being used against me by my father. I said my father had a motive
to kill me because a month earlier I had called the FBI to tell
them that my dad was doing some illegal practices. I said that his
effort to commit me was his way of getting back at me for calling
the FBI on him.

Dr. Kelly said, "I believe you're sick."

I asked, "What's wrong with me?"

He said, "You're manic."

"What does that mean?"

"That's the opposite of depressed."

"Well, the opposite of depressed is happy, so I'm in here because I'm happy?"

"Well, you need treatment, Bill. I'm going to put you on some medication."

That was the end of my session with Dr. Kelly for that day. I left with the impression that he was insane because he had me in the hospital to treat happiness. I had never heard the word "manic" before this manic episode.

I did feel happy. People generally feel great when they are manic. There was a woman who physically resembled Jennifer Weinberg on the ward. Also, being happy reminded me of my days at Camp Okranski, where I had met Jennifer, so I called her. I hadn't spoken to her in three years. I remember talking to her about my upcoming speech to the legislature, and quickly changing the topic to the hunt in South America for Nazi war criminal Joseph Mengele. I also told her that I was in the hospital, so I guess that explained to her my bizarre jumping from topic to topic. She knew about my first breakdown in Israel, so she probably just figured that being scatterbrained was to be expected given my history. Feeling good like I did at camp also reminded me of Joel Stein, so I called him. I told him about my main plan to get rich on the stock market by buying stocks in construction companies that build prisons, after convincing the nation's lawmakers to build more prisons. I also told him that the Secret Service was listening to the phone call. I felt they were still doing a background check on me so that they would know whether I qualified as an FBI/CIA/Secret Service agent.

I read now in my medical records, that Joel called the nurses station to ask what the deal was with me after I called him. I hadn't spoken to him in three years.

The nurses' notes say the first several days I was at Helgerson Hospital, I was again very guarded in conversation with them. Like I said before, I think now, that I was "guarded" in conversation with them, because I thought I was on a top secret mission. Also, if word of my great speech leaked out before I had the chance to put the rest of my money in prison construction-related stocks, I wouldn't make as much money in the stock market. After a while, I warmed up to the nurses, and there was a set of notes I wrote for them to read, and some notes I kept secret. Also, I soon realized, that they thought I was crazy, so there was no danger of them seriously leaking my speech's contents. One nurse asked what I needed. So I told her I needed a lot of police for security when I gave my speech, because a lot of criminals wouldn't like what I'd be saying.

All this while, both at Beasley Hospital, and Helgerson Hospital, I was refusing medication, and sleeping very little if at all. I was spending my time writing bizarre notes to be put in my chart. I knew that the nurses were having trouble understanding my notes, but I felt someone who really knew me and understood me could understand them. I felt the FBI was investigating me thoroughly enough so that they would understand the notes.

Let's get back to Dr. Kelly. Almost every day that he saw me up until March 5, he said, "If you don't take the medication, you'll be locked up."

To which I would say, "I'm already locked up," because I already was in a locked ward from which I could not leave. That was his chance to say that if I got committed, they would get six orderlies and hold me down, and tie me to a bed and give me shots. He never said that. I wish he would have. The nurses never said it, either. Also, neither Kelly nor the nurses ever said I'd get out in three weeks if I took the drugs. I wanted to get out. If they would have said that, I probably would've taken the drugs.

They all only said, "It depends what happens at your hearing."

Finally on March 5, I got escorted by two sheriff's deputies to my hearing. Then, my *court appointed lawyer* told me what happens if you get committed. He said, "If you get committed, and I think you will be, they will get six men and strap your body to the bed, and inject drugs into your body, and you won't be able to move. If you agree to take the drugs voluntarily, by mouth, you can avoid that and be free."

So, I told the judge that I would take the drugs, and I avoided being legally committed.

I got driven back to the hospital by the deputies, and I started taking the drugs. The next morning I woke up and was very surprised. I thought, Oops! I guess this isn't a CIA training base.

As I started taking the drugs, I got less hyperactive. I was on major tranquilizer Haldol and mood leveler Lithium. I also got the side effects of Lithium. My muscles started to twitch. Any muscle I used twitched. (This is properly called muscle tremor.) I remember people earlier had said, "Lithium is a salt, not a drug." I remember thinking they were saying it was "assault." Now that was coming true. It was an assault on my muscles. (It doesn't cause muscle tremor in most people.)

I devoted less time to my note writing, and started getting to know the other patients. There were a bunch of fourteen-year-old runaway girls. Many of these girls had, sometime in their lives, been raped, they said, when I mentioned crime including rape. There were a few people in for alcoholism, and a couple general juvenile delinquent boys. There were several people in for depression. There was one accused murderer. He had apparently stabbed a women seven times in a robbery. He was undergoing a pre-trial psychiatric evaluation. He did not belong there. He harassed the depressives.

After a week or so of taking major tranquilizer Haldol, mood leveler Lithium, and side effect drug Cogentin, I was transferred to the open ward. There they provided Occupational Therapy, Group Therapy, and Recreational Therapy.

Some of the nurses on the open ward were helpful in talking about my parents. Still, they never gave me a list of symptoms of manic depression, and they didn't talk about the symptoms directly. Their attitude was, "Well let's just get these past few months over with. Take your Lithium, it can help. It helps keep you on an even keel."

They were too honest to say that Lithium would definitely make me perfectly healthy. There was hesitation in their voice when they said, "It helps keep you on an even keel." From their tone it was clear that they were not so sure.

Once I got over to the open ward, people started visiting me and saying I sounded "much better" on the phone. I also gradually realized that I had a problem and that I would need to take Lithium indefinitely. I hated Lithium because of the muscle tremors, but I would put up with it for a while. I still wanted to save the country from crime, but I knew I couldn't do it easily. I knew I couldn't get rich on the stock market. Finally on March 27, 1980, I was discharged. I went back to my grandfather's duplex.

Let's hear it for the medicine!

15

Another Year of Depression and No Good Doctor

I left the hospital mostly thinking the manic depression was due to stress. I would sometimes tell people that it was the stress of my mother's stroke and what it did to my family. But specifically I felt it was the stress due to my dad's behavior. Dr. Kelly returned to his mute stance of failing to give information about the genetic aspect of it, the symptoms to watch for, or all the appropriate drugs.

I continued to blame my dad's behavior for all my problems. In reality, it would have been much better to change my genes than to change my father. I didn't know that then. Dr. Kelly continued to be nearly mute.

I went down to the University of Puget Sound to visit my friends. I told them I was okay now and wouldn't be saving the world and getting rich on the stock market. I remember telling Wayne, my roommate from freshman and sophomore year, that I was really upset that my muscles twitched.

I said, "I want to be the body beautiful."

He said, "You just have to live with it," or something like that.

I talked to Betsy Straka, who I had proposed to from the hospital, and she said, "To put it bluntly, I'm not interested."

I said, "Yeah, I guess I got carried away there."

I hung around campus for about a day, and then went back home to my grandpa's duplex on Mercer Island.

A few days later Stan Gold came over and helped me put all my records in their album covers. He also urged me to keep up in doing my dishes. That was nice. I needed the encouragement.

There was a bunch of old washing machines and other junk in the basement of the duplex that needed to be taken to the junk yard. So one Saturday morning I got a group of my poker buddies to help haul the stuff upstairs to a truck and take it to a junk yard. It was gruelling work, but we had made a dent in the huge pile of junk. I bought my friends lunch for helping me.

Feeling like my place was set up, my next step was a career. My career plans were now to become a computer programmer. I enrolled in a private trade school for an eighteen-month course in computer programming. I promptly quit after flunking the first four tests. I had poor concentration. I had the usual "I am a loser," depressed thoughts on my mind.

An instance of poor medical practice by Dr. Kelly that year was his failure to prescribe an antidepressant medication for me even though I made it clear that I was depressed. Antidepressants are some of the main drugs used in treating manic depression, but he never even mentioned them. I had never heard of them. Even though I always complained of symptoms of depression, he never told me it was treatable. A person can take antidepressants in addition to mood leveler Lithium to combat depression when the Lithium fails to prevent it. He also never gave me a list of symptoms of depression, and never gave me a list of symptoms of mania. When I went to see him once a month, he would hardly say a thing. I would talk and he would just sit there and take notes. If I asked a question, I would have to ask twice to get an answer. I remember once he did say there are genetic factors in manic depression. I thought that that just applied to the manic part, not the depressed part. He didn't take my depression seriously enough to talk about it. At that point, I didn't know he was a bad doctor because I didn't know what a good doctor was. Now I do, so I know he was bad. I feel he was botching the job every time I saw him. He should have told me more about my prognosis. He should have told me more about symptoms, side effects, and medication. He should have given me literature. If he would have told me more about the genetic aspects, I would know that the problem was from within me and not environmental. If it was not environmental I would have known that moving away from my dad was not the main solution.

When I flunked out of the computer school, as a victim of bad medicine, I decided I wanted to go back to UPS. I decided this when I heard a love song on the radio. It made me think of Betsy Straka and the others like her down at Puget Sound, even though she had already rejected me. So I got my name on the waiting list to get back into Puget Sound, and I registered for UW at Seattle, just in case I didn't get back into Puget Sound. This irrational mode of thinking, deciding where to go to college based on a song on the radio, was typical of this depressive time. That is just one example of my thinking I could cheer myself up through environmental change rather than through medication. It was inaccurate in this case, as it usually is for manic-depressives.

In the meantime, I usually went to bed late, after listening to Larry King or Sally Jesse Raphael. Then I would sleep late, and I wouldn't get out of bed until my mother would call on the phone. She couldn't talk, but she could dial the phone, and then say, "Dee de dee," in sentences.

Then, I got out of bed and talked to her. She would always ask as best she could, "Were you awake?" I could tell by the tone of her voice.

I would always say that I was awake, but still in bed, which I was. I would talk to her for a few minutes, and then take a shower and get dressed. Then I would get some breakfast. It was always cold cereal. I didn't cook much.

For activities that summer, I watched lots of television. I did go jogging with my poker friend Jack Johnson sometimes, because I remember complaining about my muscle tremors to him. I jogged with his sister a few times also.

I was terribly unhappy, though. Difficulty getting out of bed is a sure sign of depression. Plus, I would never do my dishes. I would just wash one dirty one from the dirty dish pile when I needed a clean one. Then, when I was through with that one, I'd put it back on the dirty dish pile. I had no energy. I still viewed the world as a crummy place because of all the crime. It still looked liked something desperately had to be done to save the world. My outlook was not rosy. It was very dreary.

This whole year, my dad would invite me over to his house for Friday night Sabbath dinner. I went because I felt I had to go, because my dad was supporting me financially. However, it was also a good chance to see my mom and my two younger brothers.

My dad's financial support saved me from being homeless. Without the cash he gave me every month I may have ended up as just another mentally ill street person. I was very lucky that he was willing and able to give me money. During this time and during many future years he gave me money for medicine, doctors, rent, food, tuition, and cars. He was really very helpful. His generosity made my eventual recovery possible. Thousands of manic-depressives are homeless and never recover. My dad was making my life livable. However, at this time and at many future times I was too depressed and upset to appreciate my dad's help.

Being depressed, I sat or lay around a lot, sometimes listening to music, sometimes not. I listened to a lot of Rolling Stones' music as well as lots of other rock and roll. I would often listen to the same song or same side of a record over and over. I did this with the song "Green Onions" from the soundtrack of the movie *American Graffiti*. Also I played the song "Brown Eyed Girl" by Van Morrison from the *Twenty Years of Rock and Roll with Dick Clark* anthology over and over again and thought of Betsy Straka.

Spending so much time doing nothing, or just listening to music or watching television, was clearly a symptom of depression. I would see Dr. Kelly once in a while, and he would say nothing. I was on mood leveler Lithium (at blood level 1.0) and side effect drug Cogentin (1 mg per day), and I was miserable. The blood level is the measure of how much drug is in your bloodstream. They take a test tube full of blood, and test for the drug. The level in your blood tells you how to adjust the dosage. I was on a full dose of Lithium, but the Cogentin was a mistake. Cogentin is for stopping the muscle stiffness and restlessness side effect of major tranquilizers. It did nothing for the tremors of Lithium. Therefore, Dr. Kelly should not have prescribed it. Cogentin even can have a side effect of its own. Depression!

As I have done before, I will give an example of my train of thought while I was depressed this entire year:

God I feel awful. I'm such a loser. If I just had a girlfriend I'd be happier. How can I attract anyone if I'm so uncheerful? How can I be happy if my stomach muscles twitch during sex? How can I have sex if I don't have a girlfriend? How can I get a job if I don't have a girlfriend to cheer me up before the interview? How can I think about interviews when the radio keeps playing this crummy music all the time?

My thoughts would go on like this all day, nonstop. They would preoccupy me so much, that I could do very little else, like build a social life, which is the only way to start a romance. In reality, of course, even a great relationship is no treatment or prevention for manic depression. It takes the proper medication. I didn't know that.

In an effort to cheer myself up, I asked Jennifer Weinberg to go to a couple of movies with me. She agreed, but made it clear that these were not dates. I didn't expect them to be. She was very nice and talking to her cheered me up for the moment.

She would always say, "Think positive, your craziness will be controlled by the drugs."

I had trouble thinking positive, because I was depressed. My drugs weren't controlling my depression.

My mother was in a nursing home off and on during this year, mainly for depression. She wouldn't eat, she was so depressed, and she wouldn't do anything. My dad couldn't take care of her so she had to go into a nursing home. I went to visit her, and she was glad to see me, but she still didn't eat. They couldn't give her medication that would help, I was told, because of her heart condition.

Winter quarter I had the chance to go back to UPS but I stayed in Seattle and went to the University of Washington, like I had fall quarter. I went to UW because they had a program with the state legislature in Olympia where a student could go to the Capitol and assist state legislators for a few days a week. In turn, the student would learn about the legislative process. There was also a one-hour-a-week class to go along with the internship. I had a car, so I could make the sixty-mile trip to Olympia.

I went to the Capitol in Olympia and filled out an application. I said I wanted to work for a Republican. I wanted someone who was tough on crime and in favor of a free-market economy. A few days later, I called back, and they said they had a legislator who was willing to interview me. His name was Andy Denslow. I had an interview with him. I told him I was a political science major, and I was having trouble getting excited about school, but I thought that some actual hands-on political experience would help get me excited about school. I believed that to a degree. I thought a stimulating environment was the key to cheering me up. Representative Denslow agreed to have me work with him for a few days a week. He was a Born-Again Christian, and was a big supporter of Reagan.

So, I started driving down to Olympia three mornings a week. I observed committee meetings, talked to lobbyists, stuffed some envelopes, and answered some letters. Andy Denslow authored one criminal law that year. It was a law making it a felony to flee a police officer in a motor vehicle. It was designed to help cut down on high-speed chases. We discussed other crime issues because I still was obsessed with them.

I decided that after the quarter was over, I would again try to lobby the legislature for tougher sentencing facilitated by building more prison space. I talked to a couple legislators about crime while I was still working for Representative Denslow, which I wasn't supposed to do without his permission.

I wrote to the embassy of every Western European country I could think of and asked them a bunch of questions about crime in their countries. By the end of the quarter, the embassies, except for a couple, came through with a lot of information. It is sort of manic to write to embassies, although in this case I know I was still depressed and thinking that someone has to do something about the depressing crime problem.

Toward the end of the quarter, in early March 1981, my mom died. Her heart valve gave way. We had a funeral, and held mourning sessions in the evenings for seven days which was the Jewish tradition. At the funeral, I thought about how this was the end of an era, and that our family could not be put back together. A new era was beginning. At the burial the only memory that really stands out is that everyone pulled up in their cars and didn't say anything. All you heard was the car doors opening and slamming. Otherwise there was silence. That was the sound of burial. Car doors and silence.

I thought, as one of my friends said, that her death was a relief for my mom and for the rest of us. My mother was usually very depressed, couldn't talk, read, or write, and was paralyzed on one side. I hoped my dad would remarry. I got very excited at the thought that my dad's behavior might improve.

I thought if my dad's behavior improved, he wouldn't be such a pest. I started getting more excited about fighting crime, also. I started to get manic again in spite of being on medication. It was April 1981.

This April 1981 manic episode is the manic episode that I described in the first chapter of this book. It was very similar to the Winter 1980 manic episode of chapter 14. This chapter 1 episode was called "KGB Bloodhounds." It was when I thought the FBI/CIA was trying to help get me elected to Congress. In the meantime, I had the delusion that I was CIA. I was down at UPS, wandering around at night. I stopped at a dorm lounge to read the secret clues in the late night Associated Press written news that scrolled up the television screen. Later, a dog was following me, and I thought it was trailing my scent for the KGB. I swam across a pond so the dog would lose my scent. I ended up in a stranger's dorm room because I thought we were all supposed to switch rooms to confuse the KGB. I ended up in the psych ward of a hospital in April 1981, just like I did in the previous chapter in February 1980. I got out again thanks to medication. Then I had a good summer in 1981.

16

The Good Summer of 1981

I got out of the hospital in late April 1981, and went back to my place in my grandfather's duplex. I was there a few weeks, and then Dr. Holley, whom I had switched to when I started to get manic, said I should move in with my dad because it was less stressful than living alone. I reluctantly agreed, thinking that my dad would behave now that he wasn't tied to my dying mother. Actually his behavior toward me didn't change that much; he still called me "honey" like I was his wife or something. Fortunately, my brothers, Steve and Johnny, were there, and for a while my brother, Rick. When my brothers were there, it occupied my dad so that he didn't demand so much attention from me.

I decided I would go back to the University of Puget Sound in the Fall, even though my classmates had graduated. My main reason for going back down there in the Fall was that they had coed dorms, and it would be a chance for me to have a good social life, and possibly fall in love. I thought a lot about Betsy Straka, and knew she would still be there.

In late May, I got a job as cashier at a convenience store. It was a minimum wage job, of course, but I couldn't handle it. I couldn't learn how to work the cash registers. I quit after three days. I was still on a lot of tranquilizer.

Dr. Holley now had me thinking I was schizophrenic. But I asked him, "What caused my episode down on campus?"

In spite of blood tests he ran that said I was not using illegal drugs, he said, "Oh, I just think you were smoking a little grass."

I said, "No, so what caused it?"

"Well, I think you were a little depressed about your mom's death."

"Well, not really, but wouldn't what I did be the manic part and not depressed?"

"Well, you can act strange when you are depressed, too."

"I wasn't that depressed."

"Well, a parent's death can be a big stress on someone."

"Maybe I'll be okay now that I got out my feelings about my mom and what it does to my dad," I said.

I somehow had picked up the idea that "Suppressed feelings pop out later, and are the cause of nervous breakdowns." This idea is not true for manic depression, but it is a common myth. It may be true for other things.

"I think you probably will be okay as we gradually reduce the dose of this tranquilizer in the next couple weeks," said Holley.

It was this assurance that made me think that the disease was behind me. I thought it would not bother me again unless I was under severe stress, like someone else's death. Overall, he maintained that I was schizophrenic, not manic-depressive, and I would probably be fine for a long time. This somehow made sense then, but, of course, it does not make sense. It made sense because I temporarily felt okay. I thought that feeling would last a while.

This is another example of failure to diagnose me properly, and failure to treat me properly. Now that I was fairly healthy, it was the time to ask me about the content of my delusions, and to figure out what the problem in April had been. If he had determined that I was schizophrenic, he probably should have put me on major tranquilizers; if he had determined that I was manic-depressive, then he should have put me back on mood leveler Lithium. Instead, in a couple weeks, he had me on nothing. He thought that talking to him would keep me stable. I recognize this as extremely poor medical practice now, though I didn't recognize it then. I've learned much since then. Misdiagnosis is a big error. I could have gotten better sooner with earlier diagnosis. However, my mood was temporarily good.

In mid-June, we had our stag party for high school poker friends Jack and Jim. They were getting married to their sweethearts of several years that summer. We had dinner in a private room in a restaurant. I was feeling very good. This feeling good was random luck, but I didn't know that. We had speeches and presentations of gifts. The speeches were to be roasts of Jack and Jim. A cousin of Jack's gave a good roast of Jack. He told a lot of funny stories from when they were little, including the time Jack startled a babysitter so bad that she almost passed out. I thought the story was funny. I was having a good time.

Jim's brother roasted him. He pointed out many escapades of Jim's where Jim ended up looking stupid. This included a time when he was so drunk he couldn't stand up. "I had to help him get his contacts out and undress him so he could go to bed," said his brother.

I wished that my manic episodes were just one nighters, yet I prided myself in knowing not to get drunk. Many manic-depressives are chemically dependent, which means addicted to alcohol or street drugs. Then they have two major mental illnesses. My avoidance of drinking was partly due to school health programs saying "Your problems will still be there when the drugs or alcohol wears off." My father, my doctors, and my swim coaches had also told me not to drink.

At the stag party, I gave the presents to Jim. I felt like I was just one of the guys. I was on equal footing with them, and I had just taken some time off school. I said, "When we used to play cards and Jim would win, we would always say, 'Will Eckhart go to college with his poker winnings?' Well, he not only went to college, he even graduated." I went on to say, "He probably paid for his condo with poker winnings, too." Then I presented him with our gift, which was a brief case. He had graduated from the University of Washington with a degree in electrical engineering.

Dave Frish presented the gifts to Jack Johnson. Both Dave and Jack were about to start graduate school at UW in aerospace engineering. We gave him a tool set because he had just bought a car. It was such a homey, middle class, typical American gift, that I felt some reassurance that I was part of it all. I had felt out of step since 1976. I also liked the idea that people my age could get married.

Jim and Jack gave some gag gifts to the four of us who threw the party. I had always been slim and trim, but I had gained twenty-five pounds since I got out of the hospital.

So Jim said, "To Bill who used to always pride himself at being a good swimmer, and being in shape, who is now so fat all he can do is float, we hereby enroll him in the Orson Welles diet plan." That got a good laugh from the group. I didn't mind.

We had about thirty-three guys there, and about twenty stayed to play poker. We gave part of each pot to Jim and Jack.

Jack's wedding was first. It was at Temple Moses and there was a dinner at a hotel afterward. His best man, who had been his roommate in college, chained up their bed in their bridal suite, and put the key to the lock inside one of many balloons in the bathtub. I thought it was pretty childish. I didn't like the idea of anything interfering with someone's sex life.

In early July, Jim got married. It was also at Temple Moses, and they had a dinner there. I was an usher for his wedding. It was a happy occasion. I thought my life could be happy now, also.

I took some summer courses at UW. There were two summer sessions. During the first session I took a statistics course. I got a B in it. In the second session, I took two business courses, and I got an A and a B. With some great luck, my mood was good that summer, which is what enabled me to concentrate. My mood was the best since the disease started. Being manic had brought me out of my depression. I felt like I would be okay, and my insurance was seeing Dr. Holley. Knowing about antidepressants and knowing that sleeplessness was an early warning sign of mania would have been better insurance, but Dr. Holley kept me uninformed. He said as long as I got B's at UW, he would tell my father it was okay for me to go back to UPS.

17

A Search for a Happy Environment

Summer ended, and my dad drove me back down to UPS. I was assigned a room and a roommate. My roommate was named Paul.

I told him I had taken a year and two-thirds off because of illness. I said I was paranoid schizophrenic, because that's what Dr. Holley had me believing. I described my letters that were considered possible threats, and my delusions about the CIA.

I said, "Now I'm okay, but I'm still seeing a shrink."

I really thought I would be okay since I *thought* the problem was mostly environmental, and now with the death of my mother, my father might behave. I was living in a dorm at UPS away from my dad, and I could get done with school and be done with my dad completely. I could get a job, so that I wouldn't have to depend on him for cash. I still didn't realize the problem was mostly in my genes.

Classes started, and I took art history, which I needed for distribution requirements, and a course on the political economy of capitalism. My plan was to major in economics.

Early in the quarter I went to my economics major advisor who was also the head of the economics department, and asked him what sort of a future there was for economics majors. In other words, I asked, "Can you get a job with an economics degree?"

He tried to tell me yes, and I asked him to name what jobs people got out of last year's graduating class of economics majors. He went down the list of last year's graduates. For some people he named a graduate school. For some he named a specific job. For others he just said, "Job."

I asked him, "What job?"

He said, "I don't know."

This was a bad sign. That meant he was just guessing or hoping that they had jobs. They probably didn't have jobs.

I started to think that I should major in electrical engineering. That way I'd be more likely to get a good job when I graduate. UPS didn't offer an electrical engineering degree, so I started considering transferring back to the UW at Seattle where I could major in electrical engineering. I really felt optimistic. I felt that now I was okay, and now I could take on something like electrical engineering. The idea that I was healthy enough to handle the toughest undergraduate major, electrical engineering, was unrealistic, and an idea given to me by Dr. Holley. That was more bad medical practice.

By the end of the quarter, I was considering the switch, because I knew my dad would not be as intolerable as he used to be. If I lived with him on Mercer Island, and went to UW Seattle to take engineering, he might not be that difficult to live with. He was in a position where he could date, so maybe he wouldn't be so mad if I dated.

That quarter at Puget Sound, I started jogging every day until I sprained my ankle playing touch football. I gradually lost weight when I was jogging. I thought I was losing weight because of the jogging. I'm sure now that the real reason I was losing weight was because I was becoming depressed again. Changes in appetite are a symptom of depression. I was eating less and was glad about that. I didn't know it was related to the other symptoms I was developing.

In the evening, I would lie on my bed trying to read my art history book, or my economics books, and I would just gradually put my head down on my bed and fall asleep for a half hour at a time. This wasn't normal, because I was sleeping well at night. This was the sleep disturbance symptom of depression, which can include sleeping too much.

I was also becoming concerned about crime again. This time, though, it wasn't in a manic way, it was in a depressed way. I didn't think I could save the world from crime, I was just worried about the crime that could happen around me. I heard that there was someone being allowed back on Puget Sound campus for winter quarter. He had been kicked off for a year, for breaking into people's rooms. I heard that he was also a rapist, although that was unproven. I went to the president of the university to complain about his being allowed back on campus.

He said, "Thanks for telling me. You've done the right thing. I'll check into it."

He talked to the dean of students, who just assured him that the guy was going to be on probation.

I also wrote an anonymous letter to the editor of the Puget Sound school newspaper saying the student being allowed back was a rapist and shouldn't be let back on campus.

As the quarter progressed, my mood was getting worse, I was getting more depressed. I was driving up to see Dr. Holley in Seattle every three weeks. Once in a while he'd say, "I've got a new drug I want you to try."

I told him, "No, I don't use drugs." I figured, as many people do, that all drugs for the mind are addictive and dangerous in other ways also.

"It'll help you sleep."

"I'm sleeping too much as it is."

"Oh, this is a fun drug, you'll like it. A lot of people like it."

I assumed he was speaking of burned out druggies who liked getting stoned. "No. I don't do drugs."

"This is a lot better than the ones I had you on last spring."

"No. I don't ever want to be on drugs again."

"Well this one is different. It will help you sleep."

"I'm sleeping too much as it is."

He may have been trying to give me antidepressants which would have been right, but he didn't tell me what they were, or what they were for, or what they would do. I now consider his failure very poor medical practice. I thought they were sleeping pills. I had never heard of antidepressants. He didn't tell me that they could *cheer me up.*

I will again provide an example of one of my depressive streams of thought. These depressive streams of thought are significant because *they were my activity most of the day:*

I'm such a loser. The majority of women at this school are taken. If they aren't taken, they probably still don't want me. I'm a loser. I am grossly inexperienced. How will they like me? I have to date an unpopular woman or steal one from some guy who has a normal family, transcript, and life knowledge and experience. I can't compete with normal guys. I crack up under pressure. How manly is that?

I thought a girlfriend was the key to being happy. Of course, this was unrealistic. What I really needed was treatment for manic depression.

As the quarter progressed, thoughts like that preoccupied me more and more. They interfered with normal daily activities like talking and flirting. I often ate alone. Sometimes I'd eat with Paul or with one of the guys who lived on our floor. With women, I was at a loss for words. I wasn't in a good enough mood to talk to them and I didn't know how to tell them about my illness.

The quarter ended and I got a C in economics and a D in art history. I went home to Mercer Island, not knowing I was medically depressed, and not knowing there was treatment for depression that worked. I thought my problem was simply that I was just not motivated or excited by economics, and I didn't have a girlfriend.

I got a temporary job as a Christmas rush helper for United Parcel Service. I rode around with a regular driver, and ran up to the houses with the packages. It paid $7.80 an hour which was outstanding pay back then and doesn't sound bad now. The whole time, I was agonizing about whether or not I should go back to Puget Sound, major in economics, and graduate in '83. The other option was to switch back again to UW and major in engineering and graduate in '84. I did a passable job as a delivery helper in spite of this dilemma preoccupying my mind. It wasn't that hard a job.

I thought if I was unhappy while majoring in economics, economics was a problem. It didn't occur to me that there was a *chronic,* built-in problem with my brain chemistry. Nobody had said that yet. Not a single doctor. Nobody. I thought the problem was environmental. I thought my episodes that required hospitalization were temporary, and due to high stress. I didn't have insight into the chronic depressed phase.

I remember jogging with Jack Johnson in December and discussing with him the idea that I could make $26,000 a year as a first-year electrical engineer, or $17,000 a year as a first-year average economics graduate. I remember even taking into account the interest on the money I would save by graduating sooner. In the end, I decided that the pay differential for engineers was overwhelming, so I decided to transfer to UW School of Engineering. I did this even though it meant waiting until 1984 to graduate. I thought the lure of high pay would motivate me, and keep my spirits, concentration, and energy up. I planned to live at home with my dad, brother Johnny, and Grandpa, and I planned to commute to UW.

18

Getting Diagnosed and Ascending from the Depths of Depression

Winter quarter 1982 started and I had a physics class, a physics lab, and a calculus class. Things were okay for about a week. Then my depression grew worse. I started to be obsessed with guilt about the letter I had written to the UPS school newspaper saying that the guy who was being let back on campus was a rapist. They never printed the letter, but I thought enough people may have read it so that I could get sued for libel. I had not even signed the letter, but I had told one person on the newspaper staff in person that I wrote it. Realistically, the letter was thrown away and forgotten about, but depression was not realistic. My guilt feelings were exaggerated greatly. They preoccupied my mind so much that I couldn't pay attention in class. I couldn't study either. I did really poorly on some tests.

This whole time Dr. Holley was prescribing *nothing*.

When my guilt got so bad that I wasn't getting out of bed to go to school, and wasn't sleeping at night, Dr. Holley said, "Well maybe you're getting depressed again."

It was true, I was getting depressed, but when he said "again" I'm sure he meant that to mean manic, the opposite. Somehow, he confused the two, as he had confused them before. He prescribed some major tranquilizer Thorazine for me, which is the treatment for mania. It is the opposite of the treatment for depression. *It drags you down!* I took the Thorazine and I'm sure it made me worse. I went back to him in a week. *That week I spent eighteen hours a day in bed feeling paralyzed with guilt.* When the phone rang, I was afraid that it was the police wanting to question me about the crime of defamation of character.

This time, my depressive string of thoughts made me worry so intensely that I could not sleep at night. Then, I would stay in bed during the day to catch up on sleep. As before, I will show my thoughts. They went something like this:

Oh, why did I write that letter? I'm such a criminal. Here I am trying to say I'm against crime, at least I'm a good guy, and then I go and pull something like this. I'm going to get arrested for defamation of character. I am going to get sued. I'm going to get attacked by the asshole who really is a rapist, but I can't say so because the world is such an upside-down, unfair, crummy place. The innocent go to jail. The guilty go free. What a rotten place the world is. There is no hope. I shouldn't have written that letter. I am a dirtball. I'm an unusually disgusting person in a disgusting world.

I managed to make it to Dr. Holley's office.

Holley said, "Let's try Lithium."

I knew I felt awful whenever I had been on mood leveler Lithium, so I asked, "Is there something besides Lithium that you can give me?"

"Lithium is the drug of choice."

"Is there something *besides* Lithium?"

"Lithium is the drug of choice."

Of course, mood leveler Lithium is not the drug of choice for depression. One of the twenty antidepressants along with Lithium is. So the Lithium prescription without antidepressants was a serious mistake, as was the prescription for major tranquilizer Thorazine. Thorazine is designed to pull you down towards depression from the highs of mania. It doesn't lift you up.

I made it out to campus one day around then, and I ran into an old friend that I used to hang around with in junior high. His name was Carl Paige. I told him how awful badly I was doing. Later he called me up and invited me over to his apartment to try to cheer me up. That was nice. I still was staying in bed for eighteen hours most days.

I thought of someone cheerful who could maybe cheer me up. It was Jane Eggers, who had been the resident advisor of my dorm floor sophomore year. I knew she was in town. She seemed always in a good mood, so it seemed like a good idea. I called her and we made plans to have lunch. On that day, I struggled out of bed and made it there. I told her of my situation, my guilt feelings, and so on.

She said, "You can't get sued if they don't print the letter." We had a good talk and she said I could call her again.

Lunch with Jane still did not relieve my total preoccupation with the idea that I was going to be sued for libel. My dad was getting concerned at this point. The mood leveler Lithium was doing nothing. The next time I went to see Dr. Holley, my dad came with me.

He said, "I want Bill to get a second opinion. I want him to see an expert on this condition he has."

Dr. Holley referred us to Dr. Edward Haglund. He was a professor of psychiatry at the University of Washington Medical School. He also saw patients himself. When we first went to see him, he talked to both of us for a while, then he talked to my dad and me separately.

When I told him I was spending all day every day lying in bed feeling guilty about the letter I wrote, he said, "You need an antidepressant."

I had never heard the word before! Dr. Haglund ordered a dexamethasone suppression test. It tests for chemicals in your blood that change in amount when you are depressed. He said he would give me an antidepressant next time I came. He also said, after asking several questions, that I was manic-depressive, and that the illness was mostly genetic. He asked me questions about the episodes during which I had been hospitalized. He asked if I had been on a crusade to save the world.

I said, "Well, yes. I was going to save the world from crime."

Dr. Haglund asked, "Did you sleep? Did you have high energy?"

"I didn't sleep much. I had a lot of energy."

He went on to ask more questions about these episodes and concluded they were manic. He then asked me when I had been depressed in the past, when the depression started, if I had felt hopeless, and other questions along those lines. He concluded that I certainly had a pattern of depression.

He said, "Well it looks like you have a clear case of manic depression."

This definitive diagnosis of manic depression was five years late, and desperately needed. I was upset to hear that it was largely genetic, because you can change your environment, but you can't change your genes. In a way, though, I was relieved to get a definite diagnosis. At least there was a word for my disease, which meant someone somewhere must have had it before. I had never met another manic-depressive in my life outside the hospital. The exception to this was my mom, but I wasn't clear about her disease, and we hadn't been able to talk about it because she couldn't talk. At least it was a specific disease. It meant it wasn't my fault, and I was glad there were medications designed for it.

I went back to see Dr. Holley, because I had visited Dr. Haglund just for a second opinion. When Holley asked what Dr. Haglund had said, I said, "Haglund says I need an antidepressant."

Dr. Holley said, "I'll give you an antidepressant."

So, he wrote a prescription for guilt-stopping, cheer-inducing, energy-inducing, tear-stopping, sleep-normalizing, antidepressant Asendin. I think he gave me fifty milligrams to start. That night I took some before I went to bed. *I slept for the first time in weeks, and I woke up feeling better, less guilty, and more energetic!*

About the second or third day of my treatment with antidepressant Asendin, my dad had a second date with a Jewish widow named Connie Palmberg. He got home at about 11:30 P.M. I asked loudly and sarcastically, "What are you *doing* out this late, Dad?!"

He came bursting into my room and asked loudly, "Do you feel okay!?"

I yelled, "Get out of my room!" Then I went into his room.

He followed me into his room, and then he yelled, "Is it this new medication that is making you act disturbed?!"

I walked back into my room and yelled, "This new medication makes me feel better! I slept the last two nights for the first time in weeks!"

He walked back into my room and I yelled, "Get out of my room!"

My dad yelled, "I'm going to call your doctor!" and left my room.

My dad did call Dr. Holley the next day. Then Dr. Holley's office called and said Holley wanted to see me. So the next day I went and saw him and I asked him a lot of questions which he didn't answer, but he did say to increase the dose to 100 mg per day. That helped even more. Now I was even less depressed. It was just in time to sign up for spring classes, so I signed up for accounting and an economics course. Engineering was out, because of course, I had failed every class winter quarter. I got Dr. Holley to sign a form excusing me for flunking because of illness.

Meanwhile, my dad was seeing a lot of Connie Palmberg, and I was starting to give him a lot of trouble. I wasn't giving him a hard time about Connie, because I was overjoyed that they were together. I was glad that now my dad had someone his own age to play with. Now he wouldn't have to rely on me. I gave my dad a hard time by questioning him repeatedly about all the hard times he had given me. I did this so he would finally be able to realize that he had to let me do what I wanted, and though I had to put up with his intrusions or he'd cut me off financially, I now expected him to get his companionship from Connie. My dad had mistaken my forced acceptance of him as genuine, and now I wanted to tell him to get lost when he had somewhere else to go. When he had nowhere else to go he wouldn't listen, and would just yell back at me. Now things had changed, and he would not promote an anti-romance attitude. Now if I would yell, he would walk away from me. I followed him around the house yelling, "Do you think I enjoyed it when you told me not to go out with a girl who wasn't Jewish?!"

He would say, "I don't remember saying anything like that."

I yelled, "Do you think I enjoyed it when I had a steady girl-friend who *was* Jewish, and you told me to quit seeing *her*?!"

He said, "I never said that."

I wanted my dad to really dislike me, so that he would never dream of coming to me for attention. Now he had no excuse not to dislike me. I yelled at him a lot. At least by his responses, I knew he heard me. He denied ever being anti-girlfriend, but at least in saying that, he was acknowledging that that was the wrong way to be. Now that he was in love with Connie, accusing him of being anti-romance really hurt his feelings. That was good. I wanted to hurt his feelings.

I remember when Connie and my dad first started dating. I got the feeling I got when I was twelve years old and my parents first told me that I could ride my bike on *any* street. I was free at last!

I was seeing Dr. Haglund and Dr. Holley that spring and summer.

The problem with my treatment was that I was still on only 100 mg of antidepressant Asendin in the middle of June of 1982. I eventually learned that the best dose of Asendin for me was 400 mg. So while I was better, I was still depressed. However, my concentration *was* improved enough for me to get C's in the accounting and economics classes I took in the spring. I quit feeling guilty. I stayed in bed only eight hours. I got up and went to school.

In late May my dad and Connie got married. At the reception, I gave a big trophy to the couple that fixed them up. It said, "For Excellence In Matchmaking."

I kept giving my dad a hard time much of the summer. I told him I hated him, and wrote letters to some of his business partners saying what a jerk he was. Finally, one day I ransacked his and Connie's bedroom. It worked just great. I didn't wreck anything, I just emptied out all the closets and drawers and dumped everything on the floor. My dad yelled at me. It was great. For the first time since 1970, he yelled at an appropriate time. He even threatened to kick me out of the house. That was a big switch from always trying to lock me in the house. My dad's behavior was now relatively close to normal. I had given him a hard time. I felt he needed it. After my dad threatened to kick me out of the house, I quit giving him a hard time. He had then come to the realization that he didn't need me. I had taught him how to behave. I had conditioned him to not expect so much attention from me. Some parents are very difficult.

Now that he doesn't depend on me as much, we get along well. *He never came into my room after his remarriage.* I could say things like, "I'm going *away* to do *things* with *people*. I'll be back *later*."

He almost never protested.

The antidepressant Asendin that I was now on gave me new life. I felt like I had emerged from a cocoon to discover that the world was still there. The world had gone on without me, but was waiting for me to return to it. I felt I could understand people better and do more. Just walking around campus to my classes felt like a privilege and a joy. I felt so good on 300 mg of Asendin toward the end of the summer, that it reminded me of the summer of 1976. (Dr. Haglund had eventually increased the dosage.)

I was reminded of people like Jennifer Weinberg, Joel Stein, and Lisa Mudek from camp. Those were fun times. I wrote Joel Stein and told him that a new day had dawned in my life.

I would often make hand flexing motions like I was swimming without even consciously thinking about swimming at first. This was because I swam when I was happy and the feeling I had now was fairly happy, so it reminded me of swimming in high school. Thanks to antidepressant Asendin, I had energy and started jogging to get ready for an Outward Bound backpacking trip. I felt adventurous. This was way better than lying in bed eighteen hours a day feeling guilty over nothing. Asendin had saved me! Let's hear it for the medicine!

Antidepressant Asendin made me feel so much better, and my dad being married to someone healthy made me feel so much better, that I got up enough confidence to call Melanie Carson. We talked for a while and had a decent conversation. I told her I had manic depression, but was okay now. I told her that it was now very clear that it was jealousy that made my dad scream when I went out with her in April 1977, not her religion. This was based on his new behavior. She told me that it was multiple sclerosis that she had referred to in her letter to me in 1979. This was her one letter, in response to my one letter, which had been prompted by my talking to the psychologist once. The letter was during the quarter of school that I had flunked out of UPS.

Melanie said, "I have no symptoms of MS right now."

I think we also mentioned that we both knew Doug Bossard. He was a Puget Sound classmate and swim teammate of mine and had gone on a round-the-world trip with Melanie and a large group of others from Pacific Lutheran University.

About a week later Dr. Haglund made an astounding recommendation. "Try going off your antidepressant Asendin," he suggested.

This was bad advice, because I just got depressed again. He should have told me to go back on it immediately if I got depressed again. I started obsessing about Melanie Carson. I wished she would be mine so she could cheer me up. This is the same as the depressive, obsessive wishing that I did in 1977. Also, when a person goes off antidepressant Asendin, there is a sudden increase in sex drive. Asendin causes impotence (impaired erections) in some people. I consider it the worst non-life-threatening side effect a person could have. Asendin is the worst tricyclic anti-depressant as far as one's sex life is concerned. It caused partial impotence in me. Being suddenly off it caused a bizarre reaction. All I could do was think about sex, generally with Melanie. I called Melanie but she wasn't home. I left a message. I called four times in one day and left messages. I was obsessed. She didn't return the calls.

Dr. Holley and Dr. Haglund both said something to the effect of, "If phone calls don't work, write her a letter."

I said, "No, she didn't call me back. She doesn't want to talk to me. Besides, she thinks I'm crazy anyhow."

I was seeing the doctors separately but they both said something like, "Oh, it can't hurt to write her a letter. She doesn't think you're crazy. Everyone has some strange disease."

I said, "No, most people are way healthier than I am."

"Oh, that's not true. You're better now."

"I'm not better."

"Yes, you are. You're fine."

"I'm not fine, and I can still get manic."

"Just tell her you like her and you want to have coffee."

"No. She doesn't like me."

"Just try it."

This is a common flaw in psychiatry and psychology. They tell you to express your feelings regardless of how inappropriate. They were encouraging sexual harassment. This is an example of more extremely poor medical practice, in my opinion.

I wrote Melanie love letters. I didn't put a return address on them because I was afraid she would throw them away without reading them if she knew they were from me. I also didn't sign them thinking that would make her read them. I thought they were so great because they rhymed. I sent her one letter one day and another the next. They would've been good in 1977, but it was 1982. Suddenly going off antidepresssant Asendin made me act this strange. I didn't realize how inappropriate I was being. A few weeks later I reached her by phone and she said I was very annoying, and should not try to get in touch with her.

A short time after writing Melanie, I went back on antidepressant Asendin, because I was having concentration difficulties in class. In spite of the side effects, Asendin was good because it could make my mind work. It stopped me from always thinking about crying; it gave me some energy; and it stopped the topic of suicide from crossing my mind. This was as long as I was on at least 300 mg of it.

In early August, Mercer Island High Class of 1977 had our five-year reunion. I went and thought it was reasonably interesting and enjoyable. I did feel bad that at this point I was neither a college graduate nor married. I talked to some people I knew and caught up on what they were doing. I tried to approach Melanie and she just avoided me. I spent a lot of time staring at her. I'm sure she thought I was rude. The reunion was interesting, but I wished people knew that I had been through the twilight zone and was not quite back. I wanted some sympathy. On the other hand, I didn't want people to know all the crazy things I'd done. I wanted to fit in like I had in high school. I didn't talk to too many people at length, but I did tell people I had manic depression.

Elsewhere in my small social life, my cousin Laura Felber convinced me to join the Jewish Dating Service. It felt stupid for two reasons, one because it was a dating service, and two because it was Jewish. I didn't particularly want someone Jewish, and I didn't want to get involved with someone who was prejudiced against non-Jews.

I went out with a couple of women from the dating service once each, and one woman about three times, but all I could talk about was what a jerk my dad had been, and nothing romantic ever happened. I was still thinking about my dad because I was not yet on quite enough antidepressant Asendin to make me think of something pleasant. Later, a full dose of it made me think more happy thoughts. Because I still had some depression on these dates, I probably came across as strange.

I had been on enough antidepressant Asendin throughout the summer that I was able, for the first time in a long time, to get a full quarter's worth of credits for my summer classes. I got C's in four economics courses. C's were better than I had been doing, but they were unlike the A's I had gotten in high school.

19

Learning that Antidepressants Can Be for the Long Term

During the fall of 1982, I lived in a dorm on UW campus. I managed to pass two classes because I usually stayed on my antidepressant Asendin.

This antidepressant Asendin seemed like such a miracle that I thought I should have gotten it sooner. I asked Dr. Haglund if he would testify in a medical malpractice trial against Dr. Kelly and Dr. Holley for not giving me Asendin sooner.

He said, "No."

I said, "Why not?"

He gave a limp excuse for the other doctors, saying, "Manic depression is hard to diagnose."

No, it's not. The list of symptoms is in the back of this book.

I guess doctors won't testify against each other because they fear some form of retaliation. They fear being shunned by the medical community. That is my guess.

I figured that if I couldn't get my current doctor to testify against my old doctors, I didn't have much of a case. I'd have to go hunting for another doctor to be an expert witness. I was afraid I'd get the same negative response.

I was on 300 mg of antidepressant Asendin, 1200 mg of mood leveler Lithium, and the side effect drug Cogentin. After many complaints of drowsiness like the following, I quit taking the Lithium and Cogentin. I continued to take the Asendin.

When I saw my psychiatrist Dr. Haglund, he said, "How are you?"

I usually said, "I'm drowsy."

He asked, "Are you dating?"

"No. How am I going to tell women that I have a mental illness?"

"You don't have to tell them right away."

"But what do I say when I *do* tell them, and what do I say when they ask why it's taken me so long to graduate?"

He'd say something useless like, "Just say you were sick."

"Besides, I'm partially impotent."

"Does that mean it takes you longer to reach orgasm?"

"No. It means it doesn't get as hard as it is supposed to."

"Well don't you think that would go away with heterosexual activity?"

"No. It's from the drug."

"How's your dad?"

"My dad didn't want me to have a girlfriend," I said. (His behavior had improved markedly, but he still had never said anything positive about me having a girlfriend.)

I said, "I'm drowsy, very drowsy."

"I know."

The dorm I was living in was an all guys dorm, but we ate our meals with a dorm that was coed. I usually sat with the guys on my floor. One day I got up enough nerve to sit with one of the prettiest women at the dorm. There was an empty space next to her and I just sat down and said, "Hi."

Her name was Bridget Cassady. I developed a big crush on her almost immediately. She was smart and pretty. She already had a boyfriend though.

Before the end of the quarter, I just happened to have to go lap swimming. I went so I could talk to Bridget where she worked at the check-in desk. She was sitting there studying, and we talked a little. I went and swam about 1500 yards. Then I came out, said a few more things to Bridget, and left. She was sweet.

Still, I wanted a steady girlfriend of my own. I made arrangements to move to a coed dorm on the other side of campus for winter quarter. Dr. Haglund approved of this. Neither he nor I realized how impossible it would prove to be attractive while I was on antidepressant Asendin. Still, I knew Asendin made my mind work.

I knew antidepressant Asendin made a big difference because I tried going without it a couple times during this Fall quarter of 1982. I bombed some tests those days without Asendin and ended up with two C's and two D's for grades. I did well when I stayed on the Asendin.

During Christmas vacation, my father Lee, stepmother Connie, and brothers Rick, Johnny, Steve, and myself went skiing for four days. Skiing was okay the first day, but then I ran out of antidepressant Asendin, and I started to feel like doing nothing. Without Asendin, depression returned immediately. I skied maybe one hour the last two days.

We got back in town a few days before school started. When I finally got to see Dr. Haglund, classes had already started, and I hadn't been to class yet. I was sitting in my new dorm room doing nothing. I was that depressed without antidepressant Asendin. I was feeling so badly unmotivated that I was not going to class. I was also thinking about the argument I had with my dad when I went out with Melanie Carson in 1977. Either that, or I'd think about the arguments I had with him when I went out with Angie Spiess in 1976. This preoccupation with past trouble was a symptom of depression. I was having trouble getting out of my bed in the morning because I didn't have Asendin to treat my depression. However, the impotence side effect of Asendin had gone away.

When I saw Dr. Haglund, he asked how I felt, and I said, "Not *too* bad."

I didn't feel too bad because I was glad that the sexual side effects and the drowsiness were gone.

Haglund asked, "Do you want to die?"

I said, "No, I want to live."

"You don't need any more antidepressant."

"Yes I do. I need some more Asendin. I haven't been going to class. I'm not motivated!"

"Try going without it. I'll give you some next time if you need it."

"Please," I begged.

"No," was his only reply.

The next time I saw him was in about two weeks. Meanwhile my depression got worse. I went to a few classes, but I couldn't concentrate. All I could think about was how much I hated my dad for having demanded so much attention, and for being so

jealous of my relationships with others. When I went down to
meals in my dorm, I often sat with some women and introduced
myself, but I said that I was manic-depressive, and I was having
trouble in my classes, because all I could think about is how much
I hated my father. I got a reputation for being very weird.

There is a problem when people think you are weird. People
don't differentiate between different types of weirdness. There was
a woman in my dorm to whom the worst thing I had said was,
"I'm against the Equal Rights Amendment because it could put
women in combat."

Later she got an obscene phone call, and my roommate told
me that he heard she suspected it was from me. Of course, it
wasn't from me. Often people equate mental illness with criminali-
ty, even though most criminals aren't mentally ill and most mentally ill people aren't criminals.

My roommate was getting sick of my depression, too. He was
sick of hearing about my father. I was obsessed. He was ready to
kick me out and find a new roommate. Just after that, on my third
visit to Dr. Haglund that quarter, he finally gave me a prescription
for some antidepressant Asendin which was great, but he should
have done it sooner.

When I started to take antidepressant Asendin again, I *immediately* felt better. I quit thinking about my dad so much. I started
going to class. There were about four weeks left in the winter
quarter, and I managed to get a C in one of my three classes. I
dropped and flunked the other two.

I still was going to see Bridget and swimming. Her mother had
had a stroke in February of the same type that my mother had. We
talked about that for a long time and became good friends. She
was the first good friend I had made in *years*. I fantasized that we
could be lovers. She was so beautiful. I was still disappointed that
she had a boyfriend. He was from her home town and went to a
different school. Still it was an honor and a joy to be her friend.

My roommate, Walter, convinced me, after I was feeling better
at the end of winter quarter, to go to Mazatlan, Mexico, for a
spring break vacation. Because I *was* feeling better, in spite of the
fact that I didn't have anyone to go with, I signed up to go by
myself. I wouldn't really be by myself, because they would assign
me roommates, and the town would be loaded with other American college kids, partying up a storm. I went and met some people
on the plane, roomed with them, hit the beach and the clubs for a

week, and had a good time. I didn't drink because I figured I shouldn't because of my antidepressant Asendin. I met some people from all over the United States, but had no romance thanks to some lingering depression, and some definite impotence, a side effect of the Asendin. Asendin helped a lot, but it didn't help enough.

Also in Mazatlan, I ran into Doug Bossard. He was the guy from the University of Puget Sound, whom I knew from the swim team there. He knew Melanie Carson from his trip around the world with the group from Pacific Lutheran University. We discussed her for quite awhile. Also I told him about my manic depression and how it would have been nice to be able to talk about it freshman year, but my dad had ordered me not to do so. Doug was encouraging and said I had been, and still was, an interesting guy.

All in all, Mazatlan was a success. I had finally gone on a vacation in a decent mood.

I went back up to Seattle and started spring quarter. My classes were on abnormal psychology, statistics, and expository writing. I was on the full 300 mg of antidepressant Asendin and no mood leveler Lithium. I started to sit for meals with the guys on my floor. We had single-sex floors, and there was a lot of self-segregation of the sexes in the cafeteria. I quit trying to sit with women.

There were some women that I had sat with the previous quarter, and when I looked at them too long, even from way across the room they would yell, "Aaah!" and then start laughing. Then I would look away and they'd be quiet. Then I'd look at them again, and they'd again yell "Aaah!" and then start laughing. Then I'd look away. In a way I liked the attention, although it was negative attention. I was considered weird, not smooth.

When I was on antidepressant Asendin, I looked at women too long, and it was rude. There is a social convention that says you are only supposed to look at a member of the opposite sex for a half second, or you will be considered staring and rude. I think that men look at attractive women in order to get a touch of physical arousal. However, most men, when they get this little touch of arousal, hear a little voice inside that says, "Not here, not now, look away."

When on Asendin, it takes longer for that inner voice to speak. For me, it took five seconds whereas for other guys it took half a second. I hate to put this so crudely and bluntly, but given the nature of the subject matter, I have to. My penis was totally shrivelled up all day. Impotence does not just affect you in bed.

When I'm not suffering from this side effect, it is instantly obvious that women are sexy, so I look away quickly. I don't want to be rude and inappropriate.

It was a miserable existence. People thought I was strange. Still, this was better than being massively depressed. I was a lot better off with antidepressant Asendin than without it. My intellect worked. My sexuality didn't. Without Asendin, neither worked.

I did have a friend named Rachel Moeller. She was a woman I knew from UPS. She lived in Seattle now. We went to a lot of movies. We were just friends, and that was fine with me. A person needs friends.

Bridget, the gym and pool check-in clerk, had a long distance relationship, but she was starting to get interested in another guy who hung around and talked to her while she was working at the gym desk. His name was Todd. He had been a big swimmer for the UW team, and he was smart, too. He was going through the application process for being an Air Force pilot. Bridget finally dumped her hometown honey, Jack, and started going out with Todd. I was a little jealous that she didn't pick me, but I was realistic in knowing that I had told all my serious problems to Bridget, and I therefore wasn't as attractive a candidate for a boyfriend. I came to see Bridget twice a week when she worked, and I talked to her a lot. I told her she was my best friend, even though I knew I wasn't hers.

A typical conversation with Bridget might go like this:

"Hi, Bridge."

"Hi, Bill. How are you?" she'd say with a smile.

"I'm okay."

"How are things over there in Johnston [the name of my dorm]."

"Actually okay. I'm caught up in my work."

"That's good. I'm doing okay too. I'm looking forward to gymnastics after I get done here. It feels good to work out," she'd say smiling and stretching out.

I'd say, "Yeah."

I felt working out didn't really make a difference. Only antidepressants made a difference. I didn't usually say so, though.

She'd say, "How much are you going swim today?"

"Probably 1500."

"Now do you swim breaststroke or freestyle?"

"Freestyle."

"Is it very crowded in the pool?"

"Usually not."

"Yeah. I guess most of these people are going to the gym. I'm looking forward to this weekend. Some of my friends are coming to see me."

"That's nice."

We would keep up this small talk for a while, and then I'd say, "You're my best friend."

She'd say, "Thanks, Bill."

We'd talk a lot more, and then I would go in and swim. I'd only go there on days when she was working and she knew that. She was my best friend because she would talk to me more than anyone else would talk to me. Most people would hardly talk to me because I didn't smile.

I was still seeing my friend, Jane Eggers, once a month for pizza. She was the one who had been my resident advisor sophomore year at UPS. I had called her when I was really depressed in the winter of 1982. I saw her once a month and it helped give me someone to talk to. She was also the head of the Seattle Mental Health Association. She told me about the Washington Manic-Depressive Association. They had support groups.

When I went to some of the support groups, in a way I was glad to hear other people's stories about what they did when they were manic, but I sure didn't want to be like them. I was usually one of the youngest in the group, and I sure didn't want to end up like the other group members when I was their age. These people were divorced, unemployed, broke, and on welfare. I didn't like going to the meetings, because these were not the type of people I liked to hang out with. I did go several times, though, and I got some literature about manic depression, read it all, and learned a little about the medications.

The end of spring quarter came, and I had stayed undepressed enough to get two B's and a C, thanks to 300 mg of antidepressant Asendin. Let's hear it for the medication!

20

Lousy Medical Practice Leads To My Contemplating Suicide

In the summer of 1983, I asked my psychiatrist, Dr. Haglund, if I could reduce my antidepressant Asendin dose to 200 mg per day. This would cause less severe sexual side effects and less drowsiness. There would also be less of the dry mouth, dry nose, and dry eyes side effect. The main thing I was concerned about was getting rid of the impotence side effect. Haglund said I could reduce the dose. This would later prove to be a big mistake. The side effects were reduced, and I didn't get more depressed right away. At least, I couldn't tell that I had somewhat increased depression right away. The impotence on 300 mg was just partial, but it was enough to interfere with normal functioning. A dosage of 200 mg was not as bad.

Since March, I had been seeing a psychologist named Donald Mulcrone in addition to seeing Dr. Haglund who was a psychiatrist. Psychologists are not medical doctors and therefore cannot prescribe drugs. They believe in talk therapy called psychotherapy. I went to Mulcrone with the idea that he could help me forget about my dad, and that he could help me to know how to start a relationship with a woman, in spite of the fact that I would have to tell her that I was manic-depressive. Also, in March when I first started seeing Mr. Mulcrone, he said that it would be good to treat my depression with psychotherapy, instead of medicine. That way I would not have the side effects of antidepressant Asendin.

Mr. Mulcrone seemed to have no system except to tell me to ask out any woman I mentioned. He was of little use. However, he did listen to the stories of the arguments I had with my dad, and he did take my side.

As the summer wore on, I began to get depressed and started having some trouble in my classes. I became obsessed with the depressive fear of getting manic. I was depressed about the possibility of getting manic in the future! Dr. Haglund, the psychiatrist, and I thought the fear was legitimate. Mr. Mulcrone, the psychologist, thought the fear was not legitimate. He thought he should get rid of my obsessional fear of mania by arguing with me.

Mulcrone said, "You're not going to get manic."

I said, "I could."

"You will not."

"I could."

"You will not."

"I could. I have before."

"I doubt it. *I've* never seen you manic."

"You've only seen me for four months, I was manic two years ago in 1981."

"*I* never saw you that way."

"I was manic."

"I don't *know* that."

"I was manic. Don't you believe me?"

Mr. Mulcrone said, "That's a matter of opinion."

Dr. Haglund, the medical doctor and psychiatrist, thought the fear of mania was legitimate so we started to discuss putting me on mood leveler Tegretol which is supposed to prevent mania. It is an alternative drug to mood leveler Lithium. Both are supposed to help prevent mania. I didn't like Lithium because of the drowsiness and muscle tremors it gave me. *Nobody realized that my fear of mania was just a symptom of depression.*

So I started to take mood leveler Tegretol to prevent mania in addition to my antidepressant Asendin for depression. I had feared Tegretol because it had a bunch of awful things listed as possible side effects, including impotence. I felt I had to have it to prevent mania. I didn't want to get manic at a job and get fired. I didn't want to get manic in a marriage and get dumped. I was really obsessed with these fears. I thought I would be financially dependent on my dad or welfare for the rest of my life, unless I prevented mania. It was fairly strange being worried about being dumped by a hypothetical wife, when I hadn't even had a date in a year or so.

I was also worried about getting manic in front of my friend Bridget. She went home for the summer, but we were writing letters back and forth. I was obsessed with her as well as obsessed with my fear of getting manic.

Finally Dr. Haglund said, "Just try Tegretol to prevent mania for a while and if it's too awful, you can go off it."

When I first started mood leveler Tegretol, it put my speech on one-second time delay. It was some weird neurological phenomena that made my words come out one second after I told them to come out, caused by the combination of antidepressant Asendin and Tegretol. I had to not listen to myself or I would get confused. It was like calling a radio station and being on seven-second time delay, only this was just one second. The disc jockey always has to tell callers, "Turn down your radio!"

I had to give a short speech in front of a class with my voice echoing a second later. I was really nervous. Afterwards, I asked the teacher if I sounded clear enough. She said I sounded clear but nervous. I was nervous because I had never spoken in front of a group with my voice on echo.

Later, mood leveler Tegretol made me uncoordinated, so Dr. Haglund told me to get off it. I still had the depressive, obsessional fear of getting manic. This obsession was a symptom of depression due to not enough antidepressant Asendin, but neither Dr. Haglund nor Mr. Mulcrone nor I knew it. I didn't realize this until later, when I went back on the full dose of Asendin. Once Tegretol was disqualified, I reluctantly went back on mood leveler Lithium. Lithium helps prevent mania.

Mr. Mulcrone continued telling me that my fear of mania was unfounded because, "I've never seen you manic," he said. Also he said, "One survey in a rural area showed that there was no mental illness there in a six month period." He also said, "Lithium has never been proven to work. It's just a theory someone has, so there is no use taking it to prevent mania." Last but not least he said, "Some experts believe there is no such thing as mental illness, so you don't need Lithium." Of course, I knew it then, and I know it now. He was a terrible psychologist. I went to him a few more times, though, hoping he would straighten out.

So I was on mood leveler Lithium and 200 mg of antidepressant Asendin, and I was pessimistic about my future. It was August and I had gotten C's for the first summer session of school. Now I needed only two classes in order to graduate. Mr. Mulcrone had encouraged me to call the Jewish Dating Service to get some dates. I did that, and I got a date with a woman for lunch on campus. I was feeling really awful and pessimistic about everyone and everything at this time. The exception was my friend Bridget. We were writing to each other. I thought about her when I wasn't obsessing about future mania. I went to lunch with the woman I had met through the dating service but I hardly said anything because I was so depressed. She talked and I pretended to listen and care. Then I went to my dorm and contemplated suicide.

I thought about the impotence from antidepressant Asendin and the way I felt and the fact that I could get manic, and I felt like the future was hopeless. This blind date was a stress. I kept comparing how the theoretical healthy me would have handled it. I would have been so charming and lovable. Actually, I thought, the healthy me would've been married by now. I felt the healthy me would never return. I thought of better drugs, but I was sure that would never happen. I thought the healthy sixteen-year-old me would have been able to attract a girlfriend like Bridget, but I thought that healthy me would never return. I feared I would never be able to hold a job for long because I would get manic too often. I thought I would never have sex again as long as I lived. Therefore, there was no use living. I thought about killing myself with a gun, because that would be the surest way. I was thinking about the location of some gun stores, and I decided I should kill myself in the parking ramp where I parked my car. Then I thought, I didn't want to be a mess for someone to clean up, so I better not do it. Also, I thought I should leave a will so my $20,000 (Bar Mitzvah money plus eleven years' interest) would go to my friends and not my father. Then I thought about the fact that my friends had never asked for money, and they would rather have me alive, so I shouldn't do it. Also, maybe they *would* have better medications someday. I was doing this contemplating in the lounge of my dorm. I decided not to do it, thinking maybe there would be better drugs one day. Then I went back to my room and cried.

I was crying at the thought that I almost died. I decided to call Glenn Simco when I was through crying. He was the head and founder of the Washington Manic-Depressive Association. I told him I was suicidal, and he said I should call my doctor.

He said, "Remember, you want to kill the disease, you don't want to kill you."

So I called Dr. Haglund at home, and after reassuring him that I was not going to do it, he said, "Come to my office in the morning."

Knowing I was on 200 mg of antidepressant Asendin and that 300 mg worked better, I took 600 mg of Asendin that day, because according to the package insert which gives prescribing information for Asendin, 600 mg is the most you can safely take of Asendin in one day. For anything above 400 mg, you are supposed to be in the hospital, but I thought I better take it anyway. It is because of my reading of package inserts, the *Physicians' Desk Reference*, and other books about medication that I am fairly healthy today.

I went the next day to Dr. Haglund's office and after talking for a while he said, "I'm going to switch your antidepressant around."

I said, "No, no, just give me some more Asendin, I was on 200 mg and that's what caused the problem. I was fine on 300 mg. Just give me some more Asendin."

Dr. Haglund said, "Oh no, let's switch. That Asendin is a bad drug."

After a few more minutes of arguing like this, I said, "No, give me Asendin or I'll go to another doctor."

He said, "Okay."

Of course, given that my life was at stake, and given that Asendin works at 300 mg, giving me something else at that point would have been extremely lousy medical practice.

I got my prescription for antidepressant Asendin filled, took 500 mg for a few days, and felt much better after only three days. During these three days, I felt bad that I had nobody reasonable to talk to. I knew that I had many old friends and a few new friends who cared about me, but I didn't tell any of them that I was suicidal. I knew they would help me if they could, but I knew they could not help. I didn't want to ruin their day by making them worry about me. I didn't want to be a bigger chore than I already was.

I remember going to my classes and thinking the people there don't realize that I almost died. I figured some day I would have people who care and I would be healthy, so I could tell the story, but it would be past tense, so it wouldn't upset them. I knew the antidepressant Asendin would work. Those three days I had lots of dry mouth, dry eyes (I had to wear my glasses instead of contacts), and drowsiness, but I knew Asendin would work. After three days I lowered the dose back to the usual 300 mg and felt okay. Let's hear it for the medicine! After a week, suicide was far from my mind. This clearly shows that manic depression is a biochemical illness. The medication restored my brain chemicals to a more normal level.

Later I went to see the psychologist, Mr. Mulcrone, and I told him about the afternoon when I contemplated suicide. In the evening of the same day that I contemplated suicide, I had gone to a movie with Rachel Moeller.

Mr. Mulcrone asked, "Did you feel better when you were with Rachel?"

I said, "Yeah."

He said, "Well that should tell you something."

I said angrily, "Like what? I'm supposed to have people around me all the time or I'll commit suicide? It was the drugs not working at too low a dose."

Mr. Mulcrone said, "Well this incident should show you the value of personal relationships."

He was saying, it seemed, "I told you so, I told you so. I told you you need to make friends. Suicidal thoughts are a normal reaction to being stuck by yourself for twenty-four hours. This is what you get and deserve when you don't make more friends."

I didn't need him to tell me to make friends.

Of course, his statement was extremely lousy medical practice, and I knew it then. I quit seeing Mr. Mulcrone shortly thereafter.

Later, over a soda with a psychiatric nursing graduate student who lived on my dorm floor, I said, "Happiness can be found in a bottle of Asendin."

He said, "No, no, you have to create a life for yourself that is rewarding."

This conversation went on for awhile, but I wouldn't budge from my point of view that happiness can be found in a bottle of antidepressant Asendin.

I finished my classes and passed, so I graduated with a B.A. in economics. I didn't bother attending the graduation exercises.

I quit worrying about mania once I was back on 300 mg of Asendin instead of 200 mg.

After I asked my Aunt Brenda Felber if I could live with her, and she said, "No, because you can live at your father's," I moved back in to my father's house. I moved in reluctantly and with the idea that I would only be staying a few months, until I could find a job, so I could support myself.

All summer long, Bridget was the only bright side of my life. I didn't tell her about my suicidal thoughts. I didn't want to seem like more of a problem. Just having her for a friend was wonderful though. She was a great listener.

It was really a symptom of the disease that I thought of Bridget so much that summer, even though she was not my girlfriend. These thoughts were interspersed with my fear of future mania. They both go with the general theme of pessimism. It was pessimistic to think that I had to stay close to Bridget because nobody else would ever like me.

Lately I am better. A lot of people like me. If one person doesn't like me, other people do.

21

Brains Yes, Personality No

Sweet Bridget came back to Seattle from her home town of Ellensberg. She had gotten back together again with Jack after breaking up with Todd the fighter pilot to be. I was having lunch with her shortly after she got back to Seattle, and I told her I had gotten a job that didn't require a college degree, but it at least was a job. I figured I would do it and still look for something higher paying that used my degree. The job I got was as a pizza delivery driver for Dave's Pizza near the UW campus.

In December 1983, I started a year-and-a-half course at Seattle Area Technical Vocational Institute. I had sent out a bunch of resumes, but after getting lots of rejection letters, I had given up at finding a job using my economics degree. I had heard a lot of stories of some high school classmates of mine getting jobs repairing computers. So I signed up for the computer technician program at the Vo-Tech. I had always looked down on Vo-Techs as the place people go if they aren't bright enough to get into college. Now I saw it as a practical option. My biggest fear was that I would be too drowsy to stay awake in class. Luckily I stayed awake in class in December, and made it to January when I was not on mood leveler Lithium, and therefore was less drowsy. I dropped the Lithium because Lithium plus antidepressant Asendin caused too much drowsiness.

I asked one of the two women in my class, Cheryl, to be my lab partner. She was engaged, but she was a great lab partner. We were the two brightest in the class the first two quarters. Antidepressant Asendin actually made my brain work. I was on a full 300 mg dose of Asendin. Asendin stopped me from feeling like crying;

suicide didn't occur to me; my mind was not clogged with worries; and I had energy and motivation for school. I was the smartest in the class the first two quarters. The first two quarters, Cheryl really respected me for being smart and for being a gentleman. We pretty much would restrict our conversation to the lab at hand, but sometimes we would talk about other stuff. I looked forward to seeing her every day. She was fun to work with.

Third quarter I experimented with 275 mg or 250 mg of antidepressant Asendin instead of the usual 300 mg. I liked the greater sexual feeling and did not realize right away that I was spacey and irritable. Spaciness meant my memory and attention span were much worse. Irritability meant that I talked to everyone in a meaner tone. I talked to other classmates and Cheryl about the labs we had to do. I sounded unfriendly because of the decreased dosage of Asendin. Finally I realized that Cheryl was drifting away, and went back up to 300 mg every day.

Class was from 8:00 A.M. to 2:30 P.M. five days a week. I continued to deliver pizzas for Dave's Pizza on Friday and Saturday nights.

When I saw Dr. Haglund once a month, the conversations still started off like this:

Dr. Haglund asked, "How are you?"

I said, "On drugs."

"What do you mean by that?"

"Drowsy and partially impotent."

"Does that mean it takes longer to reach orgasm?"

"No. It means it doesn't get as big or as hard as it is supposed to."

"Are you dating?"

"No."

"How's your father?"

"My father didn't want me to have a girlfriend. He has still never said anything nice about me dating."

"Are you meeting any women?"

"Not really. What am I supposed to say to them about manic depression?"

"You don't have to tell them."

"I'm not gonna lie. What am I gonna tell them?"

"Well, you don't have to tell them right away. Tell them after you've slept with them for the third time."

"It takes a long time to get it up, and it is difficult to act interested."

"Well, you can say you are tired or nervous."

"I'm not gonna lie. When are you gonna get me better drugs so we don't have to keep having conversations like this?"

"We can try antidepressant Aventyl if you want."

"Okay, next vacation."

"Why not now?"

"If it doesn't work immediately, I won't be able to concentrate and then I will flunk like I did last winter, and everyone will hate me, and my lab partner will get pissed at me and dump me."

"Okay."

We would then talk about other stuff. The appointments were a half hour, once or twice a month. We both sat in chairs; couches are pretty much out of date.

Additional evidence of lousy medical practice, is that in the search for an antidepressant without sexual side effects, Dr. Haglund failed to tell me that the new antidepressant drugs need to be tried for six weeks. They sometimes suddenly start working the sixth week. A two-week vacation is not enough. He should have told me that, so something could have been arranged to try the antidepressants for six weeks. I learned this later when I read the book, *The Good News About Depression* by Mark Gold, M.D.

Antidepressants, by the way, are not addictive. They are safe, legal, prescribed, non-addictive, mind-altering drugs. They cheer you up. Also, they are not anesthesia. They do not numb you. They make you more alert and more conscious. They cheer you up. In addition, antidepressants have no street value. I was hoping that I could get an antidepressant that would make my whole body work at once. Then I could have a job, a social life, maybe a girlfriend, and I would feel good like I had a normal life.

Once I had realized that I could do well in school on the current antidepressant, Asendin, and I wouldn't be falling asleep in school, I decided I shouldn't mention my medication or manic depression to anyone. I didn't even tell Cheryl. I decided that talking about it would seem like whining, and therefore would be a bad attitude. Also, I didn't want anyone to know. If the students didn't know, our teachers wouldn't know.

If my teachers didn't know about my manic depression, they wouldn't be able to give a recommendation to a prospective employer that went something like, "Yeah, Bill does very well in spite of his mental handicap."

In the beginning of the program, I had told two fellow students about my manic depression. This is because they noticed my drowsiness. One of them quit the program, so the only person in my class that knew was the other. I don't think he told anyone, but for the rest of the program, I was sure that I was nice to him because I was afraid otherwise he would tell people.

Throughout these years of 1984–1985, during vacations from computer repair school, I tried different antidepressants, hoping for no depression while decreasing the impotence side effect. They didn't work. It was very lousy medical practice to try them for less than six weeks, without mood leveler Lithium, and without taking blood levels. However, my Dr. Haglund failed to follow these guidelines, and I didn't know how wrong it was at the time. None of the alternative drugs worked during the vacations, so I went back to antidepressant Asendin so I could get A's (or at least C's) in school. Also, on Asendin I felt better. Trying a new antidepressant for only two weeks was two weeks of misery for nothing. It was two weeks of being fairly close to crying all day. Thankfully, Asendin worked the first day. So, the Sunday night at the end of a vacation, I went back to Asendin. I woke up Monday feeling okay.

I keep mentioning lousy medical practice. I feel that maybe 30 percent of psychiatrists currently practicing should not be practicing. They make too many mistakes. I think the problem is that the 70 percent of psychiatrists who are good, fail to testify against the 30 percent that are bad. Probably because they are friends with the bad ones. I think what we need is a team of good psychiatrists to testify against the bad ones. Incompetent psychiatrists should have to face malpractice lawsuits and risk losing their licenses. In order for this to happen, undercover patients would have to be wired for sound. Or, undercover professional actors could pose as patients.

Psychologists, who cannot prescribe drugs, who attempt to treat manic-depressive patients without drugs, need to be sued and have their licenses removed also. Manic depression needs to be treated by psychiatrists who revere medication, and know how to use it.

During a two-week vacation, while trying a new antidepressant medication, I had strings of repetitive thoughts. I felt like crying. I was waiting for my new drug to start working. This time, similar to previous times, my preoccupying thoughts went:

Shoot, I'm in a lousy position. If this drug would just work. I could be healthy and bright. This is the pits. I'm stuck. If only I were healthy, I could get a girlfriend. I feel awful. The eleventh grade Bill Hannon could attract women. This stupid drug will probably make me only partially well if it works at all. Then I will be able to attract a woman who is only partially attractive. It probably won't work at all. It is not working yet. I'm stuck. I'll get back to school and not be able to say what I did all vacation. Here I am lying around listening to music. This sucks. If this drug doesn't work, I can't try another drug until the next vacation. I'm really in a hole. This stinks. I wish I could live my life over again, knowing everything that I know now, without the manic depression. That is impossible, but it is the only way to happiness.

After about the twelfth day of thinking thoughts such as these all day long, crying would be crossing my mind frequently, and suicide would cross my mind for a second. Then I would switch back to antidepressant Asendin. It would immediately cheer me up. Asendin was different than the other antidepressants I tried because it worked the first day. School usually started again the next day. I then regarded the new drug as being no good, even though it had not been given a fair six-week trial.

At one point, I boosted my dose of antidepressant Asendin to 350 mg up from 300 mg to get rid of some negative feelings. I felt better right away. I was less irritable. At 350 mg, *the side effects were all worse, but they bothered me less, because I was in so much of a better mood.* I decided to stick with 350 mg because I was mentally so much better. There was one problem: I got hungrier. I gained about twenty pounds in two weeks, and ten more in the next month.

I tried to be nicer to all my classmates now that I was in a better mood.

Bridget was back at her job at the check-in desk at the UW gym and pool. I still went to talk to her and swim. There were a couple of other guys who would talk to her also, and it made me very jealous. One of them was a student named Don, and given that he was healthy and normal, Bridget liked him better, and would kind of ignore me when he was around. It made me pretty mad. A more normal thing for me to be doing would have been to go out and find other women, but I felt people who would talk to me were so rare, that I had to stick with the ones I had.

I needed a girlfriend, although by this time I was aware that having a romance was not the way to treat or the way to prevent manic depression. In the winter of 1985, I had three dates with a woman I met who was a waitress at a restaurant I went to. Her name was Patti. We went out to dinner, had a good conversation, then I drove her back to her apartment and we kissed in my car. I remember telling myself to try to act like I would be acting if only I felt normal, but of course, I didn't feel normal. I thought, act like you're enjoying it, but I wasn't. It just seemed stupid. This kissing was way less exciting than the kissing I had done when I was normal. It was also less exciting than the kissing I had done while depressed and untreated. At least with antidepressant Asendin, I could get A's in school instead of F's. My intellect worked.

After five minutes of this unexciting kissing, I said, "Goodnight" or something and we called it an evening.

I would guess now that she would've preferred more enthusiasm and for me to ask if I could come up to her apartment. On our next date, I forget what we did, but then I kissed her again unenthusiastically. On our third date, she walked out on me in the middle of a racquetball game, when I tried to tell her she had to get out of the way to let the other person's shot hit the front wall. That was the end of that.

During this period of my life, I went to support groups of the Manic-Depressive Association once in a while, but I usually considered myself too well to go there. I did ask other men whether they had the impotence side effect. Actually, most did not. Asendin is the worst antidepressant for the impotence side effect. At group meetings I talked about the other side effects of Asendin, and got a reputation as someone who tries a lot of different antidepressants. They called me Mr. Antidepressant.

Things at my house were calm. My dad and his wife, Connie, were well-behaved. They didn't bug me about where I was going or when I'd be home. Still, I didn't talk to Dad much. I didn't want him to get attached to me.

In June 1985, I graduated from computer repair school with the highest grades in the class, but the lowest popularity because of my irritability. I didn't talk much, didn't smile or laugh, and didn't talk about women with the guys. I had a brain, but no personality.

It was around this time that I started thinking often of what I would wish for if I had magical wishes. First, no manic depression, second, no hay fever, third, the best possible eyesight that humans can have. I'm very nearsighted. In another version of the same wishes, I'd be able to go back in time knowing everything I know now, and I'd have the three good health wishes, and my mom would be perfectly healthy, too. Then I wished I would meet Bridget again, and she would fall in love with me. I really thought about her all the time. She was so fine. These wishes came to mind often. I guess that was a sign that I was unhappy at that time. Asendin stopped depression, but not totally, and of course, not without the annoying side effects. I saw room for improvement. I still second-guessed myself all day. Things like: What channel on television would I be watching if I was healthy? Which brand of soap would I be using if I was healthy? What would I be eating right now if I was healthy? What would I be saying right now if I was healthy? Having so many questions was a symptom. Never mind the answers to the questions.

Now that I am healthier, I don't second-guess myself all day.

Another female friend I had was Rachel Moeller. I knew her from the University of Puget Sound. We went to movies or on walks. We were just friends, but we saw each other about every other week. Among our many conversations was one that went like this:

I said, "Oh man, I'm so drowsy. I just hate these drugs. I don't know what drug to try next."

She said, "I am so *disgusted*. I am so fat. I've gained five pounds in the past week. This is ridiculous!"

She was not fat.

After thinking about it for a few seconds, I said, "Okay, Rachel. I won't talk about my drugs, and you don't say you're fat."

22

I Want a New Drug

In June 1985, I waited for the new antidepressant Merital to be put on the market. Dr. Haglund had told me about it. It had been approved by the Food and Drug Administration, but wasn't at drugstores yet. I also applied for a few jobs and wound up getting hired as a photocopy machine repairman. I was under pressure from myself, my father, and others to use my electronics diploma. I, and especially my dad, didn't want me to sit around the house waiting for an antidepressant to be marketed when I should be jumping at the chance to put my electronics diploma to use. I was offered the job on June 25, 1985 and I said I'd start after July 4. On June 27, I saw Dr. Haglund and he said antidepressant Merital would be at drugstores July 1. Then I was torn. I wanted to forget the job and try the drug until it started working, but Dr. Haglund convinced me to start the job. The new drugs take a while to work. During that period, I can't concentrate on work. I'm lucky if I can get out of bed.

In my free time, before I started the job, I was spending some time with my cousin Laura Felber, and her friend Diane Estenson. Diane was then dating my cousin Kevin Felber, and was lots of fun to be with. Diane was very outgoing and friendly. Laura and Diane talked about Laura's attempts to find a husband, and both told me to start dating, rather than sitting around doing nothing. When Kevin was around, he told me that being partially impotent should not stop me from having a girlfriend. I never believed him.

I also talked some with my cousin Burt Felber. He was a follower of a spiritual leader from India who said that sex was only to have kids, so Burt basically believes sex is wrong except for those

few times you want to conceive. He said that just the companionship of a girlfriend should bring me pleasure. He didn't understand that when I was partially impotent, most women seemed
unattractive to me. Companionship was usually no thrill. Impotence does not just happen in bed.

On July 5, 1985, I started the job repairing copiers. I was slow
to learn. My drowsiness, poor concentration, and irritable mood
were a problem. After about six weeks on the job, I asked for a
leave of absence to try the new antidepressant Merital. Luckily
they gave me the leave of absence for up to six weeks to try the
new drug.

Dr. Haglund had said, "You should try this particular drug for
six weeks, because it can take that long to work." In the past,
about other drugs he had always said, "Two weeks is enough."

After about five weeks of sitting at home obsessing, antidepressant Merital started working, and I went back to work. For a few
weeks, I was happier, more energetic, a better worker, and less
impotent. Women seemed a lot more attractive. After a few weeks
though, Merital gradually wore off. I started making more mistakes at work and I was sadder. I almost started crying at work one
day. So, I switched back to the old antidepressant Asendin, and
improved a bit. Still my work on the copiers was not good
enough, and I got fired in January 1986.

At the manic-depressive support groups, I was continuing my
reputation for being Mr. Antidepressant. People at the meetings
went on and on about how unhappy they were, and often others
would say nothing, so I would say, "Try an antidepressant."

Sometimes, people said they were thinking of suicide, and
everyone else in the group would just sit there. I would say, "Get
your doctor to prescribe an antidepressant."

I may have saved some lives.

I learned later that antidepressants can sometimes lift your
mood up too high, and cause you to get manic. Still, they have to
be tried if you are depressed, and especially if you are suicidal. I
got on some people's nerves for giving too much advice. I didn't
emphasize that you had to check with your doctor before switching medication. I thought people knew that. I liked going to the
support groups to help other people.

If I saw people doing better than I was doing, I asked them what
medication they were on. In that way, the support group helped me.

23

Hanging Around

I applied for unemployment compensation, and in March I got it.

For recreation, my cousin Laura Felber had convinced me to go to international folk dancing. Laura had decided I needed to be more social, so I should try dancing. I started going in October 1985. There were some attractive women there, so I decided to keep going. I had trouble learning the dances, but I tried.

The dancing was set up so that there was teaching from 7:00 to 8:00 P.M. and requests from 8:00 to 10:00 P.M, every Tuesday night. There are about 200 different dances.

Two women I liked seeing at international folk dancing were Jenny and Debbie. They were students at the University of Washington. They talked to me a lot, unlike most of the people there, and when I told them I was manic-depressive, they didn't seem to mind. Sometimes we'd go out to eat after dancing. I really liked Jenny, but she wanted to only be friends. That was all right. Friends are important.

During the week, I started volunteering at the office of the Washington Depressive and Manic-Depressive Association (WDMDA). The office was all volunteer except that Glenn Simco, who was in charge, got about $200 a month. All the money for the organization was donated, and nobody donated very much. My big project was typing the names of everyone who had ever been at a support group meeting into the computer, so that we could have a mailing list. Also, there were many other assorted manic-depressives who hung around in the office that I got to know.

I was in better shape than most of the other manic-depressives who worked at the office, because I was on an antidepressant that worked. However, I wouldn't usually stay in the office very long because I couldn't stand it. This is because I was still unhappy. I didn't want to make a big commitment to WDMDA, because I didn't want manic depression to be my full-time job. I didn't want working on it to be my sole purpose in life or my sole source of social contacts.

Meanwhile, Dr. Haglund was bugging me to try an MAOI antidepressant. I was balking because a person was supposed to be on no drug at all for a while in between a tricyclic antidepressant like Asendin and an MAOI antidepressant. On no drug at all, I could kill myself. Dr. Haglund said it was not *that* risky to take one a few days after the other, but I refused to risk my life for another antidepressant that probably wouldn't work. Once, I was going to try to make the switch from Asendin to MAOI antidepressant Nardil, but after a few days off Asendin, my fear that I would be suicidal made me go back on Asendin before I ever took any Nardil.

Then Dr. Haglund made a classic stupid statement, "If you weren't so pessimistic, it would be easier to treat your depression."

I was still living at home with Dad and my stepmother Connie. They didn't bug me. It wasn't that bad. I tried to stay distant, and that worked okay. I usually ate dinner with them. However, I ate quickly and did not talk to them or listen to them. They spoke to each other. I was glad they didn't demand attention from me. My dad's behavior was really just fine at this time, but I felt I should stay distant so he wouldn't get attached to me.

I had taken the written test to be a mail carrier about two years earlier, and the post office had finally gotten to my name on the list. I started work as a mail carrier, in May 1986. The job has two parts, sorting and delivering. I was on 350 mg of antidepressant Asendin. Even though Asendin helps a lot, my concentration was still not very good. I still thought a lot about the arguments I used to have with my dad, instead of paying attention to my work. Thinking about the arguments was just a symptom. My dad had been a nice guy since 1982. I got fired after a couple months for being too slow.

In September and October of 1986 I continued to volunteer for WDMDA, and answered phone calls from people who said things like, "Hi, I just ah, took the CPI (California Personality

Inventory) for the fifth time." (The CPI is a very long personality test. It takes a long time to fill out, and is not necessary once a person has been diagnosed as depressive. A much shorter test is appropriate once a diagnosis has been made.)

I asked, "Why did you just take it again?"

The caller said, "Well, I just moved in from out of town, so I went to a new psychiatrist."

"What did your new doctor say?"

"My doctor said I was depressed."

"Did he give you any antidepressants?"

"No."

"Have you been given antidepressants by previous doctors?"

"Yes, but they didn't work."

"Well, I can give you the name of a group of doctors who will give you antidepressants. One of them might work." (I still failed to emphasize trying all the antidepressants for six weeks. This is because I still didn't know better thanks to Dr. Haglund failing to tell me.)

"Well, all I do is go from doctor to doctor and get these drugs and they never help."

"Well, there are sixteen antidepressants, and you have got to get blood levels, and if one doesn't work, you've got to try another. Just try these doctors, they will make an effort. Call 555-3498. You probably haven't been on a large enough dose. The blood levels will show if you are on the appropriate dose. Also, come to our support groups. I'll send you some literature."

"All right, I suppose. Bye."

We got about one phone call per half hour, and we usually told them about our support groups, and mailed them literature. I still felt stuck in a crummy phase of my life. Working at the office was fairly boring. I did get some satisfaction from telling the caller about getting blood levels of antidepressants. That was a help, I felt. Psychiatrists often fail to get blood levels.

For recreation I was now hanging around with a guy named Howard Schultz. He was a healthy individual I had met at a Jewish singles party.

We were hanging around at the party, and I said to Howard, "I am out of work because I was fired for being too slow, because I am manic-depressive."

He said, "I have trouble holding jobs too, because my bosses are jerks. I think my *bosses* are manic-depressives," he said jokingly.

The day after the party Howard called me and asked, "What are you doing?"

I said, "I'm just sitting at home watching the news. What are you doing?

"Oh, I just got off of work. I'm just doing this job until I find something better."

We talked for a while, he about his jobs, me about manic-depression.

We started doing a few things together like eating at restaurants. Howard also was a collector of 78 RPM records, and lots of other old stuff. He went to estate sales to buy these old things. On a couple weekends, I went with him to estate sales and looked at the stuff for sale while he looked at the old records. He liked the music on old records from the 1930s and 1940s.

24

I Really Need a New Drug

In September and October of 1986, I sent out falsified resumes in an attempt to get another job in the electronic technician field. I had to lie so that they wouldn't know I was fired from my last two jobs. I had no luck really, so in November I took a near minimum wage job at a photocopy shop. I was already twenty-seven, so my co-workers and boss were a few years younger than I, but I didn't mind. I was working 6 P.M. to midnight on weekdays. That was thirty hours per week. I would mostly ring stuff up at the cash register, and clean the place at closing time.

Then an electronics firm that I had applied to, called. They wanted to interview me for a job repairing circuit boards.

With the lies from my resume memorized, I went to the interview, and luckily, the interviewer didn't really ask me any questions about my past. He just told me about the company and asked me when I could start. He said I would be permanent part-time, and then I could work my way up to full-time. My hours were 1:00 P.M. to 5:00 P.M. So I could still work at the photocopy shop.

For a few weeks, I was working both jobs, a total of fifty hours a week. That's the most I ever worked. I started to displease my boss at the electronics job, because I was not repairing enough boards per day. There was homework I could have done to learn the circuit much more quickly, but I never found time to get that homework done. When I knew I was in trouble at the electronics job, I quit the photocopy job in order to have time to study the circuits, but it was too late. In mid-January, I was fired from the electronics job for being too slow. Much of the problem was not the lack of doing my homework; it was mostly a case of poor concentration. Three hundred and fifty milligrams of antidepressant Asendin only works so well.

In March I raised my dose of antidepressant Asendin from 350 mg to 400 mg. Immediately I felt better than I had ever felt on 350 mg. *The dreaded side effects, including the impotence, were a little worse, but I didn't mind them as much, because I was in such a better mood.* I also didn't mind any of life's problems as much. People noticed that I was in a better mood. Things seemed easier and more fun. Dr. Haglund was upset that I changed my dose on my own, but he agreed I was in a better mood, so he let me continue.

About this time, at the WDMDA office, I got to know Jeanne Loomis, a single mother. She had gotten pregnant while she was manic and gotten engaged to two guys at once. They both dumped her when she ended up in the psych ward. She was on Aid to Families with Dependent Children.

Jeanne and I would get together and compare our moods. We would talk about manic depression and I'd usually tell her she needed an antidepressant. She wasn't usually on one, and she was usually a bit pessimistic and spacey.

Besides visiting my few friends, most of my time was spent just hanging around watching television. I watched the news several times a day. I watched talk shows. Often I would try a new antidepressant for two weeks as I have described before.

Not being on great drugs, I had trouble making friends. Being a little depressed all the time made me a little irritable all the time.

I did have a few friends. Howard Schultz called me every day or I called him. We'd go out to eat sometimes or rent a video. He was still struggling to find a job he could hold.

My father on whom I was still financially dependent for rent and food, again pressured me to quit trying new antidepressants and get a job.

I said to him what I always said at support groups, "I am in search of the magical antidepressant without side effects."

Dad said, "It's not good to sit around without a job."

He did not believe that medication would make me better. I think he thought that I would never get better.

I thought that I would never improve to the degree that I have. Depression makes one pessimistic about everything. I was pessimistic about my recovery from depression. I *did* think I could improve to a degree. That's why I kept trying different medications.

My doctor never said anything that indicated that he thought I was going to get as much better as I have. He did think I could improve to some extent. That's why he kept prescribing different medications.

In August 1987, I applied (false application info, of course) at the Dave's Pizza on Mercer Island. I had worked there before, but the turnover was so high that nobody there was recognizable. I applied to be a phone order taker. It was a job I already knew, and at $4.00 per hour, it paid better than delivering. When you deliver, you destroy your car and that subtracts greatly from your pay. I told them I just wanted to answer phones, and I'd consider making pizzas (although I didn't think I could make pizzas fast enough), but I did not want to deliver. They hired me and I started working there answering phones. I worked about four or five nights a week during the dinner rush, answering phones. It was dreary, but I did the job well enough.

Dreary thought patterns were preoccupying my mind and slowing down my work, in spite of antidepressant Asendin's help. These were the same sorts of strings of depressive thoughts that I mentioned before. I would hope for "magic wishes" or miracles by God coming to earth and totally curing me.

In September, Mercer Island High School Class of 1977 held a ten-year reunion. It was reassuring to know that all these people still existed out there, and that most were having fun and progressing through life normally. People still looked pretty much the same. I talked to a lot of people, and they were friendly. It was good being with a group of people who remembered primarily the healthy me. A few expected me to be a doctor or a lawyer, but I had to tell them the truth. People listened and many told me that their boyfriend, father, or brother-in-law was manic-depressive. Melanie Carson wasn't there. That was good because I had planned to avoid her.

A few days later, Dr. Haglund again wanted me to try the antidepressant Nardil. But before I went through weeks of depression, probably for nothing, I wanted to talk to some other people on Nardil who were doing well on it. Dr. Haglund said, "I have hundreds and hundreds of patients on Nardil."

I said, "Name three."

He could only name one, so with that patient's permission, Dr. Haglund gave me her number and I called her.

She went on and on about how depressed she "had been," but said she was now happy. I was hoping to hear more about how good life was now, but instead I got gory details of how horrible life "had been."

I decided her life now was not so happy, because she was preoccupied with the past.

I told Dr. Haglund that when he could find me three manic-depressives who were doing well while on antidepressant Nardil, who had jobs, significant others, and an active sex life, then I'd try it.

I was working about twenty hours per week at Dave's Pizza, answering the phones. My concentration wasn't very good. I couldn't take an order while walking over to put up the previous order. The phones had long extension cords. However, I couldn't remember the second order long enough to write it down ten seconds later, rather than right away. While walking over to put up the first order, I would forget the second order.

Most of my co-workers were younger than I, but I didn't mind. I was a little bit depressed all the time, so I wasn't too popular. I wasn't cheerful enough. There were a couple guys who were friendly to me. In February 1988, I mentioned to them that I was manic-depressive. That was the first I had spoken of it. I didn't give them the gory details, but one of them said his girlfriend was on the antidepressant Elavil. That was nice to know. It was nice to know that a depressive had a boyfriend.

For recreation, I still went to international folk dancing, but my concentration was so bad, that I could still only do the easiest dances.

I continued to attend WDMDA meetings, and sometimes helped type the newsletter into the computer. Support group meeting space was donated by a hospital. They let us meet in a conference room or cafeteria for free.

The meetings were free, and conducted on a self-help and peer-led basis. At a support group meeting, first we read the group guidelines, then we went around the circle of about eight, one by one, to introduce ourselves. Then it was open for free-flowing discussion. We wore nametags. Most people wore them with first name only. A couple people chose not to wear them. I will describe a typical meeting.

A middle-aged guy dressed neatly in blue jeans, but not smiling said, "Hi, I'm Joe. I'll be the facilitator tonight. I've been diagnosed with this illness for about ten years. I've had some manic episodes, and now I'm in sort of a depression. My work is going more difficult and I think the stress from work is making things worse. My ex-wife is giving me a hard time also. With that I'll pass." (Looks left, looks right.) "Jill, do you want to go next?"

Jill opened her mouth, took a breath, but didn't say anything.

Todd said slowly and hesitantly, "I'll go. I'm Todd, I've had this illness for a while. I, um, think it is serious because it has slowed down my memory and, um, energy." Sadly he continues, "I don't know if that is from the illness or side effects of the medication. Otherwise I'm ah, um, doing okay. I'll pass."

Next to Todd sat Ann. Ann was grossly overweight, and was wearing big stretch pants.

Ann said upset, "Ooh, I didn't know if I was going to make it here tonight. I've been having such a rough time. I was so depressed, I've been crying all day (sob) and my doctor hasn't even called me back yet." Ann was silent for a moment and stared at the floor.

Joe the facilitator said, "What happened?"

"I just got kicked out of my apartment. Now I have to go live with my mother."

Joe said, "Okay, we will come back to you after introductions and talk about it more."

I said, looking at my watch, "Hi. I'm Bill and I've been manic-depressive for eleven years and two months. I'm not sure on the number of days" (slight laughter from the group). "I'm stuck in the depressed phase, so I'm looking for the magical antidepressant without side effects. I'm on Asendin now, and it helps, but it doesn't help enough. It also has a lot of side effects. Right now I'm just working at Dave's Pizza, answering the phones. That's all for now."

We then moved to the next person. It was Kelly. She was in her early thirties and dressed neatly in blue jeans, but didn't smile. Kelly said, "I don't really know what to do. I'm worried about my fifteen-year-old daughter, Andrea. I think my illness is affecting her. See, she doesn't have a father, just like me. She might be taking after me. I never knew my real father. Then my stepfather abused me until I was about twelve, when my mother kicked him out. Then a year later, my mother committed suicide. I went to live with my aunt and uncle. They were very religious and I couldn't stand it. I ran away with my boyfriend when I was sixteen and pregnant with Andrea. Things were okay for a few years, but we really had a co-dependent relationship. We were really dysfunctional parents for Andrea when she was little. We both drank. We never got legally married. My boyfriend got killed in a one-car accident when Andrea was just ten. I know he was drunk. I started to get depressed somewhere around that time. Then I freaked out and was in the hospital for being manic, except I might be schizophrenic. Now Andrea likes *boys* and stays out late. She goes to *parties*. She doesn't listen to me. I'm afraid she is depressed. It's dangerous for kids these days."

We finished going around the circle, and then we opened things up for discussion, going first to Ann to try to help her. As I often did, I said, "You need an antidepressant, and get a blood level of the antidepressant."

A few people argued with me and said that drugs are not the solution. People said that there are things in Ann's environment that need changing, because that is what is making her unhappy.

I said, "If we weren't so biologically depressed, we wouldn't mind our environment so much."

Usually everyone there was in one degree of depression or another. Basically they all needed to boost the dose of their antidepressant or find another, I thought. At that time I didn't pay much attention to the fact that antidepressants can often make a manic-depressive go up too high, beyond normal, into the manic phase. Still, antidepressants need to be tried.

People at the support groups usually just spoke up in no particular order after the introduction. Sometimes one person would state a problem and several would comment on that. Then another would state a problem and several would comment on that. A good facilitator would not talk much more than anyone else. He would maybe call on someone who was being quiet to make sure the quiet person got a chance to speak.

Our support group meetings lasted about an hour and a half, once a week. I went to learn from other people, to teach other people, and to be sociable. It was better than television, I thought.

In March 1988, my antidepressant Asendin quit working. It had worked for six years, and now it gradually quit working. Four hundred milligrams had been my usual dose. I started to feel worse. I worried more and thought about crying more. I boosted the dose to 450 mg, then 500. It didn't help. I went to see Dr. Haglund.

I said, "We have a major problem. Asendin has quit working." This was a major problem because I had tried most of the other sixteen antidepressants and they hadn't worked. I was afraid I would be suicidal in two weeks. We agreed I would try antidepressant Norpramine again, and I said, "I should try it for six weeks."

Dr. Haglund agreed.

As I have said, over the past five years I had tried about twelve of the antidepressants for two weeks. This was in an effort to find one with a less severe impotence side effect. I would lie around obsessing about the past and listening to music. I was unable to work during these two-week periods because my concentration was so poor. Crying would start crossing my mind towards the end of two weeks. Suicide would also start crossing my mind at the end of two weeks, partly because I thought this important drug trial had failed, and partly because suicidal thoughts are a symptom of depression itself. I would then switch back to antidepressant Asendin. It was too bad, because antidepressants can start working the sixth week. Dr. Haglund had failed to emphasize this fact about six weeks. That was extremely poor medical practice, in my opinion. The hope for what could happen over the course of an additional four weeks could have kept me going until one of these drugs kicked in.

I told my manager at Dave's Pizza that I had to quit due to inevitable poor concentration and irritability. I told him that I had manic depression. I had worked there six months and hadn't told him yet. The poor concentration had already set in. I knew I had to quit, or eventually I would be fired because of the poor concentration.

I waited for antidepressant Norpramine to work.

25

Finally Trying Antidepressants for Six Weeks

I tried antidepressant Norpramine and a great thing happened. I found I could stand being depressed for more than two weeks without committing suicide. Actually, I had had depression untreated for years before without committing suicide, but in recent years I had thought about suicide after just two weeks without antidepressant Asendin. Suicide crossed my mind the first thirty-nine days on Norpramine, but not after that. Norpramine kicked in suddenly on the fortieth day. I felt less depressed than during the first thirty-nine days. The fortieth day and beyond, I had more energy, I was more optimistic, I had better concentration, and I didn't feel like crying. I woke up the morning of the fortieth day feeling much better.

Also, this time that I tried antidepressant Norpramine, I insisted on getting a blood test. This is something Dr. Haglund had neglected in the past for most of the antidepressants he had prescibed for me. There is no way to tell whether or not I was on the right dose of all the past antidepressants I had tried. I have a second cousin who is a psychiatrist, who also recommended that I get blood levels. I would have talked to him more and sooner, but he lived out of town.

Antidepressant Norpramine helped a lot, but I was still somewhat depressed. However, Norpramine did not have nearly the side effect problem that antidepressant Asendin did. The sexual side effects were much less severe. Therefore, the women at international folkdancing looked much more attractive. They seemed harder to talk to, though, because I was more depressed than on Asendin. The dances were harder also, because my concentration was worse. I used international folkdancing as sort of a measure. Did the women look more attractive than before? Are the dances easy to learn this week? Do people come up and talk to me? In other words, am I smiling?

I still talked to Howard Schultz every day. We would hang around together, maybe rent a video or go out to eat.

One day a manic-depressive named Paul Crosby walked into the WDMDA office. I knew him from a year earlier when he was on the board of WDMDA. He was a friendly, undepressed kind of guy. He asked me if I was on social security disability. I said no and that I thought I had to be broke to be on it. I had $40,000 from interest, dividends, and the appreciation of money my dad had given all us kids in the past. Paul said that you just have to be disabled, you don't have to be broke. That was useful information. Paul also asked if I knew Kenneth Boreen. Kenneth Boreen was a corporate raider.

I said, "Actually I may have met him at my father's wedding, because my father did some business with him."

Kenneth Boreen was really rich. His mother had been manic-depressive, and he knew that I was manic-depressive because my dad had told him. Paul Crosby would play a key role in my next manic episode. In my imagination, so would Kenneth Boreen.

After a few months of tricyclic antidepressant Norpramine, I stopped it on July 11. Now, in my battle to be healthy, I was going to try the dangerous monoamine oxidase inhibitor (MAOI) antidepressant Nardil. Dr. Haglund had been bugging me for two years to try an MAOI, but I had always refused because I thought they were too dangerous. Because Norpramine was a tricyclic antidepressant, and Nardil was an MAOI antidepressant, it was safest to wait up to two weeks on no drug at all before switching from one to the other. It can be fatal to mix an MAOI with a tricyclic. I, with good reason, was afraid that mixing the two drugs would kill me. I made Dr. Haglund sign a contract that said if I got suicidal, I could be put in the locked psychiatric ward, and left there until it was safe to go back on Norpramine. That would be in case of feeling suicidal while having Nardil in my system. Also, I would *not* be given electroshock. Electroshock is a last resort treatment for depression, but causes some memory loss. I sent a copy of that contract to a commitment defense lawyer and sent the lawyer $100 with it.

I also memorized the list of foods you can't eat while on antidepressant Nardil. There is a long list of common foods, that if you eat while on Nardil, you are fairly likely to have a stroke and die. The stroke can happen within an hour of eating these foods. The foods are cheese, pepperoni, yogurt, bananas, raisins, caffeine, chocolate, and alcohol among many others. If you can get to an emergency room fast enough upon getting the headache which is the warning sign of the stroke, you will live. Otherwise, you could die or be badly brain damaged.

Dr. Haglund had always said that the waiting period between the two drugs is really unnecessary, so on July 15, I started antidepressant Nardil. I had gotten Dr. Haglund to say that this was his idea for me to try this drug, and that he would take the blame if anything went wrong. We had taken many precautions. One precaution we hadn't taken, was to make a plan for what we would do if I got manic.

26

Manic Lawsuit Aided by Secret Agents

The first couple of weeks on antidepressant Nardil, I got a slight lift in my mood, and a stimulant side effect, so I couldn't sleep very well. I had to take the sleeping pill Halcion to get to sleep. I still didn't sleep very much, so I experienced what I called the "wired but tired" effect. This is the feeling of being very tired and wanting to sleep, but having in you too much stimulant to fall asleep. It would be similar to a normal person who is pushing himself to stay up late and get little sleep, and is taking a lot of caffeine to stay awake. It is a very weird feeling and gives you poor concentration and energy. I continued to go to the WDMDA office and answer phones. We didn't get much done there, but we played a mean game of phone tag.

On August 2, 1988, my brother Steve, my brother Johnny, and my niece Dana arrived from Israel. Steve and Dana lived there, and Johnny was visiting. My sister-in-law Amy would be coming in a couple weeks. Our house would be full for awhile.

I was feeling very excited and optimistic. I bought a *Wall Street Journal*. I saw Dr. Haglund later that day and he was afraid I might be getting manic because I was laughing more than usual, and the *Wall Street Journal* also was a sign that I was getting manic, because manics often plan on being big business tycoons. Dr. Haglund gave me the name of Dr. Harry Dellwo to call in case he was out of town.

The next day, I did another thing to prepare for possible mania. I gave my safety deposit box key to my cousin, Kevin Felber. I told him not to give it back if I was crazy.

On about August 3, I started flexing my hands alternately like I was swimming freestyle, or together like I was swimming butterfly. It was a very exciting feeling. Feeling this good reminded me of when I was healthy and swam. I thought about my old teammates and our meets. It was very pleasant, much better than depression.

On August 5, I went car shopping with my cousin Laura Felber. I couldn't stop laughing. It was so much fun. Car salesmen were so funny. One tried to sell her rustproofing plus fabric protection for $1000. Rustproofing should sell for about $300, so she would be getting $700 worth of Scotchguard for her seats. I thought that was hysterical.

Also, we went to a Honda dealer who said, "Because Hondas are imported, we only get X amount."

Laura said later that the term "X amount" was used in a Steve Martin movie, and it was a big joke because Steve thought "X" really meant something specific, rather than being a variable. When she said it was from a Steve Martin movie, I just couldn't stop laughing. I laughed for about twenty minutes straight. I really did.

I was optimistic because I hadn't laughed that much in years. During this time, I was writing electronic mail letters to Dave Frish, my old poker friend, and I told him all about the new drug. I finally sent him a funny letter that talked about the sprinkling bans that were in effect. I told him that if you violate the sprinkling ban, they fly over your house spraying agent orange. Then your grass won't be green for a long long time.

By August 6, Dad was starting to get concerned about me. He saw my hysterical laughter, and started to think I was getting manic.

On the morning of the seventh, I babysat Dana, my niece. I carried her around the house singing "Twist and Shout" and other Beatles songs. I said to people later, "The more Beatles you teach them now, the less you have to teach them later."

My concentration was very poor. I was busy thinking of funny or successful things to say in the future so much, that I was not paying attention to the present. I was manic, but I didn't recognize it in myself, mostly because manics don't usually recognize their own mania, and also because in my previous manias, I didn't laugh so much. I was sure it couldn't be mania, because of the laughter. I also was sleeping only about four or five hours a night, because of the drug. I couldn't pay attention to dinner table conversation, my concentration was so poor. I just stared into space thinking funny thoughts. Everyone else was eating, but I ate much slower than them because I was so distracted.

On the ninth, I called Dr. Haglund and asked permission to take less antidepressant Nardil. It was the first time I wanted to take less of an antidepressant in my life.

Dr. Haglund agreed that that would be a good idea.

On the tenth, I had an appointment with Dr. Haglund. I came about twenty minutes late, instead of the usual ten minutes early. This was because I was laughing so hard that I left the house late, and then I missed the exit off the freeway. This again, was because I was too busy thinking about funny things. Dr. Haglund said I was manic and should start mood leveler Lithium. I said in a very angry voice that Lithium makes all my muscles twitch. He never seemed to listen to me say that in the past. Then he said that I should try Mellaril, which is usually used as an antimanic major tranquilizer.

I said angrily, "Dr. Haglund, do you read your own literature?" (I read lots of literature, including some written by him.) This was because Dr. Haglund had come out with some literature saying that antidepressants are for depression, while the drugs usually grouped with Mellaril, major tranquilizers, were for mania. I didn't think I was manic.

Dr. Haglund often prescribed Mellaril for depression, in apparent contradiction to his own writing. I felt he was misprescribing Mellaril again. This time he was right, he was prescribing it for mania, but I felt I was still depressed. I didn't think I was manic. In spite of the laughter, I still thought I was in the depressed phase. I was out of touch with reality. Dr. Haglund brought in Dr. Dellwo for a minute to see me, and he saw me laughing, and he started naming drugs I should have. I refused all medication changes except to quit the antidepressant Nardil, and agreed to come and see Dr. Dellwo on Friday the twelfth. Dr. Haglund would be out of town.

On August eleventh, I called Dr. Haglund in the morning and asked him, "Will this be a new chapter in a psychiatry textbook?"

He said, "No. It's just hypomania." (Hypomania means a little bit of mania.)

I said, "Good *guess.*"

I felt this was a new phenomena, because I had never laughed so much during mania, and I had never heard of a situation where anyone laughed so much. It annoyed me greatly to have Dr. Haglund say I was manic, because he wanted me to go into the hospital, which would be no fun. I was having fun on the outside, and I felt the drugs for mania would bring me down to a deep depression. I felt they would turn me into a zombie, like some of the people at WDMDA support group meetings who were on major tranquilizers, when they didn't need them. I thought antidepressant Nardil would just wear off in two weeks and I would be okay.

The next day I went to see Dr. Dellwo. Diane Estenson, my cousin by marriage, had told me not to drive while laughing constantly, so I took a cab. I told the cab driver to drive anywhere on campus that would sell a small portable tape player. I was going to record the session with Dellwo, so if he said anything wrong I could sue him.

I got to one of the drugstores on UW campus, and hurriedly bought a tape recorder, batteries, and tapes. I then ran to the University Hospitals building where Dellwo has his office. I hoped that he would just give me some more sleeping pill Dalmane. I thought, just some Dalmane to get me sleeping eight hours again, along with the wearing off of the stimulant and antidepressant Nardil, would make me okay. I was expecting, though, that Dr. Dellwo would say I was manic, so the tape would be evidence of malpractice. I didn't think he should call me manic, when I was sure it was just too much antidepressant Nardil lifting up my mood.

I later summarized my visit with Dr. Dellwo in a letter to Randy Harold who I knew from University of Puget Sound, but hadn't talked to in six years. I also sent the letter to Phil Holland. Phil was one of my Mercer Island poker buddies. Both were lawyers, but by sending letters to them, I was showing the symptom of excessive letter writing which comes with mania. Here is how I summarized my meeting with Dr. Dellwo in the letters. The unbracketed parts are part of the original letter. The symbols "( )" also show part of the original letter. The symbols "[ ]" show my notes added here for clarity:

Enter Bill: (tape rolling) I say, "This is Bill Hannon, manic-depressive as usual." (Assumes immediate misdiagnosis of mania, assumes correctly, and we know manic people don't think they're sick.)

[Let me explain. I had the tape recorder rolling. I was expecting to be called manic. I didn't think I was manic. I meant that if I was manic, I wouldn't even go to a doctor. Manics generally don't go to a doctor. Manics are generally irresponsible. I was doing something responsible by going to a doctor. I thought that if I *really was* manic, I would not be at the doctor's office. Given that I was there, I must be healthy.]

Dr. Dellwo: "You're manic." (Basically insane.)

Bill: "It's just too much Nardil." [Too much Nardil was the best name for my diagnosis that day, I thought.]

Dr. Dellwo: (Asking someone he judges insane for their own medical history.) "How much Nardil are you taking?"

Bill: *"What did it say on my chart?!"*

Dr. Dellwo: "I don't have your chart, I've never seen it, and medical records are totally irrelevant to the practice of medicine anyway." [Actually he said they were not always necessary to medical practice, because he could just look at me. I was clearly in a manic state given that he knew a little of my history from talking to Dr. Haglund.]

Bill: "Sounds like malpractice already."

Dr. Dellwo: "Let's go have a look at the locked psychiatric ward."

What does this sound like to you?!

I meant at the time that I wrote the letter, that it sounded like malpractice. It seemed like he would want to put me in there and dope me up and take the tape recorder to destroy the evidence that he didn't have my chart. A week later, I inflated my fears to the paranoid level that he wanted to put me in the hospital and deliberately overdose me and kill me, to shut me up forever.

I still have the tape of that visit. Being in the hospital would have been right. I told him I wasn't sleeping much and was laughing all day. I told him one thing I was laughing about. The training program for Dave's Pizza drivers. I said, "As soon as you're hired, you get together with upper upper management and they spend eight hours telling you, "Don't speed, stop at red lights, and *don't* speed, and so on."

"When you get to your store, managers won't say, "'Speed.'"

"However, senior drivers can tell you, "'Yeah, you can go forty-five miles per hour down 76th Avenue no problem." (76th is a thirty-mile-per-hour zone.) The managers can be standing right there, and they just won't say anything. This is the Dave's Pizza Hot Rod Society."

Dr. Dellwo didn't think that was funny.

At the end of the session, I told Dr. Dellwo that he and Dr. Haglund were fired from my case. I told him that Dr. Haglund could call me to get his job back, but Dr. Dellwo could not call me.

Saturday and Sunday August 13 and 14, we were planning to go up to the mountains, but my dad cancelled the trip when I told him that Dr. Dellwo thought I was manic. My dad wanted us to stay near a hospital so I could check into it if necessary. I was planning on staying home so I could be near my WDMDA friends, and my dad wanted to stay home with me and have everybody else go up to the mountains.

I said, "No, if Lee (my father's name is Lee) is home alone, I'm at a friend's house, or in a hotel. I'm not staying alone with him!" So, everybody stayed home. I figured this cancelled camping trip was another part of the damages claim that I could use in my malpractice case against Dr. Haglund and Dr. Dellwo. Dad had talked to Dr. Dellwo, and I had told Dad that Dr. Dellwo thought I was manic, so I thought his misdiagnosis was unnecessarily worrying my dad and the rest of my family. I thought that the obvious answer was for me to stop taking antidepressant Nardil and keep taking the sleeping pill Dalmane. I thought that would straighten me out and we could go to the mountains and have fun, but Dr. Dellwo wouldn't even give me any more Dalmane. I felt it was Dr. Dellwo's fault that the camping trip was cancelled.

Dr. Dellwo was really right; I was very manic. On the fourteenth, I was home alone. (Everyone else was just out somewhere locally.) The phone rang, and now I'll quote from the letter I wrote to Phil Holland and Randy Harold, who were my lawyer friends in distant cities:

> Sunday, I get a phone call that sounds a Hell of a lot like Harry Dr. Dellwo. He said, "Howard Greenberg high school classmate of Lee Hannon calling from Albany, New York." He gave some area code like 518 or 519 which was right for Albany. Then he gave a local number. I called Albany long distance information (a free call) and said, "You got a Howard Greenberg?" A couple of Greenbergs, no Howards, no initial "H". No Greenbergs whose local number matches the one he

gave. Talk about annoying telephone calls! It was Dr.
Dellwo trying to get through to my dad to tell him that
I'm insane, when I'm not! Haven't I had enough
trouble getting along with my dad already? 911. The
Mercer Island police were there in about twenty
minutes. They've got his name and they know where
he works. Nuisance phone calls! Also, I happen to
know that there weren't all that many Jews in
Spokane Central Class of '44. If there were, my dad
probably didn't hang out with them anyway. He was
only slightly Jewish. Actually, Howard Greenberg is a
very good Jewish name for a non-Jew to think up. Did
names like Noah Aaron Goldstein ring a bell
anywhere at the University of Washington? Guess
who?

I was really annoyed. I called to get a trace put on our line like
the cop told me to. This was so that I could prove that it was really Dr. Dellwo posing as Greenberg. However, the line was in my
father's name, so I needed his permission for the trace. Obviously,
that wasn't going to work.

I decided to fight fire with fire. It was Sunday night, so I
decided the only part of the hospital that was open was the emergency room. I called there and said, "This is a friend of Noah
Aaron Goldstein, and he just got an extremely annoying phone
call from what sounds like Dr. Dellwo."

They said, "Oh, really."

I said, "Yes, so could you take a message?"

"Well, who is the message for?"

"For everyone at the hospital. Just tell them that Dr. Dellwo
makes extremely annoying phone calls and the police have already
been notified."

Months later I found out that Howard Greenberg was really
Howard *Grenberg* and was a real person living in Albany, New
York. He really was a high school classmate of my dad. He spells
his name with only one "e" in the first syllable.

On the fifteenth, I called the information line for Trenton
Hospital that they always advertise on the radio. All I knew was
that Trenton Hospital had nothing to do with the University Hospitals. It was private and was not a teaching hospital, so I'd have
fair odds of getting a good psychiatrist there. All my laughter was

fun. It just wasn't practical. I knew that, but I didn't think I was manic. I hadn't laughed so much in previous manic episodes. I wanted a new doctor to prescribe the sleeping pill Dalmane, and to testify that I was not manic, in my lawsuit against Dr. Haglund and Dr. Dellwo.

That night I walked around a lake with Laura Felber, Diane Estenson, and my brother, Steve. I absolutely could not pay attention to what anyone was saying. I was lost in space. I do remember that the colors seemed so much brighter than they did when I was depressed. The grass seemed intensely green, and the lake intensely blue. In my mind I was rehearsing testimony for my big lawsuit, that's why I couldn't pay attention to the conversation. Later, Kevin Felber joined us, and I told him some Dave's Pizza jokes. Like, when does a Dave's Pizza chef wash his hands? Only after making an anchovy pizza, or when he's getting ready to go home. I thought that was very funny, and it was true.

On the sixteenth, I called some local malpractice lawyers. They said they'd call me back. That night I took some hay fever drug Benadryl to help me sleep. It is for hay fever and has a drowsiness side effect. It is the only hay fever drug you can take by mouth when antidepressant Nardil is still in you. I had run out of sleeping medication, so I had to take the Benadryl for the drowsiness. I still knew I should be sleeping and that would eventually save me. I was in possesion of some mood leveler Lithium, and that had a drowsiness side effect. However, taking Lithium could be construed as a treatment for mania. Therefore, I didn't want to take Lithium, because if I got better by taking it, that would suggest that I *was* manic, and my lawsuit hinged on the idea that I was not manic.

I was talking on the phone every day to my manic-depressive friend Paul Crosby. He really didn't like his previous doctors, and was glad I was planning to sue some.

I was also talking to my healthy friend Howard Schultz. He knew I was not normal because of all the laughter, and he thought I was paranoid. He was right. I was paranoid.

Being manic feels really good. I was getting intense feelings which reminded me very vividly of being back in eleventh and the first part of twelfth grade. Those times were fun, and were really the best times of my life. I started thinking a lot about Melanie Carson. In my five-page letter to the lawyers, Randy Harold and

Phil Holland, I mentioned that I had been out cutting the grass with no shirt and no suntan lotion. I said that I came in and got a glass of orange juice, and noticed something in the paper about fewer babies being born in May because of the heat in August. This article reminded me to put on some sunscreen. The whole thing was reminding me of my high school senior class trip to Jamaica, where I got to know Melanie Carson, and where I got a massive sunburn. This time, at least, I didn't get sunburned. The memories were intense even though Jamaica was eleven years earlier. It was fun and exciting.

I also continued alternately flexing my hands like I was swimming freestyle, or simultaneously like I was swimming butterfly. It reminded me of summer camp in 1976.

On the seventeenth, I was watching the news. They said the Hispanic FBI had walked off the job. This fact has to do with law enforcement, which meshes with my idea that the world needs to be saved from crime. A month earlier, also on the news, it was reported that in North Miami Beach, a gang of black teenagers was grabbing women up off the beach in broad daylight and raping them. People would just stand there and watch, afraid to do anything. None of the perpetrators was ever arrested. I had been thinking, that in my testimony at the malpractice trial of Dr. Haglund and Dr. Dellwo, I would say what it was like to be really manic and obsessed with fighting crime. I would talk about my delusions during my mania of 1980 and 1981, that I could save the world from crimes like these. I knew I had been manic then, I just didn't think I was manic currently.

On the eighteenth, my brother Steve's friend, Scott, was over at our house. Steve and Scott were talking in our living room and I was across the room. I picked up the *Seattle Jewish World* (a weekly newspaper) and Scott turned to me quite suddenly and said, "There is nothing for you in the *Jewish World* this week."

Then Scott's six-year-old daughter repeated, "There is nothing for you in the *Jewish World.*"

I found it odd that Scott interrupted himself to say that. One thing about Scott was that he had the same job that Melanie Carson did. He was a surgical nurse. I thought there was a big conspiracy tying Scott, Melanie, myself, and dozens of others together to help me win my lawsuit. It was a delusion of grandeur.

I opened the *"Jewish World"* to the only section I always read, the section on weddings, births, and deaths. There it was, a death notice for Lee Gross of North Miami Beach. This notice had to be fake for about four reasons. Lee was my dad's first name. Hadn't I been saying that he was gross for years? Secondly, I had just seen on television that North Miami Beach was an all-black neighborhood. There are very few black Jews. It was a Jewish newspaper. Third, whoever put that in, as a secret clue to me, would know that I had only heard of North Miami Beach in the context of crime. Fourth, who in Seattle would care about someone in North Miami Beach? I knew then that enough people had heard about my situation so that they were trying to help me by putting secret clues in the newspapers. The "Death of Lee Gross" obituary was a secret clue. There was really no such person, I thought. They were just trying to encourage me by saying my father was gross and should die. This was encouragement because I still thought a lot about my dad's anti-girlfriend yelling of the past.

In my delusions I figured that the malpractice trial would be a big enough media event that I could say, "Build prisons and keep them full," on the witness stand, in the context of the malpractice trial, and it would make national news. It was very exciting. I was crazy, but I didn't know it. I was having fun. It was great having a sense of purpose.

I decided that there was a giant conspiracy of people getting together to try to help me win my malpractice case. It would be a big case because Dr. Haglund and Dr. Dellwo were professors of psychiatry at a university. I decided that the help I was getting was financed by Kenneth Boreen, the corporate raider friend of my dad. He was being assisted by the FBI and a lot of people who knew me. The phones were tapped, the house was bugged, I was being followed, and my letters were being read, I was sure. This was all in an effort to help me, to know what clues to leave for me, and to know how I would react to certain things. It was all secret so people would not know that the FBI was helping, I thought. This was a laugh riot. I thought this was great. This was certainly the euphoria and grandiose delusion symptom of mania. Also, manics think they are going to be rich, so that was another symptom. I thought I would get rich from my lawsuit.

Also on the eighteenth, when I sent the letter to my old friends who were now lawyers, Phil Holland and Randy Harold, I included something which alluded to the fact that I thought that "Dear Abby" was aimed directly at me. There was something in "Dear Abby" about defamation of character. I decided this meant I should try not to cut down my family in my testimony for my lawsuit. It would've involved taking the Fifth Amendment a lot, I thought. Now I understand that just saying something negative about someone is not necessarily a crime. You can say anything that is true. Anyway, "Dear Abby" also had a letter about forced hugs, and I thought that was directed at me. My dad had forced me to hug him from 1977 through 1982 by threatening to cut off room, board and tuition. By putting these things in my letters to Harold and Holland, I thought I was confirming that I read "Ann Landers" and "Dear Abby" every day. If they were a part of the secret conspiracy helping me, they would need that information. At this point, I was through writing to Dave Frish. He kept writing back, calling me manic, so I was angry with him. The letter was originally intended for him also, but then I decided the letter contained so much anger towards him that it was better to just let Randy and Phil read it.

On the nineteenth, I had an appointment with a new psychiatrist, Dr. Ken Stark, at Trenton Hospital. My cousin, Laura Felber, drove me there because I still wasn't driving. I told her that she should come in and talk to my shrink with me so that the shrink could gain more information that I might forget to give him. We headed towards the hospital early because there were some stops Laura wanted to make. First we stopped at a temple where Laura was teaching Sunday school in the fall. She was to meet with a rabbi there.

Laura introduced me to the rabbi and he said something like, "I have to have a meeting with Laura."

I said, "Speak it in Spanish."

To me this was a code word in honor of the Hispanic FBI that had walked off the job, and in honor of the first psychiatrist I had in Israel whose first language was Spanish because he was from Mexico.

Laura and the rabbi went in to the office for a meeting, and I sat out in the hall right under the fire alarm. I thought, when in a Jewish temple, act like a Jew. Always assume that someone is about to come burn the temple down. Always have Holocaust paranoia if you are acting like a Jew. To me it is "Holocaust paranoia" when American Jews say that there could be a Holocaust in the United States. This very unfairly insults America. I thought, pretend to have Holocaust paranoia. Don't pray, just sit by the fire alarm. So, I sat there, and when anybody walked by me, I stood up and got my hands ready to hit the alarm if they tried anything funny. It was a fun game. As people were walking by I said, "Hello." I did this to show I was not truly paranoid. I was just spoofing Holocaust paranoia.

A young woman walked by and I said, "Hi, what's your name?"

She said, "Stacy, what's yours?"

"Bill," I said. "Well, maybe I'll see you around here."

"I doubt it," she said. "Where are you from?"

"Mercer Island,"

"Oh that's good. Bye."

In my delusions, I decided she was an FBI agent sent to follow me. I was trying to be flirtatious. I thought that was the best I could do to encourage the secret private investigators and FBI agents helping me.

After playing the fire alarm game for a while, I walked around the temple looking at the art and other displays.

Laura got done with her meeting and then we went to a frozen yogurt place. We sat outside and there was a man with dark sunglasses sitting behind me, alone. Clearly, he was FBI. In order to clue him in that I was picking up my clues, I started to mention to Laura the story about the gang rapes in North Miami Beach. As soon as I said rapes, he belched. I decided that burping was now a signal.

We went to see Dr. Stark. I was in there mostly myself giving my medical history, in a hyper tone of voice. I also told him that I thought Dr. Dellwo and Dr. Haglund had motives to kill me right now because I was going to ruin their career by suing them for malpractice. I told him that I had the tape of Dr. Dellwo calling me manic for no reason. I told Dr. Stark that I was not manic and they were calling me manic, and that was the basis of the suit.

Dr. Stark also decided I was manic, and told me to go back to Dr. Haglund. I told him that Dr. Haglund was out of town, so he said, "Go back to Dr. Dellwo."

I told him, "Dr. Dellwo really wants to kill me."

So Dr. Stark said, "Well then I'd like to put you in the hospital here, and treat you for mania."

I said, "No, could I just have some sleeping medication Dalmane?"

He said, "No."

"Well, I don't want to go in the hospital, because you're misdiagnosing me also. I haven't displayed any symptoms of mania here."

"Well, I can't treat you then."

"Okay," I said. "I hope this works out for both of us." We shook hands and I left. He talked to Laura for a minute and then we left.

Then Laura said, "You need counseling."

I thought, yeah, wouldn't that be funny, and it would appease my family a little bit. A psychologist for manic-depression, and no psychiatrist, what a laugh. I believed then, and I still do, that psychologists are not good for manic-depression. Psychologists should always refer their manic-depressive patients to psychiatrists. Psychologists do not usually revere the drugs as they should. They also do not usually even understand manic-depression, from what I have seen. My family was worried about me, so at least I'd be seeing someone by seeing a psychologist. That way I could see a mental health professional until MAOI antidepressant Nardil wore off. I felt that my family had some undue faith in psychologists, so if I saw one, they wouldn't worry or scream as much as they would if I saw nobody. Once the dangerous Nardil wore off, I would be safely depressed again. I could go on a safe tricyclic antidepressant. That's what I thought.

I said to Laura, "Yeah, I'll go to a psychologist. Which one?"

She said, "They probably have some here."

So we turned back around and made an appointment for the twenty-fourth with a psychologist named Brad Maiers who worked in the same office as Dr. Stark.

You see, I knew I was not well. I had made up a name for what I had. It was P.O.M.E.L-N.E.S., "Phenomena Of Much Extra Laughter, and Not Enough Sleep." I thought this was different from being manic. In my other manic episodes I didn't laugh so much. Somehow I didn't equate laughter with the euphoria symptom of mania. I didn't want the treatment for mania, because I felt I had something different. I felt it was just too much antidepressant Nardil causing Pomel-nes. The major tranquilizers, which are the treatment for mania, would just make my concentration worse, I felt. Actually they would have really helped. They do interfere with the concentration of normal people or depressed people. Of course, I was neither.

As Laura and I walked to her car, two people walked by us and one said to the other, "I was listening to Suzanne Vega . . ."

I figured that he was another FBI agent giving me the clue that my tape of malpractice by Dr. Dellwo was valuable, just like tapes by the singer Suzanne Vega. She had a hit song named "Luka" which is about child abuse, which is a crime that often goes unreported. Mistakes by psychiatrists also are often unreported. It is the duty of the good doctors to help bust the bad doctors.

I was feeling very excited and mostly happy. Most hours of the day my happy, grandiose delusion of looking forward to the lawsuit outweighed my paranoid delusion that Dr. Dellwo and Dr. Haglund wanted to kill me. I was extremely glad the FBI wanted to help me with my lawsuit. This excitement was causing me to sleep only three hours per night, but I didn't mind. I didn't feel tired. I was looking forward to the lawsuit very much and was enjoying the thought that I'd be rich. By this time my fear of being killed was less than it had been.

At the dinner table that night, my sister-in-law Amy was talking about the hassle and red tape they were running into in trying to get a new passport to get Dana back out of the country with them. She was a year old and they made babies get a new passport each year. They were talking about how some piece of paper had to be mailed from somewhere and stuff like that, because Dana was adopted. Amy said that she felt like she was being forced to stay in the country. She said it was like *The Sound of Music* where the lead man is being forced to stay in Austria, because he is being drafted into the Nazi navy. Amy and Steve were going to a play that night.

Amy said, "We could walk out at intermission like they did in *The Sound of Music*."

To me this passport red tape was part of the conspiracy to help me. If they were forced to stay longer, they would be around to help stop my dad from getting me committed, so I could be killed. My dad didn't want to kill me, but he didn't realize that Dr. Haglund and Dr. Dellwo did, I felt. Amy and Steve, I thought, did not think I was as committable or as sick.

Manics like rhymes and puns. After dinner that night I went into our computer room and the windows were open. Amy and her brother Aaron (who was also visiting) were in there and I said, "I think there's a draft in here." I meant a navy draft and a wind draft.

Amy said, "Okay." I don't know if she understood the pun.

Later that night, my dad came into my bedroom and said in what seemed like a overbearing voice, "Howard Grenberg just called."

I said, "There is no such person! Get out of my room."

Like I said before, much later I found out that there is a Grenberg, but there is no Greenberg. There is a difference by one "e."

My dad then took another step into my room and said, "Let's talk *privately.*"

I then screamed, "You don't have the right to talk to me without witnesses!" I then left my room.

He came out of my room and screamed, "Keep your voice down!"

I then yelled, "You don't have the right to talk to me without witnesses!"

He screamed, "Keep your voice down!"

"You shut up totally and I'll keep my voice down!"

My dad then shut up, and then my brother Rick asked, "Do you want to go for a walk?"

I said, "No. You've never been a good listener. I tell you things about Lee and you don't believe me."

Rick said, "Those things never happened."

I screamed, "Listen Rick, we have a damn abusive father. He used to go into a jealous rage every time I had a date. You didn't believe me, and you still don't believe me! You may never believe me! A lot of help you've been!"

Rick's best friend, Hal, who had heard everything, then started crying. He counsels adults who were physically and sexually abused as children.

I didn't feel that it was safe to be at my house. I walked away from our house carrying my tape recorder with "Luka" by Suzanne Vega playing loud enough for our neighbors to hear. A song about unreported crimes was appropriate for the reason I explained before. I was being abused by my dad in a way that usually goes unreported. My dad wanted to put me in the hospital with Dr. Dellwo alias Greenberg, I thought. My dad wanted to help me, but he didn't know that Dr. Dellwo would kill me, I felt.

With "Luka" playing, it would be a clear enough signal to the private investigators and FBI what I was doing. When I got far enough away, I switched to "Parents Just Don't Understand" which is a rap song by D.J. Jazzy Jeff and the Fresh Prince. I went to a hotel about a mile from my house, but it was closed. Then I went to a convenience store and called 911 again to report what I thought was a nuisance phone call. I meant the call to my father earlier that evening from Howard Grenberg. I thought it was Dr. Dellwo saying he was Greenberg. The 911 people said that it was no longer a police matter.

I told 911, "I am an abused mentally ill person. Could you give me a ride to a hotel?"

They said, "No. We don't give people rides. Call a cab."

I called a cab, and when I was out by the street waiting for a cab to go to a hotel downtown, somebody on a three-wheeled moped drove by playing a rap tape. I thought this was a clue from the FBI that they liked my taste in music.

Also, as I was waiting for the cab, somebody lit a firecracker behind the convenience store. I didn't flinch. I thought the secret agents wanted to see if I would flinch.

The cab pulled up, and I hopped in. I told him to go to the Holiday Inn downtown. He said, "Sure."

There was another passenger also in the cab going downtown. I asked, "Where are you going?"

He said, "I'm going to the bottom of the Davis Street Bridge."

I decided this was a suicidal tendency check. My antidepressant Nardil was wearing off, so they were checking for suicidal thoughts. I calmly asked, "Why are you going to the bottom of the Davis Street Bridge?"

He said, "Well, from there it's just a short walk to where I'm going."

I said, "Okay." I thought he was either joking, or I didn't know the layout of the bridge. At least I didn't have to talk this guy out of a suicide attempt. If he was joking, then he was FBI checking on me for a reaction to see if I was suicidal. I left it at that, and changed the subject.

Months later I learned that the Davis Street Bridge slopes downhill.

I got to the hotel and checked in. I felt it was an ordinary hotel room, but the cable channels on the television were numbered unusually so I thought that they would be playing shows and commercials specifically altered to give secret messages to me. One commercial about fixing up houses got to me. It made me think about possibly buying a house. I had $40,000; you could get a house in rural Washington for that.

I didn't sleep that night, but I lay awake in bed for about four hours, thinking how much fun this was, and I really thought it *was* a fun adventure. I was in a very good mood. Then I got up, took a shower, and left the hotel. I went down and had some breakfast at a restaurant. I was sure the other customers in the restaurant were some good guys there to watch me.

I placed my order by saying, "Four eggs *scrambled,* and four glasses of orange juice." The reason I emphasized the word "scrambled" was to signify to anyone listening that I knew that I had to unscramble the clues coming off the television set and elsewhere. This was a riot.

Then, I went shopping downtown. I thought it would be funny if I worried my family just enough for them to notice that I was gone, and that they didn't know where I was. I thought this was appropriate because they didn't really listen to me about manic depression. I thought maybe if I just showed up at 10:00 A.M. seeming just fine, they would listen to me when I told them I was all right. I shopped and bought some things, all of which had some symbolic meaning. I bought a shirt that was close to my high school colors. There were shirts exactly my high school colors, but all they had was mediums, the size I wore in high school. I now needed an extra large because I was so fat. The whole time I thought the stores had been prepared for my shopping trip. The colors were a little off to fit me, because high school was a long time ago. I was thinking intensely of high school, because I felt good like I had in high school. Some thoughts of the present were mixed in. I went to a science museum and bought a book about the Plains Indians eating buffalo. This was to show the vegetarians in my family, Rick and all the Felbers, that eating meat is natural. They always gave me a hard time and said that I was depressed because I ate hamburgers. I thought they were out of touch with reality. There were little messages I was supposed to pick up in each store, I thought. These messages made it clear that the secret agents helping me had researched me carefully by talking to a lot of people who knew me in the past or present. These were questions like, "Is this book for you?"

To me this was a secret message that I shouldn't be too hard on Rick and the Felbers when I presented them with the buffalo book. Now I realize they were asking if the book was for me as opposed to being for a little kid.

I got home around 10:00 A.M. in a cab and nobody had noticed I was gone.

That night, in order to get my father further off my case, I called up three of his friends and told them what I thought was going on. I told them, "I think my psychiatrists want to kill me. I know that sounds paranoid, but it could also be true. They gave me a drug that makes me kind of hyper and makes me laugh, so suddenly they diagnose me as manic. This worries my father, makes him impossible to live with, and going into the hospital would mean three weeks racking up a big bill for nothing. Because of their mistake, I want to sue them, so now they want to kill me. Dr. Dellwo has been calling my dad under disguised names so that he can get me into the hospital and kill me. So please help get my dad off my case. Also, keep me out of the University Hospitals. If I'm sick, get me to Trenton Hospital."

They mostly just listened and tried to agree with me. A couple of them were going to be at a birthday party for Dana the next day.

Overall at this time, when I wasn't feeling paranoid, I was feeling good. I still at times flexed my hands like I was swimming, or turned my head like I was doing a flip turn. Swimming comes to mind when I feel good.

Sunday, August 21, 1988 was the birthday party for Dana. My parents invited a bunch of their friends, including some that I had called. They spoke to me saying things which I thought were supposed to be clues. One of them said something very direct. He said his wife and her twin both work at Trenton Hospital. That was reassuring.

I was still talking to my manic-depressive friend Paul Crosby. I was now sure that he was my direct FBI contact. He burped periodically and I starting thinking that was a clue for emphasis. He denied being in the FBI, but I thought that was part of his job. We talked for a long time. I forget all that we said. A couple times he mentioned that I should do the crossword puzzles in the paper. I thought nothing of it, and I didn't do them.

I was still talking to Howard Schultz every day. I kept telling him that I would be okay in a few days when the antidepressant Nardil wore off.

The next day, I was able to watch the news without laughing. I do remember, however, that on *The Dating Game*, I figured the bachelor who won was supposed to be playing the part of me. Imagine! A *Dating Game* show just for me!

On the twenty-fourth the fourteen days since I quit antidepressant Nardil were up, so I started driving again. I also quit eating the restricted diet for Nardil.

Too bad I was still manic.

Now that I was driving, wherever I went, I kept noticing tons of young, half-Asian women. Melanie Carson was half-Asian.

That week, I saw the psychologist Brad Maiers for an hour and he let me tape record the session. His conclusion was that I should also see Dr. Stark and take the medication that he prescribed. So then I made an appointment to see Dr. Stark.

One night, a bunch of my family was going to rent a video and watch it. I decided to go out to Ted Anderson's house and see if he was home. He was my manic-depressive friend who I played Monopoly with sometimes. He wasn't home, so I decided I wanted a night on the town. I figured I'd be feeling good for a while, so I would simulate a date. I wouldn't tell my family where I was going. I'd stay out all night, and come home mid-morning. I drove to a hotel and asked for a room.

The desk clerk looked Hispanic and I thought that he was working there to say I was right for telling my cousin Laura to speak to the Rabbi in Spanish. He gave me a room. Before I went up to the room, I stopped and looked at the pool for a while. It had a calm relaxing effect. It reminded me of my friend, Bridget, who used to check the identification of people going to the university pool.

My mood continued to be happy most of the time. Still, there is a difference between excited happy, and relaxed happy. The pool helped.

I went up to the room and tried to go to sleep. I didn't sleep that much. Instead I just lay there and made plans to use all of my money to buy a house to live in. That way my assets wouldn't count against me, so that I could get welfare.

I got up in the morning and bought a newspaper. I walked to a McDonalds for breakfast. The articles in the paper made me laugh. I thought it was printed especially for me, for my entertainment. I was laughing so hard in the McDonald's that I had to throw the newspaper away so that I didn't cause a scene. I was wary about doing anything unusual in public, because I didn't want to get arrested, declared a danger to myself or others, and put in a psychiatric ward. If I received any treatment for mania, it would blow my lawsuit.

I took the bus back home. (I had loaned my car to my brother, Johnny, the night before.) My stepmother was quite annoyed with me for not saying where I had been. My brother, Steve, also was upset with me.

Later that day my brother, Johnny, asked me if he could come look in my closet for shirts of his. He looked and didn't find any. Then I looked in his dresser for my clothes and found, where I knew a bunch of my t-shirts were, two of my old Camp Okranski t-shirts. They had sentimental value, and had been missing for years, I thought. Now they were back. I decided my friends and relatives had a big game of taking my t-shirts on long trips. I thought they figured, if Bill doesn't get around, at least his t-shirts will. I figured these shirts had been to Israel, Europe, and the Soviet Union, because relatives of mine had been there. Now that I was feeling good, they brought all my t-shirts back. It was so much fun.

That evening, we were getting ready to have a Sabbath dinner, but then my dad started talking to me in an angry tone, so I left in my car and went to another hotel. I told Laura Felber, who was also at our house, that I would call her and tell her where I went.

It was a Friday night, so I went for a long cruise. I went up and down and all over the metro area. I finally stopped at a hotel downtown, and got a room. I was sure I had been followed on my whole drive by the FBI who would be leaving clues for my big malpractice suit.

When I got to my hotel room, I was sure that it was bugged and that the phone was tapped. I also figured there were hidden cameras looking back at me through the television set. I thought this was all in the scheme by the FBI and other investigators to help me with my lawsuit.

I couldn't sleep. I was too busy thinking funny thoughts in my head. I wanted to go to sleep. I hadn't slept much for four weeks. I turned off the lights. I couldn't figure out how to shut off the television set. I thought of unplugging it, but I decided I was supposed to leave it on for some reason. There were two doors on the front of the television, so I closed them. There was still a crack down the front of the television between the two doors. The room was dark, but light from the television set was still coming through the crack. The light made an array of beams along the ceiling.

I thought the beams were supposed suggest what to talk about. I started talking about my past sex life and lack thereof. I thought an FBI sex therapist was listening. I sure hoped he would keep this confidential. I kept trying to shut my eyes and go to sleep, but then a bright beam would make me open my eyes again. After great hesitation, and talking about everyone else I ever liked first, I finally talked about Melanie Carson, wishing we could both be well and be together. I mentioned everyone I ever had a crush on that I could remember. I tried not to mention people who were married. The beams of light from the television seemed to clue me in on what to say next to the bugged walls. I mentioned Jennifer Weinberg, one of the girls I liked in 1976 at Camp Okranski when I was well. She was now married and lived in Israel. Her parents still lived in Ballard which is a part of Seattle. Finally, after all this fantasizing, I slept for a couple hours.

When I woke up, I turned on the radio. At some point they mentioned a three car accident in Ballard. I thought the radio broadcast had been altered to mention that accident in Ballard, so that I would get confirmation that the walls really were bugged, and they heard me talk about Jennifer.

Later that day I was at my dad's house and my WDMDA friend Roger Dymoke called and asked me a bunch of questions about how I was doing. He went through the various symptoms of mania, and I pretty much denied most of them.

The conversation about ended there, and I told him I would see my new doctor, Dr. Stark, on Tuesday, and I'd be okay. I guessed Roger was in on the conspiracy to help me with my lawsuit. It was all handled in a way so that people could deny their participation, I guessed, because this was outside of the FBI's jurisdiction.

That night I went over from the hotel to my Aunt Brenda Felber's house with Laura Felber and Amy and Steve Hannon. I told Laura that I wished there was a way for me to calm down. I was no longer afraid that Dr. Dellwo would kill me, but I was still nervous about it.

I asked my cousin Laura to give me a backrub, and she did. She gave me a backrub for about an hour. While she was, I was thinking very sexual thoughts mostly from my past, not so much about her. I was thinking about my lack of dating since 1979 and that I wanted to date some more. I couldn't exactly make up for lost time, but I sure wanted to try. I thought most people, including Laura, had continuing love lives and it was a whole area of existence that I wanted to start again.

We watched a video of some movie, and then we watched *Saturday Night Live*. I thought some of the *Saturday Night Live* skits were made just for me. I went back to the hotel and slept better because of the back rub.

On Tuesday I went to international folk dancing. I didn't know many of the dances, so I often sat and read some of the magazines that were in a lounge area near the dance floor. I looked at one of the magazines, and it was addressed to Mercer Island zip code 98040. The "4" had two prongs going straight up, rather than being a closed "4". I was sure this was a clue to me to read the whole magazine and check for more clues. I went to another room and read most of the magazine. I figured the FBI knew I didn't do many of the dances and often read the magazines. I found especially interesting some statistics that were being used as a joke that included "99 percent." I thought this was supposed to remind me of the time that Melanie Carson was impressed when I told her of my 99th percentile SAT scores. There were some other statistics about people dying from something, and I thought that had to be secretly referring to multiple sclerosis which Melanie had.

I went back down to the lounge near the dance floor. A woman named Grace who danced with me sometimes came up and asked me to dance. She had long straight shiny blonde hair. However, today I thought this was another secret message. Jennifer Weinberg had long, straight, shiny, blonde hair, and my first doctor in Israel also had straight, shiny blonde hair. The name of the international folkdance that Grace and I did was choreographed by a guy named "Cansaywho." I interpreted that as "Can't say who." This meant that Grace couldn't say who told her to do the dance with me to give the message that Jennifer Weinberg was really a spy helping with my case long distance from where she lived in Israel.

One night at the end of the month, in my hotel room I decided that just for that night, I would watch the Johnny Carson show. Melanie Carson had a brother named Johnny, and I had a brother named Johnny. It seemed like the right thing to do.

The next morning, I drove to a small town to check out real estate prices. I didn't get farther than picking up a local newspaper and concluding that all the ads in there were actually secret clues saying that the FBI wasn't ready for me to move out of the hotel yet, so I drove back down to the hotel.

One day, I had another appointment with Dr. Stark. He convinced me that major tranquilizer Thorazine would help me sleep. I had just wanted sleeping pill Dalmane, but he got me to leave with a prescription for Thorazine which is a sedating, calming, delusion-erasing, sleep-inducing, major tranquilizer, and therefore the treatment for mania. He wanted to put me in the hospital, but I refused. On August 31, I talked to my manic-depressive friend and, I thought, secret FBI contact, Paul Crosby. I was laughing about the fact that Dr. Stark was attempting what he called outpatient treatment for mania. If you are manic, you should be in the hospital. I was jumping to the idea that if you are manic, you *would* be in the hospital. I was out of the hospital, so I must be okay, I thought. I was laughing with Paul about that, and I told him that I hadn't been sleeping much. I hadn't slept for six days.

Paul said, "Look, this is serious now. Take the medication, since you haven't been sleeping."

I said, "Really?"

"Yeah."

"Is that an order?"

"Yeah."

So that night I took some major tranquilizer Thorazine, and some side effect drug Cogentin, and slept for about six hours.

In my hotel room I had some manic depression literature. I started reading some of it and decided that the private investigators and FBI had substituted alternate versions of the books in order to give me certain messages. I threw the changed versions out in the hall to show I had got their message. There was also *The Book Of Questions,* which I started writing answers in, and then when I thought the questions were getting too personal, I threw it out in the hall. I thought it was a different version and was part of the scheme to see what I was thinking. I was thinking about Melanie Carson.

One article about depression had a picture on the cover of someone who looked a lot like Karen Piel. She is one of the married women who went to international folk dancing. I decided to get rid of this article also. I didn't want it to look like I was carrying around pictures of married women to whom I was attracted. I didn't want any scandals.

There was also the question of my cassette tapes. I had some with me that were store-bought, and I had some that were recorded off records. I figured the ones recorded off records were taped illegally, and therefore against federal copyright law, and it seemed they kept disappearing. I figured, when I left the room, the people secretly helping me took the pirated tapes as a signal to me that I had to stay law-abiding or they wouldn't help me.

A major issue was that somehow my tape of my session with Dr. Dellwo had apparently been sabotaged. It was wound around itself many different ways, and was off its spool, so I thought Dr. Dellwo had hired someone to wreck it. I still had a copy of it in my dad's house, and I thought the wrecked version could be fixed, so I started carrying around the wrecked original version in my pocket.

I felt better from the major tranquilizer Thorazine. I felt calmer and I slept.

The major tranquilizer Thorazine was starting to bring me down from mania, but I still had a long way to go. On the fifth, I finally figured out how to turn off the television in my hotel room. (Hold the button down for a second.) I still didn't think I was manic, I just needed the Thorazine to sleep as a result of the stress of almost being murdered by Dr. Dellwo, I thought. I would get an apartment, apply for welfare, then after a while, put my assets in the form of a house so I could get more welfare. One law firm had already turned down my medical malpractice case, but they said I had three years to file suit. I would have three years to shop for a lawyer. Being on welfare (mainly social security disability) would relieve me of having to rely on my dad for money and of having to get along with him.

Overall my mood remained mostly good. I was optimistic about the lawsuit, about no longer living with my dad, and figured I had told so many people about Dr. Haglund and Dr. Dellwo that they didn't dare do anything to me.

On the sixth, I heard the song on the radio, "Downtown." I thought this was deliberately put on the radio to tell me to go downtown and rent a safety deposit box in which to put my tapes of my session with Dr. Dellwo. So I went downtown and rented a safety deposit box at a bank, and put the tapes in it. I thought the number of the box they gave me had some special meaning. It was a number like 2004 which was, I guessed, the first year I could reasonably be a grandparent if I got busy right away.

Delusions were still forming with ease. I went from the hotel to stop by my father's house on the sixth, and there was a message for me to call M.S. Realty. I thought, did this mean call Ms. Reality? I thought it did. Who was Ms. Reality? Wait. Ms. could be MS. MS is multiple sclerosis. Who had multiple sclerosis? Melanie Carson. Wait. What was the reality part for? Maybe in reality, she didn't have it. Maybe she just said that to get me to quit thinking about her. Wouldn't that be great? I sent a letter to Phil Holland, one of my distant lawyer and high school classmate friends. The letter included my delusions about Melanie. Phil was also the former boyfriend of a friend of Pattie Kingston. Pattie was now a lawyer and used to be friends with Melanie. I liked writing to lawyers—after all, there was still someone around who wanted to kill me, because I was going to sue him and wreck his career. I also wrote to Melissa Jenkins. Melissa was Melanie's lab partner back in eleventh-grade physics. Melissa was now a lawyer. I mentioned my current situation, and made references to Melanie like I was wondering if we could be fixed up. Or was I flipping out? I also wrote to Doug Bossard, my University of Puget Sound friend whom I hadn't seen in years. He used to know Melanie, and in my letter I wondered if it was true that she had MS.

Early in September, when I came out of the hotel to the parking lot, I noticed something strange on my car. There was a little piece of masking tape on the lower left hand corner of my windshield. Of course, I took it as a sign that meant that my car was bugged, I was being followed, and I shouldn't have any contraband in my car because it was visible. Also, things could get stolen out of my car, so I should be careful. I decided that I could leave the towel I stole from the hotel in the car, because everybody steals towels from hotels and I needed it to wipe the dew off my car in the morning. A little piece of masking tape meant all that.

On the ninth, I was in Seattle, looking for an apartment to rent, and I came to an avenue that ran east and west. In Seattle, the avenues go north and south, and the *streets* go east and west. I took this as a clue that the FBI had scrambled the street sign in order to tell me not to rent an apartment on that street.

One day that I was at the hotel restaurant, I decided to spoof good nutrition. For lunch I had a beer and a chocolate malt.

By the thirteenth, the major tranquilizer Thorazine was working well enough for me to carry on the conversation necessary to rent an apartment. I didn't think the want ad or the caretaker were using a secret code. I rented an apartment in Kent. I thought that would be a good suburb to live in because there were hardly any Jews there, and my father and stepmother hardly ever went there. Something strange happened in Kent that day. The Kent Shopping Mall was evacuated because of a poison gas leak of unknown origin. I saw that story on the news. For a few seconds I thought about it. What kind of gas could it be? Natural? No. If it was natural gas they would know what it was. Chlorine? No. There was no swimming pool there. It's a shopping mall so they had no other gases there. It had to be a joke. Yes. It was a holocaust paranoia joke. A Jew, Bill Hannon, moves to Kent, suddenly people are being gassed at the Kent mall. The FBI had a sense of humor, and it agreed with mine! Making fun of the Holocaust is not funny, but making fun of people who think it can happen in the United States is funny! I was sure the FBI pulled off the evacuation as a hoax for my entertainment.

The night of September 13, was the last I spent in the hotel. The morning of the fourteenth, I drove to my apartment to move in more stuff, and there was broken glass all over the apartment building steps. In the late thirties in Germany, when Hitler was getting ready to exterminate the Jews, there was a night called the "Night of Broken Glass," when Hitler asked Germans to go around vandalizing and burning Jewish businesses. I decided that the broken glass on my steps was just another Holocaust paranoia joke, and a way for the FBI to say that they would still be with me in my new apartment. I also looked on it as a bit of a threat. I would have to do things their way, or they could vandalize my apartment.

On the news that day my guess was confirmed. There was no poison gas leak at the mall. An eighteen-year-old kid had sprayed some mace on a wall and someone smelled it and thought it was a gas leak. I figured the whole thing was for my entertainment.

That evening, I rented a truck, and with the help of Kevin Felber, Carl Paige, Jim Eckhart, and Howard Schultz, I moved my furniture from my dad's place to my apartment. I slept there that night.

Also on the fourteenth, I saw the psychiatrist Stark. I asked for permission to increase the dose of my major tranquilizer Thorazine. He said okay. I also told him of my plan to write to the medical licensing boards of all fifty states, the District of Columbia, Guam, Puerto Rico, the U.S. Virgin Islands, and American Samoa to tell them to never let Dr. Haglund or Dr. Dellwo practice there. I had the addresses, and I was working on the letters. Dr. Stark said he wanted to talk to my dad. I assume this was to get my dad to tell me to stop writing the letters. I told Dr. Stark that if he spoke to my father, I would no longer be able to speak to him. So Dr. Stark shut up.

That week I had applied for Social Security Disability. I had to come up with the name, address, and dates worked for every job I ever had. I also had to describe the job, and why I left. They said they'd let me know in five months.

I also wrote another letter to Melissa Jenkins, Phil Holland, and Doug Bossard, inquiring about Melanie Carson's health, and should we be fixed up? Or was I having delusions?

I was feeling very good. I could win a big lawsuit and be rich.

On September 22, I was talking to my WDMDA friend, Paul Crosby. I also thought he was my secret FBI contact. I talked to him every day. For a while he had been telling me to do the crossword puzzle in the Seattle paper every day. Also for a while, when he burped, I thought that the burping was supposed to be a clue for emphasis. I hadn't really worked on the crossword puzzles, but today he said, "You really have got to do today's crossword puzzle, there are important things you need to know for your life."

I finally caught on: there were clues in the crossword puzzle! I got the paper. It was unbelievable! The answer to one across was "Carson" Paul said, as he burped. The clue was "Johnny namesake." I have a brother Johnny, and so does Melanie Carson. I couldn't stop laughing. There was more in the crossword puzzle. Five across was "Kingston." The clue was "Capitol of Jamaica." Pattie Kingston had been Melanie Carson's roommate on our high school senior class trip to Jamaica. Jamaica was where I got to know Melanie. I was just rolling with laughter. This was too good to be true! I wrote to some distant friends about Melanie, and they got back to me through the crossword puzzle! Was my mail being read by the FBI? Or was one of my distant friends an agent? How did they get the job of writing the crossword puzzle? The hows and whys didn't matter. It sure worked pretty well. I was ecstatic. I wrote to Melissa Jenkins, Doug Bossard, and Phil Holland again, and asked about Melanie and me. They had never written back so far.

Late in September, I saw Dr. Stark. We decided I would switch to the major tranquilizer Loxitane which I thought might have fewer side effects than major tranquilizer Thorazine.

Early in October, there was some candy piled up on the doorway to my apartment building. There is a Jewish tradition of throwing candy at a bride and groom rather than rice. So, I thought the possibility for me to get married was there, according to someone. I thought the implied bride was Melanie. After all, I felt better sexually now that I was not depressed.

In October, I continued to go to international folkdancing, WDMDA, and a few restaurants. The women wherever I went looked much more attractive than when I was depressed. Also, colors seemed brighter. At WDMDA, I got fired from facilitating support groups because I kept telling everybody to sue their doctors.

I went dancing at a bar once. Something I thought may have been a clue was that most of the women I danced with that night were named Lynn, Lynnette, or Linda. I decided that thinking those names were a clue, was a manic symptom, so I shouldn't be ridiculous. I decided I should only accept information that was clear.

I anonymously sent the hotel I stayed at $10 to pay for the towel I stole. I felt that this way in my lawsuit, if I ever was asked the question, "Did you commit any crimes against the hotel?" I could say no. I told Paul Crosby about this, and he started chewing me out for being so honest, so I started to wonder if he really was an FBI agent. I had already made a list of my secret clues that I thought I could prove were messages. If they were really messages, I could win my lawsuit. The basic premise of my lawsuit was that Dr. Dellwo and Dr. Haglund called me manic, even though I was not. This false diagnosis caused me a lot of problems, was my story. As long as these things were clues and not delusions, then I hadn't been manic, and I could win my case.

I told Paul about some of the incidents I have just written about. He said, "They were due to human error and coincidence, not to anyone trying to send you a secret message."

The next day, Paul and I went over the whole list of delusions, and he told me they were just coincidences. I had been manic. Shoot! I was annoyed. I wrote Phil Holland, Doug Bossard, and Melissa Jenkins and told them to kindly disregard my letters.

I finally recognized my delusions as delusions. I finally could separate reality from fantasy. I was near normal. The major tranquilizer Thorazine and then the major tranquilizer Loxitane had brought me down to normal. Let's hear it for the medication!

27

Conclusion

On October 28, 1988, I saw Dr. Stark and said, "I realize that I've been manic."

He said, "Well, I think that's a major breakthrough."

I then agreed to start taking mood leveler Lithium because by going on Lithium, you can gradually get off of major tranquilizers like Loxitane without getting manic again. Lithium helps prevent and treat mania and it has fewer short term and long term side effects than Loxitane. Loxitane caused some impotence. Lithium caused less, I thought.

I learned from my last manic episode to take a tape recorder to every psychiatric session. Dr. Stark won't let me record the whole session, but he records a two minute summary at the end of the session. This will make it easier to sue him in future if I have to. It's not just my medical history, it is also his work history.

Speaking of my medical history, it is my memory that we use for my medical history. Dr. Stark has my history written down, but he doesn't know it and never reads it.

I've also started keeping a log book of every time I take a pill. I also write down any change in mood, any change in side effects, and I write down how much I slept.

Dr. Stark has been good but he made one mistake. He left me on major tranquilizer Loxitane when it causes more impotence and staring than major tranquilizer Prolixin. I had to ask him which one has the least sexual side effects, and then he told me about Prolixin. I had thought they were all the same. He should have told me sooner.

By January 1989, my mania went away and I tried just mood leveler Lithium by itself with no tranquilizer. I had determined that Lithium was worth a trial by itself, because in the past I took side effect drug Cogentin with it. By reading the *Physicians' Desk Reference* I determined that one of the side effects of Cogentin is depression. It doesn't do anything for the side effects of Lithium anyway.

Anyway, mood leveler Lithium by itself didn't work for preventing depression. After a few weeks of just Lithium, I got depressed. I decided Lithium plus an antidepressant should be tried. In the past, Lithium plus antidepressant Asendin didn't work real well. But there is a rule, if drug A plus drug B doesn't work, that does not rule out drug A plus drug C. It does not rule out drug B plus drug C. It does not rule out drug A or B by themselves.

So I tried mood leveler Lithium plus antidepressant Wellbutrin. That combination made me manic in four days. However this time there was a difference. *I recognized mania in myself!* I had gone to bed at 11 P.M. and was wide awake lying in bed until 4 A.M. in the morning. I was thinking happy optimistic thoughts. I was excited about the future. I knew this was the lack of sleep of mania. The antidepressant Wellbutrin lifted my mood up too much. I started myself back on major tranquilizer Prolixin, side effect drug Cogentin, and stayed on the Lithium. Cogentin stops the muscle stiffness and restlessness of Prolixin.

It was a major breakthrough to recognize mania in myself. *The lack of sleep was the sign I could consistently recognize.* For a couple years, when I slipped into a depression, I again deliberately induced mania with mood leveler Lithium and antidepressant Wellbutrin.

CAUTION TO MANIC-DEPRESSIVES IN THE READING AUDIENCE: INDUCING MANIA IS HAZARDOUS. INDUCING MANIA IS BREAKING ALL THE RULES! THE DRUGS THAT INDUCE MANIA VARY FROM ONE MANIC-DEPRESSIVE TO ANOTHER. GET YOUR DOCTOR'S PERMISSION BEFORE CHANGING ANY MEDICATION! SOMETIMES YOU CAN GET STANDING PERMISSION TO VARY YOUR DRUGS WITHIN A CERTAIN RANGE.

It felt better to be under treatment for mania than it did to be under treatment for depression. By 1991, I was fairly well convinced that being in a controlled mania was more fun than being in a controlled depression.

I did okay for a while on major tranquilizer Prolixin, side effect drug Cogentin, and mood leveler Lithium, but I still had some side effects. These side effects were impotence and the staring that goes with it, and also some dry mouth, dry nose, and dry eyes. Also the drugs made me drowsy and made my muscles stiff.

The combination that worked for a while was anti-manic major tranquilizer Prolixin at bedtime to make me sleep, and side effect drug Cogentin when I woke up in the morning. The Cogentin also got rid of some of the main effect of Prolixin. So, I was less sedated during the day when I took Cogentin in the morning. I learned that Cogentin gets rid of some of the main tranquilizing effect of Prolixin by reading *The Handbook of Psychotropic Agents* (Compendium Publications Group, Ltd., of Secaucus, New Jersey). Reading psychiatry books has helped me a lot. Knowledge is power.

There is a problem with having this prolonged drug-controlled mania. Most of the major tranquilizers, like Prolixin, that you need to control mania can eventually cause tardive dyskinesia, a strange muscle disease. It causes involuntary movements. I was at risk for that.

I got rid of the mood leveler Lithium in September 1995, because it, in me, caused more impotence, staring, and drowsiness. I stuck with the major tranquilizer Prolixin and side effect drug Cogentin.

I should note, many manic-depressives are controlled fairly well by mood leveler Lithium alone. Many hold full time jobs and have significant others. They don't function fully normally though. Many do function better than I do.

Going back to October 1989, there was a coincidence. My friend Carl Paige, and my barber don't know each other. However, one week in October 1989, they both suggested that I write a book about manic depression. I had been unemployed for a while, collecting social security disability and getting some money from my dad. I certainly had time to write a book. I went to a support group meeting and noticed that all the literature there was written by doctors. None of it was written by patients. I figured we needed a book written by a patient. So, I started writing this book. It took many drafts and the help of many people, but I stuck with it and this book is the outcome. I joined a writers' group, and that helped a lot.

To support myself, I've been getting social security disability, some money from my dad, some paychecks from part-time jobs, and I've been spending the dividends and some of the principal of my Bar Mitzvah stocks. My dad is helping me financially and doesn't mind that I don't live with him. We get along now. He is usually quite pleasant. He can carry on a friendly conversation. He doesn't tell me what to do. I see him about once a month, and he doesn't demand more attention than that. I need his money, because I still have trouble holding jobs. I'm very lucky that my dad has had the ability and desire to help me financially. Without his help, I would probably be homeless. I tend to get fired for being too slow. I still have a few side effects of medication and a few symptoms of the disease. I still have poor concentration.

The thing is, now I feel better. Being in a controlled mania feels better than being in a poorly controlled depression. The next few pages are a sample of how my life has been better during the period 1991–1996. Controlled mania has been more fun than controlled depression.

Now that my manic depression is less severe, I more often can flash a one second smile at women, instead of a five second stare. It is so much better. A few women I know at international folk dancing will now sit next to me and talk to me, instead of avoiding me.

I had a cashier job when I was depressed, and later when I was just a touch manic. Being a bit manic felt much better. When I was a bit manic, my co-workers were really warm and friendly. The customers were really friendly. I talked to customers just for the heck of it instead of only when absolutely necessary. I talked to the female cashiers just for the heck of it and they liked it. I could cashier 40 percent faster with fewer mistakes. It was fun. During breaks from work, if I was in the bathroom, I also combed my hair instead of assuming that nobody was looking. When I did other jobs in the store, they seemed less baffling.

It used to really bug me when a customer would come up to me and say, "This will be cash."

I thought: How annoying, don't they know they don't have to say that? Don't they know that I don't care?

When I was in a better mood, I thought nothing of it.

Music seems a lot more beautiful than it did when I was depressed.

Lately my apartment seems warm, friendly, and cozy. This is especially amazing because I only clean it twice as often. I bought seven new posters, new drapes, a new stereo, and I repaired holes in the wall.

Hugging my female friends and relatives hello and good-bye now seems enjoyable rather than a pointless ritual.

I joined a Toastmaster's public speaking group. We meet weekly, and for a year, I was president of the group.

All of these happier feelings are because I'm stuck in a controlled mania, instead of being stuck in a poorly controlled depression.

One of my co-workers at the store, Ann, was a really a good friend. I've been overweight since 1984, so it is more difficult to keep my shirt tucked in. Being depressed, I just let my shirt be out, because I really didn't care. I figured nobody was looking. I figured life was such a tragedy, that an untucked shirt really didn't matter. Anyway, one day she came to work with her shirt hanging out. It really looked stupid because she usually looked so nice. From then on I realized that I should tuck my shirt in or look stupid. From then on I kept my shirt tucked in whenever possible.

Ann did the same thing with table manners. Since becoming manic-depressive, any table manners I had gradually deteriorated. Table manners seemed like a pointless ritual. Once, in the break room, Ann was eating something, and then sucked the crumbs off of every one of her fingers. I thought, gee that's gross. I wasn't used to seeing anyone else do that. Then I realized that everyone else was used to seeing *me* do that. I quit doing that. I started using napkins.

Feedback like that has helped me improve my appearance and manners.

I threw a birthday party for myself July 12. It was the first party I had thrown since 1972. There were about twenty-five people there.

I don't crack my knuckles as much any more.

I have gotten four letters to the editor printed that were on national policy issues. I may pursue more writing, or I may continue designing web pages like I've been doing for the past few months.

I have been going to more social events lately. I am more friendly and outgoing than I was when I was depressed. I talk to my neighbors. I'm not preoccupied with any one woman. I feel less difficulty going up to strangers and talking to them. I can tell people that I am manic-depressive, if I feel like it. If I don't want to, I don't, but it is no big deal.

I've started playing poker again with a new group of friends that I met through international folk dancing.

I put an ad in the singles section of a newspaper, and I answered a bunch of ads. One I answered was: "DWF, 29, seeks creative, intelligent, caring individual, to accompany me on life's adventures. You should be financially secure and know what you want out of life."

I called her voice mailbox and said a few things. I referred her to my ad in the same paper, and told her to call me if she liked it. My ad read like this: "Co-Chair My Committee, SWM, 34, is seeking someone to do my dreaming and scheming with. We can be partners in carrying out our plans for life. I like movies, skiing, hiking, dancing, rock music old and new, and cold purple grape juice."

She read my ad and called me back. We talked for about an hour. I told her I had manic-depression, but was mostly better, and she didn't really seem to mind. Her name was Dawn. She told me about her career as a fifth grade teacher, and that she really liked it. We talked for a long time.

She told me of a restaurant near her house that we could meet at. She said, "I'm five foot four, and have fairly long, curly blonde hair. No glasses, and I'll wear, um, let's see, a light blue dress."

I said, "I'm five foot nine, a little chubby, 215 pounds, light brown curly hair. I'll wear blue jeans and a blue short-sleeve shirt."

She said, "Is five o'clock okay?"

"Yeah, sounds good."

That day came and I went to the restaurant, but it was closed that day for the employee picnic. I sat outside and waited for her. After about ten minutes she came walking up and I said, "Are you Dawn?"

"Yeah, you must be Bill."

"Nice to meet you. I think this restaurant is closed though."

"Oh I didn't realize. I didn't know. Oh, that's so stupid."

I said, "There have got to be more restaurants along this street."

"Yeah, let's just drive up and look for something."

"Okay, where are you parked?"

She followed me up to a pizza place. She told me more about herself. She had been divorced for a year and was glad it was over. I told her I was writing this book. I told Dawn that some manic-depressives don't recover very much, but I had recovered to a large extent, so I needed to write the book to help others. I gave her an early draft of this book that was in my car, because she said she wanted to read it. That was about all we did that night. She gave me a hug good-bye.

We went out another time. We went out dancing, but she kept flirting with a whole bunch of other guys who were there, and ignored me. I figured that I would have to chalk this up to experience. After we left the bar, she started saying she wanted to be "My friend forever," and a lot of stuff like that. It seemed sincere, but then it couldn't have been sincere based on all the other guys she was flirting with at the bar. However, my still less than perfect mood could have still been a big factor in how I looked at the situation. Then she wanted to kiss me good-night, so I let her. It seemed stupid because it seemed so insincere. However, she did kiss me. It was my first kiss since 1985.

I called her a few times after that, but I just got her machine and she didn't call back. Then she called me a few times, but she just got my machine, and I didn't call her back. That was the end of that.

It is now January 1997. After over a year of being on just major tranquilizer Prolixin and side effect drug Cogentin, I'm finally on something even better. A new major tranquilizer Zyprexa is available. I've been on it for about three months. I'm less impotent and staring complaints have been greatly reduced. Also, I'm more soundly asleep at night and more wide awake during the day. I take the Zyprexa at bedtime and it puts me to sleep. However, when I get out of bed in the morning, I don't feel as hung over as I did on Prolixin. Life is easier by quite a bit. My mood stays closer to normal most of the time. I'm slightly depressed in the morning and slightly manic in the evening.

I'm not completely healthy, but I'm better than I've been for a long time. Every night before I go to bed, I see what I have planned for the next day, and I often look forward to the new day. That is much different than just hoping to cope with another annoying day. My plan since I was a little kid has always been to achieve maximum luxury. This doesn't mean riches, it just means feeling the best. I just want to have fun. I'm willing to work hard sometimes, or even a lot, but only if it is part of a plan to maximize fun. When I was depressed in the past, I had a difficult time even imagining how fun was possible. Now, with better medication, things are less complex and usually more fun.

AFTERWORD

Bill Hannon writes from personal experience about a life lived under the shifting mark of manic-depressive illness (also called bipolar disorder). For me as a psychiatrist, it is always refreshing to read a firsthand account of a person living with a serious mental illness. This book personalizes a frightening illness, and may encourage fellow sufferers by showing that effective treatment is available. Even in our enlightened times, mental illness is still a stigma. Books like Bill's help humanize and destigmatize manic-depressive illness. Perhaps it will also diminish barriers that others face when they consider seeking treatment.

Fortunately, our arsenal of effective medication is growing and greatly improving. We have better knowledge of the mechanisms of medications, the etiology of the diseases, the genetic patterns and inheritability, different subtypes of the illness, and so forth. Early diagnosis and intervention is critical, in part to avoid repeated failures and losses associated with hospitalization, but even more importantly to improve prognosis, as it appears each episode may kindle the brain to future and more refractory episodes. This is a great challenge because currently many patients with the illness receive multiple other diagnoses, often over many years and even by psychiatrists. This obviously can delay accurate diagnosis and effective treatment. Manic-depressive illness is sometimes subtle and not easy to diagnose.

Lithium has long been a mainstay of treatment for bipolar disorder. Yet 90 percent of bipolar patients require other medications. Bipolar patients who cycle rapidly, or have mania present with depression, do very poorly with Lithium. This is a subgroup of people who seem to do well with drugs previously used as anticonvulsants, namely Depakote and Tegretol.

Bipolar disorder is strongly genetic and is caused by biochemical changes in the brain's neurotransmitters. This means that medication is an essential part of treatment, but psychotherapy can be very useful in helping patients cope and rebuild their lives around their shifting moods. Community support programs are also critical. Case management and the help of social services can be very helpful.

Chemical dependency occurs frequently as a complication of manic-depressive illness. Approximately 50 to 60 percent of patients with this illness have coexisting chemical dependency problems, obviously complicating accurate diagnosis and treatment. Only if both are identified and treated will the patient get well.

Patients typically fail to recognize mania in themselves. This complicates diagnosis because they don't report symptoms to their doctors. It complicates treatment as well. Many manic patients will convince themselves they are well and will discontinue medication with disastrous consequences. Lack of sleep may be a herald symptom of mania. Conversely, lack of sleep may cause mania, an important consideration for patients when traveling across time zones or when accepting employment with erratic hours or shifts late into the night.

Depression is highly underrecognized, underdiagnosed, and undertreated. Patients often minimize their symptoms or fail to recognize that symptoms such as anxiety, insomnia, and poor concentration all constitute a syndrome of depression and not just isolated symptoms with other explanations. Patients often will explain or normalize their depression and attribute it to "stress," yet depression is a state of unwellness, a disease. Poets will romanticize depression and people will tolerate it, struggling and yet managing to function, not knowing why it is such a struggle. It is not uncommon for psychiatrists to see patients who have been depressed twenty years or more without having sought treatment.

Patient and family advocacy groups such as the National Alliance for the Mentally Ill and the Manic-Depressive Association with all its local chapters have put mental health issues on the national agenda. In a time when research grants and funding are dwindling on the national level, these advocacy groups bring to bear an important lobby on behalf of the mentally ill. Physicians are wisely coming to recognize families as powerful allies, which is a far cry from the days of attributing mental illness and psychopathology to poor parenting, especially poor mothering.

As our country seeks to reform health care and economize at the same time, we face special challenges. It is an anomaly that mental health insurance coverage is discriminatory. Parity in mental health coverage is a national issue that is hotly contested at the current time. Nondiscriminatory parity in mental health coverage is critical in achieving early diagnosis and effective treatment and in diminishing the negative outcome of mental illness, as well as improving prognosis. Parity is an imperative for all patients, their families, and the physicians who treat them.

Funding of research is also threatened. Obviously research into the causes of mental illness and into effective new treatments is imperative.

Patient confidentiality is threatened when managed care companies demand more and more personal data to authorize simple basic care. Traditional doctor-patient confidentiality barely exists with the multiple intrusions into this traditional domain and into the sanctity of that relationship of a patient with his or her physician. In addition, frequent shifts in the insurance plans provided by one's employer has seriously eroded the continuity of care and the sanctity of the doctor-patient relationship.

Patients switch doctors often because they are forced to and this fragmentation is unfortunate given the imperative of early diagnosis and treatment. Vulnerable patients tolerate switches in physicians poorly because of their illness. They often don't act as strong advocates for themselves or follow through in finding new physicians. A switch in physicians often triggers noncompliance with medication, especially when it runs out. In turn, it is not uncommon for psychiatric hospitalization to ensue as a result of a breech in the continuity of care. This is hardly an economic savings for anyone, neither employer, patient, nor society.

I would encourage patients and families to take strong advocacy positions to improve access to mental health care, protect confidentiality, achieve parity, and increase research funding. Likewise, patients need to be assertive with their doctors. A good alliance and rapport remains perhaps the most critical element to good outcome. It also enhances compliance which is a major issue in the treatment of mental illness.

There are many, many outside forces which threaten the special healing relationship between a physician and patient. Patients, families, and physicians will need to work together to contend with these intrusions to protect the interests of those with mental illness.

KAREN K. DICKSON, M.D.

APPENDIX A

Symptom List

Here is the list of symptoms of mania and depression that psychiatrists, psychologists, general physicians, social workers, and lay people should use to diagnose or recognize manic depression. People with the disease must be treated by a competent psychiatrist. My list comes basically from the booklet *Understanding Manic-Depressive Illness* (Clarke Institute of Psychiatry, Toronto, Canada). I have made some additions and substitutions and added some examples from my own experience, reading, and talking to others at support groups.

Mania

1. **Delusions of grandeur.** This can be thinking you are God, Jesus, John Lennon, an FBI agent, or thinking you have great powers, or talents or wealth. This includes thinking you can know exactly what people are thinking by reading their face. That was one of my delusions on the trip to Israel. You are having a delusion when you jump to ridiculous conclusions from normal sights, sounds, and smells. This is not the same as a hallucination. For hallucinations, see symptom #10.

2. **Paranoid delusions.** This can include the thought that the devil is out to get you, that criminals are out to get you, or that Israeli extremists want to force you to help them fight Arabs.

3. **Reduced need for sleep.** You may feel that you need very lit-

tle sleep, and you may only sleep a couple hours a night. You may not sleep at all. You may be lying in bed concentrating on such big plans for the next day that you don't relax and sleep. You don't really mind the lack of sleep. *This lack of sleep may be the only symptom you recognize in yourself.*

4. **Feeling very good.** Except when experiencing paranoia, everything seems fun, everything is more interesting. Colors seem brighter. Music sounds better. You are more talkative. Euphoria. This is the only disease where the sicker you are, the better you feel.

5. **Rapid unpredictable emotional changes.** You can switch from happy to angry quickly with no apparent reason. This is yelling and screaming suddenly to the suprise of those around you. This would be sitting and eating dinner with Ted the leader of the tour of Israel, and then turning on him and his supervisor moments later, calling them Nazis. They didn't know what I meant. Another example is when I was yelling on the bus ride in Israel, all the way from Tel Aviv to Haifa.

6. **Extreme irritability.** You may get very demanding and get angry when people don't jump in response to your commands. You may get angry if they disagree with your delusions. You may get angry when people interrupt you, while you are coming up with what you think are great ideas.

7. **Flight of ideas.** When talking to people, you may jump from topic to topic. In your mind there is a connection between these topics, but it is not clear to the listener.

8. **Thinking everything is a clue directed to you.** This includes thinking that dialogue and songs on the television and radio are being altered to give a special message to you. You also think that about newspaper articles and things strangers might say near you in public. You think the clues are secret and most people don't notice them. The clues are usually words that have double meanings.

9. **Overspending.** You may think you have great wealth or potential income, so you may spend or invest recklessly. You may give money away.

10. **Hallucinations.** Some people get visual, auditory, or olfactory hallucinations. You are hallucinating when you are seeing, hearing, or smelling something that is not really there. I never got this symptom. You may or may not know that they are not real. When you get major tranquilizers, the hallucinations will go away and you will probably realize that they were not real.

11. **Hyperactivity.** You may have so much energy that you go from one activity to another without stopping, or thinking.

12. **Increased sexual drive.** Sexual indiscretions. You may want sexual intercourse many times a day, and you may pick up sexual partners indiscriminately. You may flirt outrageously.

13. **Poor judgment.** You probably won't recognize that you are ill. You are likely to refuse treatment and blame others for everything that goes wrong. You may drive recklessly. You will certainly say things that you shouldn't say, ask things that shouldn't be asked, and do things you shouldn't do.

14. **Talking loud or fast.**

15. **Excessive phone calling or letter writing.** These can be to people you used to know, people you know now, or famous people. The calls may be long distance. The letters may be registered mail. Usually you want to tell these people of your great delusional plans. One woman tried to call the Pope.

16. **Excessive joking, punning or rhyming.**

17. **Excessive laughter.**

18. **Singing or dancing at inappropriate times.**

19. **Outrageous or unusual way of dressing to attract attention to yourself.**

Depression

1. **Sad, despairing mood.**

2. **Preoccupation with failures or inadequacies and a loss of self-esteem.** You may become obsessed with one negative

thought and be unable to turn it off. Your mind is clogged with worries.

3. **Feelings of uselessness, hopelessness, and excessive guilt.** These are three different feelings but are self-explanatory. You could have more than one at a time. These feelings can totally overtake your mind.

4. **Slowed thinking, forgetfulness, difficulty in concentrating and making decisions.** This is usually due to preoccupation with guilt or hopeless feelings. The poor concentration makes it hard to do your job or schoolwork.

5. **Loss of interest in work, hobbies, and people.** Loss of feelings for family members and friends. Nothing is fun.

6. **Excessive concern about physical complaints such as constipation.** Feeling overwhelmed with the fear that you have some physical handicap or disease. You may or may not really have that handicap. Even if you do have that handicap, feeling unduly overwhelmed by a handicap may be a symptom of depression. You may know you have depression or manic depression and be preoccupied with that. You may excessively fear future mania or depression. This is often a sign that you are depressed right now.

7. **Either agitation or loss of energy.** So restless that you cannot keep still, or too tired and weak to do anything.

8. **Changes in appetite and weight.** This could be a big increase or big decrease in appetite and/or weight.

9. **Sleep problems.** You may sleep too little or too much. Often you cannot sleep because you are lying in bed, worrying about negatives too intensely to relax and fall asleep.

10. **Decreased sexual drive.**

11. **Crying easily.** Or you may feel like crying but be unable to do so.

12. **Irritability.** You can be upset with everthing and everybody around you. You don't like it when others interrupt your obsessive worrying, even if it is to say something nice, or you don't like what others have done in the past to you. Or, you don't like others to ask you to participate in things that used

to be fun, but aren't fun now. This can come across as anger. You can be mad at everything and everybody who has helped you to reach this apparently awful occasion. On very rare occasions, this anger turns to violence.

13. **Suicidal thoughts or actions.**

14. **The excessive use of alcohol or street drugs in an effort to self-medicate.** Many manic-depressives become chemically dependent. Then they have two diseases hurting them.

15. **Loss of touch with reality.** Some people get hallucinations or delusions when they are depressed. I never get hallucinations, but once I was so depressed that I had the delusion that when the phone rang it was the police calling to question me. I felt very guilty about something I had done, even though it was not even illegal or wrong.

16. **Psychomotor retardation.** This means uncoordination. Taking forever to do physical tasks. Slow movements. Clumsiness. Slow speed at the 100 yard breaststroke, for example. It can even be hard to get up and get dressed.

17. **Pessimism about the future.** Fear of bad things that may happen in the future. Anxiety about upcoming events. Lack of confidence.

To qualify as manic or depressed, you usually need just four of these symptoms at the same time. There are normal depressions after a loss, but they should last only two weeks or so. If they last longer, treatment is recommended.

The reader should also know that there are other diseases besides depression and manic depression which give the symptoms of depression. These conditions which seem like depression include side effects of birth control pills, side effects of blood pressure medication, thryoid disease, hypoglycemia, and cancer. Consult your doctor.

APPENDIX B

Resource List

Finding a Doctor

To find a psychiatrist near you, ask your family physician for a referral, or look in the yellow pages of your phone book. You may also know someone who is a satisfied patient of a certain psychiatrist, so it may help to ask around.

If you or someone close to you is suicidal, call your or his psychiatrist. If the person in question does not have a psychiatrist, call the suicide hotline in your area, or call 911.

Manic people will generally not recognize that there is something wrong with them the first time they are manic. If someone close to you is manic, call a psychiatrist, and follow the psychiatrist's instructions. If you are manic yourself, and you know it, call your psychiatrist and tell his secretary that it is an emergency. If it is after hours, call his emergency number. Or, you may have standing orders from your psychiatrist to start taking a major tranquilizer like Prolixin or Zyprexa, like I do.

If you are seeing a psychiatrist for a while and you are not getting much better, or if you just have to find an answer to a question that your doctor doesn't know, don't hesitate to get a second or third opinion. Switch doctors if that seems right for you.

For Support Groups and More Literature

For support groups and more literature about depression and manic depression, call the National Depressive and Manic-Depressive

Association (NDMDA) chapter nearest you. Support groups are best when they are geared toward finding the best medication for each of the individuals at the group. Members of support groups should feel free to recommend medication and dosage changes to each other, as long as it is clear that your doctor must also be consulted before you make a change. Minimizing symptoms and side effects is the name of the game. The philosophy of NDMDA or any local chapter may vary.

National Depressive and Manic-Depressive Association

NDMDA
730 N. Franklin, Suite 501
Chicago, Illinois 60610
312-642-0049
800-826-3632

UNNUMBERED NOTES

Chapter 1

6   *"'Sinequan'... hallucinations"*—Edward R. Barnhart, ed., *Physicians' Desk Reference*, 45th ed. (Oradell, N.J.: Medical Economics Data, 1991), p. 1896.

7   *"Big, little, or short or tall, wish I could have kept them all"*—Sampson, "I Loved 'Em Every One," from the single *I Loved 'Em Every One*, T.G. Sheppard (Warner 49690, 1981).

7   *"Wham bam thank you ma'am"*—David Bowie, "Suffragette City," *The Rise and Fall of Ziggie Stardust and the Spiders from Mars*, David Bowie (Rycodisc USA Records 10134).

12   *"Save my life I'm going down for the last time"*—"Never Been Any Reason," *Head East, Flat as a Pancake*, Head East (A&M Records Inc. CS-3196, 1975).

Chapter 2

18   *"There is a study that proves..."*—P. J. Clayton, C. Ernst, and J. Angst, "Premorbid Personality Traits of Men Who Develop Unipolar or Bipolar Disorders," *European Archives of Psychiatry and Clinical Neuroscience* 243 (1994): 340.

27   *"Do you remember the times of your life?"*—Nichols, Lane, "Times of Your Life" from the single *Times of Your Life*, Paul Anka (United Artists 737, 1975).

Chapter 3

31   *"My analyst told me, that I was right out of my head"*—"Twisted," *Court and Spark*, Joni Mitchell (Asylum Records 1001, 1974).

Chapter 4

44   *"only 0.5 percent of the population gets the disease"*—John Born and James W. Jefferson, M.D., with assistance from the Lithium Information Center, *Lithium and Manic-Depression: A Guide*, booklet published by the University of Wisconsin (rev. January 1987), p. 10.

Chapter 7

84   *"Don't Stop Thinking about Tomorrow"*—Christine McVie, "Don't Stop," *Rumors*, Fleetwood Mac (Warner 8413, 1977).

84   *"We are prisoners here of our own device."*—Felder, Henley, Frey, "Hotel California," *Hotel California*, The Eagles (Asylum Records 45386, 1976).

88   *"Our minds are definitely twisted."*—Felder, Henley, Frey, "Hotel California," *Hotel California*, The Eagles (Asylum Records 45386, 1976).

Chapter 13

115   *"I am an island"*—Paul Simon, "I Am a Rock," *Simon and Garfunkel's Greatest Hits*, Simon and Garfunkel (CBS Inc. and Columbia Records JCT 31350, 1972).

Chapter 14

127   *"Let's Do the Time Warp Again"*—O'Brien, "Time Warp," *Rocky Horror Picture Show Soundtrack* (Rhino Records R1-70712).

127   *"If there's a bustle in your hedgerow"*—Jimmy Page and Robert Plant, "Stairway to Heaven," *Led Zeppelin IV*, Led Zeppelin (Atlantic Records SD 7208).

Chapter 15

145   *"Cogentin even can have a side effect of its own. Depression!"*—Barnhart, *Physicians' Desk Reference*, p. 1387.

Chapter 18

165   *"Asendin is the worst tricyclic antidepressant as far as one's sex life is concerned"*—United States Pharmacopeial Convention, Inc., *Drug Information for the Health Care Provider* (Rockville, Md.: United States Pharmacopeial Convention, Inc.).

Chapter 21

183   *"new antidepressant drugs need to be tried for six weeks"*—Mark S. Gold, M.D. with Lois B. Morris, *The Good News About Depression* (New York: Villard Books, 1987), p. 243.

Chapter 27

234   *"one of the side effects of Cogentin is depression"*—Barnhart, *Physicians' Desk Reference*, p. 1387.

Appendix A: Symptom List

248   *"there are other diseases which give the symptoms of depression"*—Gold, *The Good News about Depression*, pp. 77 (thyroid disease), 80 (cancer), 111 (birth control pills), 113 (blood pressure medications), 159 (hypoglycemia).

ACKNOWLEDGMENTS

I want to thank the following people for their countless hours spent reading and editing my book, or performing other essential tasks.

Kathleen A. John A. Debra A. Gregory B. Ellen B. Joan B. Ann B. Miriam B. Donna B. Tom C. Brian C. Jack C. Marv C. Nancy C. Sara D. Colleen F. David F. Julie F. Sheila F. Olivia G. James G. Eve G. Lee H. Jewish Community Center of Seattle. Peggy J. Dana J. Sue K. Kate K. Frank K. Rick L. Mitch L. Herb M. Yvonne M. Ivan M. Wayne M. Kerri M. John M. Freda M. Carole M. Hank M. Liz M. Geena N. Sue N. Jody N. John P. Steve P. Rex P. Patrick R. Kitty S. Sue S. Harold S. William S. Peter S. Beth S. Aaron S. Denise T. Timothy T. John U. Ben V. Bruce W. Dave W. Larry W. Mary W. Joe W.

INDEX